For
Hoke and Gracie
from Paul

December 1965

THE CHALLENGE OF INDUSTRIAL RELATIONS IN THE PACIFIC-ASIAN COUNTRIES

The Challenge of Industrial Relations in the Pacific-Asian Countries

EDITED BY
HAROLD S. ROBERTS
AND
PAUL F. BRISSENDEN

East-West Center Press

Honolulu

EDITOR'S PREFACE

We would like to extend our sincere thanks to the delegates who participated in the conference on "The Challenge of Industrial Relations in Pacific-Asian Countries" for their co-operation in the preparation of the verbatim record of the conference and the papers which are part of this volume.

Special thanks are due the East-West Center's Institute of Advanced Projects for financial and moral support of the program, and the Industrial Relations Center of the University of Hawaii, co-sponsor of the project, for assistance throughout—in the preparation for the conference, in transcribing the record, in typing the manuscript, and in helping with many other details. We would also like to extend our thanks to Joyce Matsumoto Najita, Helene Shimaoka, Norma Nekota, and Eva Lee Goo.

Although we are also indebted to many others not noted here, we would be remiss if we failed to acknowledge the help and encouragement of Alexander Spoehr and Neal M. Bowers.

HAROLD S. ROBERTS
PAUL F. BRISSENDEN

April, 1964

CONTENTS

THE CHALLENGE OF INDUSTRIAL RELATIONS IN THE PACIFIC-ASIAN COUNTRIES

INTRODUCTION AND SUMMARY

CHAPTER 1

by Harold S. Roberts

This volume is the outgrowth of a conference sponsored by the Institute of Advanced Projects of the East-West Center, and convened in April, 1962. Delegates from six Pacific-Asian countries met at the University of Hawaii for a series of discussions of industrial relations in their respective countries.[1] The selected papers which follow grew out of the conference discussions and reflect the views of the individual delegates in the particular areas of their special competence.

In attempting to examine the challenge of industrial relations, it became quite apparent to the planning committee[2] that perhaps there was no single challenge, unless one viewed the broad opportunity for people in all of these countries to develop their potentials to the highest or optimum

level and to utilize to the maximum all of the existing manpower facilities, as well as their social and economic resources.

The conference was conceived as the beginning of a continuing series of exchange programs to be developed over a number
of years. The long-range objective is to provide not only an
exchange of students and research scholars among the several
countries, but, also, to provide an opportunity for a continuing
exchange of information, books, and research, as well as to
permit the countries involved to keep themselves informed
about developments elsewhere and to utilize the best techniques
and facilities where they are applicable to their respective
countries. In addition, it is hoped to provide a clearing house
for universities, private research groups, and governmental
units. It is also hoped that each country will so define its
particular needs in the field of industrial relations as to call
upon scholars from the countries of the East and West to give
their cumulative knowledge to the particular problems after
on-the-spot surveys and subsequent review and formulation of
recommendations, possibly at the East-West Center.

In an attempt to narrow the area of discussion and to keep it
within the time limit set (three weeks), the advisory committee recommended that the scope of the conference be limited to
three major subject areas. The first week was to be devoted to
an examination of research in progress in each of the countries
and an evaluation of research needs deemed necessary by the
delegates from the countries represented. The second week was
to be devoted to an examination of the methods of dispute
prevention and settlement of labor-management disputes in the
several countries. The last week was to be devoted to an examination of the ideological backgrounds relevant to the development of industrial relations systems of the different countries.

The delegates to represent each of the countries [3] were carefully chosen, and an attempt was made to provide a group
which included those who had practical experience in the operation of the industrial relations systems of their own countries,
as well as persons who had a broad academic and scholarly

interest in and an understanding of the systems of industrial relations in their own countries.

The group was kept relatively small to permit easy exchange and informality and, at the same time, to provide a sufficiently broad area of experience and a spectrum of diversity in practice. An examination of the industrial relations systems of each of the countries represented will make it apparent that the spectrum comprehended a range from free collective bargaining in the United States to forms of compulsory arbitration in Australia and New Zealand and intermediate patterns in Japan, India, and Canada.

We will attempt in this introductory section to note some of the general conclusions arrived at by the delegates. At the end of each week, the group met to sum up the discussions, to see to what extent agreement had been achieved, and to highlight the major points of difficulty or disagreement. The delegates unanimously agreed on these summations, and, although this occasionally involved some qualification of the language, it does indicate in substance the attitude of the delegates attending the sessions. No attempt was made to resolve points of disagreement or to establish agreement. We sought merely to understand each other's points of view.[4]

It might be noted also that, as a result of the close association during the three weeks of the conference and continuing correspondence among the delegates in reviewing the transcript of the conference proceedings, as well as in the review and editing of the series of papers in the volume, a start has been made in maintaining a working relationship among the delegates who attended the conference.

Of further interest to those following the development of industrial relations in Pacific-Asian countries is the realization that a number of the recommendations made by the delegates have borne fruit in some of the countries. India, for example, is in the process of establishing a number of industrial relations centers. Some of the Australian universities have written for further information concerning the development of industrial relations programs and activities in their curricula, and some of the industrial relations centers in the United States and

Canada have co-operated in reviewing their industrial relations programs. Some preliminary discussion has also taken place with a number of industrial relations centers about an interuniversity program of American and Pacific-Asian universities.

Some of the results of our pilot conference are beginning to show. As a closer relationship is established among the participating countries, additional programs will be developed in succeeding years, not only to establish wider areas of co-operation and exchange among the six countries involved, but, also, to extend these where feasible to other countries already included within the ambit of the East-West Center program.

There is unquestionably a great need for continuing an extensive co-operation. It has become increasingly obvious that the rapid industrialization of countries in the Pacific area and in Asia has led to the rapid growth of labor and management organizations, which are playing increasingly significant roles in guiding and formulating policy in those countries.

The movement toward industrialization of large masses of people has resulted in the mobilizing of their power through labor organizations, which are beginning to play an increasingly active part in the political and economic life of their respective countries. An understanding of the basic economic and social conditions within the several countries and the development of the respective trade-union movements becomes more urgent if there is to be growth and stability within the developing countries in the Pacific-Asian basin.

The delegates noted that although there was a wide variety of ideology and practice among the countries represented at the conference, all of them were democratically oriented. In studying the processes within each of the countries, it was noted that the democratic process permits wide accommodation in meeting the problems of labor and management. We examined with great interest how each country sought to protect the democratic process and the rights of the individual within the society and, at the same time, preserve the national interest without eliminating the freedom of management and labor to resolve many of their own differences.

In reviewing the actual practices of the respective countries, apart from the statements of legislative policies set out in the laws or in statements of government leaders, it was clear that strikes did occur in all of the countries, even though legislation in some presumably prohibited such strikes. We became increasingly convinced that the strike cannot be eliminated in a democratically oriented country which practices the democratic process as well as preaches it. When protracted strikes did occur we found it was possible to utilize a wide variety of measures to minimize their impact on the community. Some of the countries were more strict in their approach to the problem and intervened more freely; others were inclined to permit greater latitude in the labor-management relationship and even in occasional breakdowns resulting in strike situations. Although all of the countries were concerned about ways to substitute industrial peace for industrial war, none of them had found easy answers to the problem. It was felt by many that it was more important to provide a better understanding of the problems than to find harsher and stricter methods of enforcing economic and social behavior to the point of eliminating the strike as an industrial relations practice.

Industrial Relations Research

In writing to the participants, the director stated that it was the hope of the advisory committee that the first week's session on research activities might serve to enhance the awareness of all of the delegates as to research enterprises now in progress in the several countries in the field of industrial relations and as to what projects are being planned. It was thought desirable to canvas the possibilities of useful exchange of information among the countries represented and the possibilities inherent in arrangements for co-operation and the exchange of such information, as well as of scholars to engage in such work. It was suggested that questions such as the following might appropriately be considered in this connection:

1) What research projects are now under way in the field of industrial relations, particularly with regard to the methods and principles of labor dispute settlement?

2) What other projects in this field are currently being planned?

3) How much emphasis is laid on research in industrial relations at the universities?

4) What projects are now under way at the universities? What others are being planned?

5) What governmental data about industrial relations and, specifically, about methods of labor dispute settlement are currently available? What further information might be usefully gathered and published by the several governments?

Following the discussion of the research in progress in each of the countries and a historical review of research efforts in some of them, it was clear that, before any major program could be developed for interchange among the countries taking part in the conference, it would be necessary to engage in very serious efforts in each of the countries to determine the research in progress there and the proposals contemplated for the coming years. It would also be necessary to make a preliminary evaluation of major research projects completed, as well as a detailed examination of the bibliographic research concluded and available in each of the countries in the field of industrial relations.

The conference recommendations on research were as follows:

Most delegates expressed a feeling for a need for wider interchange of information, for interpretation of material exchanged, and for an exchange of ideas for research in industrial relations.

A number of difficulties in the way of interchange were listed: first, any exchange should have a common focus in order that the information may be meaningful to the recipients; second, there is a need for a co-ordinating agency; third, there is a barrier of language, particularly in Japan; and fourth, there is a shortage of funds in certain of the participating countries.

It was noted that before there can be international exchange of information, each country must be informed about its own activities.

It was believed that the East-West Center could usefully serve as a co-ordinating center for the exchange of information, possibly through reports to it from participating countries outlining research activities. Reference was also made to the possibility of using the *Journal of Industrial Relations* of the University of Sydney as a source of information about Pacific-Asian countries.

The suggestion was made that the East-West Center might sponsor or co-operate in international interuniversity studies of specialized problems of specific countries by qualified scholars. The delegates might suggest to the East-West Center subjects relating to current problems which might appropriately be considered.

Specific reference was made to the possible development of a National Institute of Social Sciences, along the lines of the National Science Foundation, which through the co-operation of Educational Foundations would facilitate research and study of this kind.

Consideration was also given to the possibility of an Interuniversity Council of American and Pacific-Asian Universities to co-ordinate research and other mutual programs.

Since the conclusion of the conference, some of the delegates have made efforts to obtain more information on research in progress. Probably the most extensive effort has been made by Professor Taishiro Shirai in Japan. These materials, after translation by the translation bureau of the East-West Center, will be in the files of the Industrial Relations Center of the University of Hawaii. The Center is proposing a study of information retrieval in industrial relations which may provide data on research completed.

Dispute Prevention and Settlement

The second week of the conference was centered on the procedures and techniques of labor dispute prevention and settlement in the six countries. The discussion focused upon agreements, statutes, decisions, and awards, and it was hoped that, with further insights into the variant systems of decision making studied, it would be possible to reach a better understanding of them.

The emphasis was not on improvement and change but primarily on understanding.

Among the questions suggested for discussion were the following:

1) How is one to explain the fact that such highly "authoritarian" systems of industrial regulation have developed in the Australian and New Zealand democracies? And compulsory conciliation in New Brunswick, Canada?

2) The "authoritarian" systems of regulating labor relations in Australia and New Zealand, if "authoritarian" is the right word for them, appear to be the only such systems in the world—with the possible exceptions of India and the city-state of Singapore. How does it happen that similar systems have not taken root in the Philippines, Japan, or the United States?

3) Specifically, as to Japan, how is it that that country, with a long history of nondemocratic government, did not follow the line of Australasian labor authoritarianism, lock, stock, and barrel?

4) Is the method and effectiveness of labor dispute settlement related in any significant way to the extent of labor organization? Or to the extent of employer organization?

5) Is a high degree of industrialization a prerequisite to (a) authoritarian regulation, or (b) a pervasive system of control by collective bargaining? Does the experience of India throw any light on this question?

6) To what extent in the six countries are the internal affairs of unions subjected to regulation by government? Is the practice in this respect significant in relation to methods of dispute prevention and settlement?

7) What are the most reliable criteria for assessment of the effectiveness of a country's methods of labor-dispute preven-

tion and settlement? To what extent may fact finding be a means of prevention as well as settlement?

8) What should be the composition of arbitration, mediation, or fact-finding tribunals? Should they be tripartite? What does the experience of Japan suggest? Of the United States? Of Western Australia? Should the parties have a say as to who are to be their judges?

9) Are methods of dispute settlement (whether by mediation, arbitration, seizure, fact finding, etc.) affected by the nature of the economy, e.g., whether it is pastoral, agricultural, or manufacturing?

10) Has the growth of bargaining or of interventionary methods of settlement (fact finding, mediation, arbitration, etc.) had any effect on the extent of resort to direct action?

The summary agreed upon by the delegates as a result of the discussion of dispute prevention and settlement follows:

The principal approaches to dispute prevention and settlement may be classified broadly into: collective bargaining, conciliation and mediation, voluntary arbitration, compulsory arbitration (with compulsory arbitration for public servants as a special case), inquiry, and fact finding. Special aspects are the extent to which: (a) strikes and lockouts are illegal; (b) penalties are used to check disputes, especially those marked by stoppages; (c) legislation is used to achieve objectives normally sought through bargaining or arbitration procedures, e.g., annual holidays in New South Wales and New Zealand and "standing orders" in India. There are wide differences among the different countries, but beneath these differences one may note a good deal more in common than appears on the surface, not only in objectives but also to some extent in actual operations.

Australia and New Zealand have compulsory arbitration, under the shadow of which, however, a great deal of direct negotiation occurs; this is tending to increase slowly in both countries. India has compulsory arbitration for public utility employees, and the government (federal and state) retains the right to use compulsory arbitration in nonpublic utility serv-

ices also. The emphasis today has shifted from legal to moral
sanctions, and nonstatutory methods of avoidance and settlement of disputes are being evolved through bipartite and tripartite deliberations. Japan has compulsory arbitration for
employees of the government, public corporations, and, in
emergency cases, for employees of public utilities. Canada and
the United States have collective bargaining systems for matters of substance (i.e., new contract terms), but Canada in
effect has compulsory arbitration for grievances, while the
United States has widespread voluntary (or "obligatory") [5] arbitration for grievances (i.e., contract interpretation). In a
large proportion of unionized plants in the United States, collective bargaining is obligatory rather than "free." Moreover,
under the Taft-Hartley Act and in some states having similar
legislation, collective bargaining is obligatory under the "majority rule."

Australia and Japan have pervasive, though somewhat informal, conciliation procedures, while New Zealand and the
United States have rather more formal conciliation or mediation machinery. Canada has compulsory conciliation procedures available in cases where collective bargaining fails to
produce settlement. India also has conciliation machinery. In
Canada and the United States, conciliation is concerned mostly
with disputes over interests, but in the other countries it appears to be used in all classes of disputes.

Australia has penalties against strikes as part of its normal
machinery. Strikes are illegal in New Zealand for organizations registered under the principal statute. Penalties are also
available in New Zealand but are very rarely used. Canadian
trade-unions have been held liable for damages arising from
illegal strikes. Strikes are illegal in India in certain circumstances but in Japan are a guaranteed right, except in government services, public corporations, and certain special
categories. The United States has no restrictions on strikes in
industry except for national emergency situations—which are
covered by the Taft-Hartley Act—and some other very special
situations, but strikes by federal government employes are
prohibited.

The different systems in the several countries arise in large part from their particular social, political, and economic conditions; it is not possible at this stage to suggest with any confidence the transplanting of machinery that is successful in one country to other countries. It is even very difficult to assess a single country's procedures, as such assessment depends greatly on one's value judgments and on the weight one gives to different values. It was agreed, however, that success in dealing with industrial disputes was too narrow a criterion for most purposes, especially as there are several sources of loss that are often more important than strikes. Important factors considered were the impact of an industrial relations system upon the freedom of the individual, the effects upon the recognition and status of trade-unions, and the effects upon weaker groups of workers. The checking of inflation, a factor of great concern to economists, appeared to be related more to general economic conditions, particularly the level of employment, than to the type of dispute settlement procedure.

A social factor of particular significance is the notion of the public interest, which is regarded as important in all the countries represented. Recognition of this assumes different forms in different countries. One implicit recognition of the public interest is seen in the use of a tripartite approach to industrial relations problems as compared with an employer-employee approach. Recognition of the public interest is, of course, quite a different thing from the effects of the recognition which may be great or small, "good" or "bad." Recognition of the public interest, including considerations of economic growth, appear to be giving rise to increased government intervention in industrial relations. National emergencies, such as war, have also played a part here. As a result of these and other factors, industrial relations studies are becoming broader and more inter-disciplinary in character.

The discussion of dispute prevention and settlement was probably more detailed and thorough than the discussion of any of the other subjects dealt with by the conference. It was noted that, although most of the delegates approached the problem with open minds as to the operations of their own systems, they nevertheless supported the procedures in effect in their own countries. This, of course, was to be expected, and yet, as discussion continued, it also became clear that there was perhaps more compulsion than was apparent at first blush in the "free" collective bargaining system in the United States and less compulsion and more effort at mediatory approaches in the so-called compulsory systems of Australia and New Zealand.[6]

Impact of Ideology on Industrial Relations Systems

The last week of the conference witnessed the most philosophical and, perhaps, the least down-to-earth consideration of industrial relations. However, in many ways, it provided a deeper basis for understanding the development of the variant industrial relations systems. Dispute settlement systems and procedures, it was recognized, did not operate in a political or social vacuum. The delegates recognized that the industrial relations systems are conditioned by, and to some extent perhaps developed as a result of, the political form of government, the national folkways, traditions, and even religious beliefs characteristic of a particular country. The delegates felt that such considerations, though philosophical and ideological rather than predominantly factual, were nevertheless of great significance as background guides to an understanding of the industrial relations systems that have developed in each of the countries. Among the questions highlighted by the third week's discussions were the following:

1) Has the concept of the State had any significance in the fashioning of arrangements for settling labor disputes?

2) Is a labor dispute considered synonymous with (a) a strike or (b) a work stoppage?

3) Is a labor dispute thought of as a problem of concern solely to the parties?

4) Have labor disputes emerged only after the industrialization of the economy?

5) Has a concept of "wages justice" emerged?

6) If so, are there discernible standards for its recognition, or is it merely a phrase suggestive of "what labor wants"?

7) Does the expression "profits justice" have any tangible meaning? If so, what is it?

8) Do the expressions "wages justice" or "profits justice" have any relation to common notions about religion or democracy?

9) Does the "right" of a party to a labor dispute derive whatever sanctions it may have from the "rights" of citizens in a democracy?

Although the planning committee recognized that it might have been preferable to open the conference with an examination of the ideological foundations, the committee felt that since these delegates were coming together for the first time, with very little appreciation of each other's points of view, it would probably be more profitable to have the discussion center first on more or less neutral and factual problems. The decision was therefore made to begin the discussions with some appraisal of research progress and to follow through with consideration of methods of dispute settlement, which could be dealt with on a more or less factual basis, and to leave the discussion of ideologies until the last week, when the delegates would have become better acquainted and would feel freer to talk without restraint. As it turned out, this proved a fairly good assumption, although the group actually integrated quite well and worked very effectively and informally, and it might have been possible to handle the ideological discussion during the first week rather than the last.

The general summary of the third week's discussion is substantially as follows:

Ideologically, all significant social groups in the more highly industrialized and more affluent countries are gradually embracing the concept of the welfare state, quite frequently coupled with a mixed economy of private and state enterprise. The dominant branches of the labor movement, with some rare exceptions, have shed or are in the process of shedding either

their ultrarevolutionary radicalism or their extreme conserva-
tism. They also are beginning to accept the concept of the
welfare state, since experience has revealed that it is possible
in democracies, through moderate political and collective bargaining practices, to protect and improve, within reasonable
ranges, the living and working conditions of their followers.
Employers, sometimes grudgingly and often with demonstrations of resistance, are also accepting orderly industrial
relations through collective bargaining with varying degrees
of state intervention as the most practical procedure for maintaining workable industrial relations.

As social problems become more complex and as economic
life grows more variegated, the impact and scope of government intervention in social and economic affairs, of necessity,
increases. However, notwithstanding the increase of apparently authoritarian practices, basic human rights and individual freedoms are not significantly encroached upon. Indeed,
vital democratic practices are consciously being safe-
guarded.

The trade-unions have come to rely consistently upon political action as well as on industrial pressures to realize their
objectives. They have therefore begun to exert a moderating
influence on labor and socialistic political parties and, in fact,
to influence the attitudes of all political parties. In some countries, the trade-union movements have formed political parties
of their own, and those parties have from time to time taken
over the reins of government. The existence of labor parties
and their experience in coping with the business of government
have profoundly affected the trade-union movements. Simultaneously, they have created turbulent ideological currents in
certain areas.

In economically underdeveloped countries and regions where
poverty is still endemic, the social order is naturally unstable.
The labor movements reflect, as does all of society, this state of
affairs. The tendency is to stress political and mass action.
Under such conditions, orderly industrial relations are, at best,
in an early stage of development. As conditions improve, practices become more moderate and orderly.

RESEARCH IN INDUSTRIAL RELATIONS

INDUSTRIAL RELATIONS RESEARCH IN JAPAN

CHAPTER 2

by Taishiro Shirai

This discussion of industrial research in Japan conveniently divides itself into four parts:

I. The historical development of research in the field of industrial relations, including the social background against which Japan's system of industrial relations has developed. This phase of the subject will be subdivided into two sections, one dealing with the prewar and one with the postwar period.

II. The organization of research activities. This phase of the subject will be presented under five headings: (1) governmental organizations, (2) academic institutions, (3) management associations, (4) trade and labor unions, and (5) special organizations. The academic institutions will be considered under five subheadings in accordance with their several methods of approach.

III. Outstanding research projects in the field of industrial relations.

IV. Finally, an attempt will be made to assess the research activities that have been conducted, indicating any failures or shortcomings.

I. *Development of Research in Industrial Relations in Japan*

In giving a brief description of historical developments, present scope, and characteristics of research in the field of industrial relations in Japan, I should like to point out at the outset that in Japan there has been no uniform definition or common understanding of the exact meaning of the term "industrial relations." As a matter of fact, the terms "industrial relations" and "labor relations" are rather new and quite unfamiliar to ordinary Japanese people, inasmuch as they are introductions from the United States and have gained only gradual and still limited popularity in postwar Japan. To the Japanese, the term "labor problems" is more familiar than "industrial relations," and we may have failed so far to recognize the difference as well as the relationship between "labor problems" and "industrial relations" or between "labor relations" and "labor economics," with their specialized connotations. Accordingly, my presentation may cover more extensive fields than one might expect, taking "industrial relations" in the broadest sense of the term. This is perhaps inevitable, since it cannot be said that research in the field of labor at its present stage in Japan has shaken down into a co-ordinated, systematized framework.

It is only since the end of World War II that research in the field of labor has flourished in our country. However, to understand the characteristics of this research in Japan as it stands today, some reflection is required on the prewar days when considerable progress, although accompanied by setbacks and limitations, was witnessed in the research in this field. We can trace the development of research in the labor field as far back as the middle of the Meiji Era (around 1900), when the industrialization of our country was in full swing, favored by the powerful protective policy pursued by the government. The rapid, and perhaps premature, growth of industrialism inevitably precipitated labor problems, which, in turn, caused social unrest.

The first comprehensive research on the conditions of industrial workers was conducted by the government in 1900 as the groundwork on which the first factory legislation was to be developed. This was reported in the voluminous publication *Shokko Jijo* [1] ("The Conditions of Factory Workers"), dealing with textile, machine, metal, chemical, and other industries.

Along with this governmental research, there appeared a group of scholars whose chief concern was the study of various social problems. In 1896, the Institute of Social Policy, which is the counterpart of *Verein für Sozial Politik* in Germany, was established. This organization was opposed to both socialism and laissez-faireism and advocated middle-of-the-road social reformism. It conducted research, particularly on the conditions of industrial labor, in order to help in the formulating of governmental policy for its improvement. Research into the labor and living conditions of the working class had been made earlier by a distinguished journalist, Gennosuke Yokoyama. This was published in 1889, under the title of *Nippon no Kaso-shakai* [2] ("Laboring-Class Society of Japan"), which still retains its reputation as the most excellent work on the history of social research in Japan. Another book from the standpoint of the labor movement was *Labor Movement in Japan,* [3] written by Sen Katayama and Kojiro Nishikawa and published in 1902.

After World War I, research in the labor field developed as labor problems became a matter of increasing social concern. The trade-union movement began to grow, inspired by the democratic movement of that time, as well as by the worldwide upheaval of radical and revolutionary movements, including the Russian Revolution.

The founding of the ILO should also be counted as an important step. At the same time, soaring prices during wartime and large-scale unemployment, which were threatening the worker's living standard, tended to cause a great number of labor disputes. Under these circumstances the government felt impelled to take up research in this field. The Ministry of the Interior embarked on statistical research dealing with trade-unions and labor disputes. This was followed by monthly wage and unemployment surveys, dating from 1923.

One of the most noteworthy events in the development of research in industrial relations was the establishment of the Kyochokai (The Harmonization Association) in 1919. This organization was founded with the purpose of achieving industrial peace, but it devoted itself mainly to research on the labor movement and on labor disputes.

Research in labor problems among academic institutions also began to develop. Trade-unionism, collective bargaining, wages and hours, industrial accidents, and unemployment were their special concern.

However, research in prewar days, one might say, was limited or restricted by the following factors, which also summarize the characteristics of research in labor relations in prewar Japan:

1) The initiative for research in labor problems was taken by the government, with the purpose of maintaining the public peace. Thus, research programs on the trade-union movement and on labor disputes were developed to meet the requirements of police control or regulations set forth by the government. In most cases, these research programs were not open to scholars. Labor problems were taken up because such problems might cause social unrest, which would undermine the existing social order, or because they might affect the industrial or military policies pursued by the government in prewar Japan.

2) Academic freedom had been particularly restricted in this field. To the government, research in social problems tended to be identified with the socialist or Communist movements.

3) The trade-union movement was also largely restricted by the repressive tactics of government. There had been no protective legislation for trade-unions. In an underdeveloped country seeking rapid industrial growth and inclined to military expan-

sionism, the Japanese capitalist class and the conservative government would not tolerate the free trade-union movement. The trade-union movement was confined to the economically poor minority group, with a maximum of 400,000 members. Moreover, this group was split by the bitter struggling of ideological factions within it, and this prevented the labor unions from becoming stable social institutions.

4) Labor relations in prewar Japan followed a pattern of despotic paternalism, where the relationship between employer and employee was that of superior and subordinate, or of governor and governed, within a kind of "family" enterprise. Generally, the worker could not stand on equal terms with the employer because of lack of organization and lack of freedom for concerted activity. Labor relations was a matter of private concern to each enterprise. How to handle their workers and how to settle their grievances were prerogatives of management's autocratic power. Generally, management did not want to open the door to outsiders, whether trade-union organizers or scholarly researchers. They wanted to keep their employees from the infiltration of revolutionary or radical ideas that might undermine traditional patriarchal relationships within "the family" of an enterprise. Despite this attitude, violent and bitter labor disputes often arose. These were pathological phenomena, so to speak, which management was forced to consider. Accordingly, there developed much detailed research of the major disputes, conducted by the management of enterprises that were actually involved in the disputes or by management associations. Such was the background of industrial relations in prewar Japan, which made research in this field highly restrictive and generally unsuccessful.

After World War II many of the unfavorable circumstances were drastically changed. From the very beginning, the Occupation Forces pursued a policy of encouraging the free trade-union movement as an essential condition for democratizing Japan. The rights of workers to organize themselves, to bargain collectively, and to engage in concerted action were guaranteed by the New Constitution and by the Trade Union Law of 1945. The principle that labor and management should stand on an equal footing and that no police control should be involved in this relation was established. Freedom of speech and freedom of academic activity were also guaranteed. The phenomenal growth of trade-unions resulted in a total of more than six million members within a few years after the war. These drastic changes in the circumstances resulted in a remarkable development of research and study in the field of labor problems. Researchers in the labor field became the most popular in academic circles. In universities and colleges the chair of labor problems became one of the most important. Industrial relations specialists, with their knowledge of the requirements of collective bargaining, collective agreement, grievance procedures, personnel administration, training-within-industry, and benefit or welfare plans for employees, became more and more important in postwar management.

The need for the knowledge required in this new phase of industrial relations was also acutely felt by the labor unions. Trade-union leaders had to acquire techniques and knowledge of union administration, collective bargaining, trade agreements, dispute settlement, strike tactics, union finances, labor laws, work rules, wages, hours, and working conditions of members.

Favored by these developments, research in the labor field acquired momentum. Countless books and articles dealing with labor problems were published. However, for the first few years after the war, the political turmoil and agitation in which the revised labor movement was involved and the chaotic disorder in which the study of labor relations found itself did not permit research on any sound and stable basis.

Postwar Japan went through turbulent years until around 1950, when the reconstruction and rehabilitation of its national economy was achieved and the administrative regime of the Occupation Forces was removed. Industrial relations in Japan was at last free to stand on its own feet. With the authority of management restored and trade-unionism placing more emphasis on economic bargaining rather than on political activities, there emerged a system of industrial relations that was uniquely Japanese, a system essentially different from those developed in Western societies.

II. Organization of Research Activities

We turn now to a brief survey of the organizations which have been involved in research activities up to the present time. These organizations can be divided into the following groups: (1) governmental organizations; (2) academic institutions, including universities, colleges, and academic societies; (3) management associations; (4) trade or labor unions; and (5) other special organizations.

GOVERNMENTAL ORGANIZATIONS.

These include the Ministry of Labor, Central Labor Relations Commission, Public Corporations Labor Relations Commission, and the National Personnel Authority—each with several local branches at the prefectural level.

One of the most noteworthy events in the development of research in labor problems in postwar Japan was the establishment of the Ministry of Labor in 1947. The Ministry includes the Division of Labor Statistics and Research, which conducts comprehensive statistical surveys in the labor field and provides much of the basic data required by administrators and specialized research workers.[4] Statistical surveys have been made by the Ministry of Labor in the following areas: (a) employment and unemployment, (b) labor productivity, (c) wages, (d) hours of work, (e) industrial accidents, (f) cost of living, (g) statistics of labor unions, and (h) labor disputes.

Based on these statistical surveys, the Ministry of Labor publishes the *Yearbook of Labor Statistics* and the *Labor White Paper*, a comprehensive analytical survey of the labor situation in Japan for every year since 1949. Whereas the investigations conducted by the Ministry cover extensively the field of labor and industrial relations, the researches conducted by the Labor Relations Commission, central and local, and the

Public Corporation and National Enterprise Labor Relations
Commission are more specialized in the field of industrial relations, particularly in labor disputes. These organizations are
set up by the government, but are totally independent of governmental control. The reports of their activities, published
monthly or yearly, provide reliable data relating to labor disputes and settlements. Comparative studies of wage levels for
employees in private industries and for civil servants are regularly conducted by the National Personnel Authority.

ACADEMIC INSTITUTIONS, INCLUDING UNIVERSITIES, COLLEGES, INSTITUTES, AND ACADEMIC SOCIETIES.

There are several major lines of approach to the labor problem which academic societies may follow. It cannot be said,
however, that each line has a specialized field of its own with
clearly defined lines of demarcation. These are as follows:

Labor law group

The labor laws of Japan after the war had a decisive
influence upon trade-unionism, as well as on industrial relations. Naturally, the interpretation and application of these
statutes have involved some problems. This group is chiefly
concerned with the legal aspects of trade-unionism, collective
bargaining, union security, right to organize and fair labor
practices, legitimacy of strike tactics, labor standards, and the
decisions of courts and labor relations commissions.

The social policy group

Mention has been made of the research on labor problems in
academic circles conducted in prewar days by the scholars who
constituted the Institute for Social Policy (1896). This organization was almost defunct by the middle 1920s, but was revived
in 1950 and, with about 500 members, has become one of the
leading academic societies concerned with labor problems. Although this organization in the prewar period was directly
connected with social reform movements, the revived organization had nothing to do with such movements. The Institute is
composed of specialists in various fields, such as the labor

market; employment and unemployment; labor turnover; wages, hours, and other working conditions; trade-unionism; history of the labor movement; social security; and personnel administration. It must be kept in mind that research in labor problems is not yet systematically co-ordinated in Japan. It should be noted also that research in the field of labor is carried on through lectures on labor problems given in universities and colleges, usually under the heading of "social policy." This reflects the traditional thinking, that the labor problem, as a part of the social problem in general, comes under the social policy of the state and is to be solved by the administrative power of the state rather than by self-determination through autonomous and voluntary negotiations between labor and management.

Business management and study groups

These groups specialize in personnel administration, taking it as an essential part of business management. The characteristic of their approach is that they stand for management's interest in achieving the most efficient utilization of the work forces within the individual enterprises. In other words, their main concern is the development of techniques to secure the highest manpower efficiency at the least expense—by rationalization of personnel administration, including time study, wage administration, and so forth.

Industrial sociology and social psychology groups

It is rather recent that sociologists in Japan have turned to research in industrial relations. Their activities in this field owe much to the stimulation given them by American sociologists, particularly Elton Mayo and his successors. The Japanese sociologists are particularly concerned with human relations between management and labor and workers' morale.

The political scientist group

As we shall see later, one of the characteristics of the Japanese labor movement is that greater emphasis has been placed on political activities. Here the concern is chiefly with the political aspects of the labor movement, the relationship between labor unions and political parties, and the ideologies of the leadership of labor unions.

MANAGEMENT ASSOCIATIONS.

There are a number of employer associations in Japan, namely, Nikkeiren (Japanese Federation of Employers' Associations), Keidanren (Federation of Economic Organizations), Japanese Chamber of Commerce, and the Medium and Small Business Enterprise Association, with respective branch organizations set up on a prefectural or industrial basis. The most influential body in the field of industrial relations is the Nikkeiren. This association was established in 1948, as a national federal organization of employers exclusively concerned with industrial relations, directed to the formulation of employer policy vis-à-vis that of the labor unions. Although Nikkeiren and its affiliates have not been highly centralized organizations directly involved in actual collective bargaining, they function as research, educational, and lobbying groups for management. Most of Nikkeiren's work centers around economic policy formulation, as well as the analysis of collective bargaining issues and the study of labor administration, training-within-industry, and productivity improvement.

LABOR UNIONS.

The important national labor organizations, namely, Sohyo, Zenro, Sodomei, Shin-Sanbetsu (the four national centers of trade-unions in Japan), and their affiliated national industrial federations have research departments. Collective bargaining, particularly wage bargaining, is their chief concern. They investigate the working and living conditions of their memberships in order to help the unions formulate policy on these matters. Problems of union organization and administration, membership morale, and political and legislative demands are also dealt with.

SPECIAL ORGANIZATIONS.

Comments here will be confined to the two organizations which are most active and influential, i.e., the Japan Productivity Center and the Japan Institute of Labor, neither of which can be called strictly research organizations, but which stress research activity as one of their most important functions.

The Japanese Productivity Center

Established in 1955 by the employer associations Keidanren and Nikkeiren with the backing of the Japanese Government and financial aid from the American Foreign Operations Administration (FOA), The Japanese Productivity Center concerns itself with research in industrial relations, with the definite purpose of achieving industrial peace and rationalization and improvement of labor administration as an indispensable means to the attainment of higher levels of productivity. The research carried on by the Center has been focused on the joint-consultation system and the rationalization of our traditional wage system and wage structure as required by the development of technical innovation. The Center has invited trade-unions to participate on an equal footing with management, but up to the present time the national unions affiliated with Sohyo, the largest national labor organization, have refused to join, fearing that their participation would further undermine their efforts at collective bargaining and might lead them to endorse programs they politically oppose.

Japan Institute of Labor

The Japan Institute of Labor was established in 1958 by a special statute, the Japan Institute of Labor Law, with a fund of 1.5 billion yen (approximately $4.2 million) appropriated solely by the government. The purpose of this organization is to conduct basic research in the field of industrial relations and to promote labor education. At the time the bill providing for the Institute was being discussed in the Diet, Sohyo and the Japan Socialist Party condemned the bill, deeming its major purpose to be the promotion of labor-management co-operation and the curbing and restraining of labor-union aggressiveness. However, under the presidency of Dr. Tamon Mayeda and of his successor, Dr. Ichiro Nakayama, the Institute has succeeded in preserving its independence from any governmental control or intervention, so that it has been able to win co-operation in trade-union circles as well as in academic circles. The research activities of the Institute have a wide coverage in industrial relations, and the Institute's publications are increasingly appreciated both at home and abroad.

III. Outstanding Research Activities

In giving a brief review of research projects in the field of industrial relations, it must be noted that in Japan research in this field and in the social sciences as a whole has been largely conducted by individual scholars. At any rate, we have not been very successful until recently in setting up organized, group-research enterprises. However, group-research projects, particularly at the interuniversity level, have been developing gradually, and some comments on a few outstanding research enterprises conducted in this manner are commented upon below:

TOKYO UNIVERSITY TRADE UNION RESEARCH CENTER.

The most noteworthy achievement in this field was made by an organization set up within the Institute of Social Science of Tokyo University, with Professor Kazuo Okochi at its head. Its purpose was to examine the characteristics of the organizational structure of postwar trade-unions. This research was started in 1949, and its results were published in 1952 under the title *The Actual Phases of Post-War Trade Unions.*[5] After this project was completed, the participants formed a research group, the Tokyo University Trade-Union Research Center, which received a grant from the Ministry of Education. Specialists from other universities in Tokyo have joined the Center, and it has taken a leading role in advanced research in the field of industrial relations. The second achievement of the group was a research study on the representative national industrial unions, published in 1954. It was followed by a study of the labor market, taking Kanagawa Prefecture as a model of a highly industrialized area, the purpose being an analysis of the structure of the labor market as the basic factor affecting industrial relations. The result of this research was published in 1955. This group carried out further research on trade-union organizations and their functions at the shop or plant level. This inquiry was conducted in view of the importance of negotiations between trade-union organizations and management at the workshop level. The result of this research was also published in 1959 under the title *Structure and Functions of Labor Unions.*[6]

INSTITUTE ON LABOR DISPUTES.

The Institute on Labor Disputes is another interuniversity research group, which was formed in 1955, with Dr. Ichiro Nakayama at its head; he was joined by leading specialists in labor disputes, including members of the Central Labor Relations Commission. This group, with financial aid from the Asia Foundation, was engaged in the three-year project of making a comprehensive analytical study of the major disputes arising in postwar Japan. This research covered major industries, including coal, electricity, transportation, steel, textiles, and chemicals. Special inquiry was also made into the problems associated with labor disputes, such as unfair labor practices, collective bargaining agreements, lockouts, disputes in small and medium-sized enterprises and disputes involving national and local government employees. Their reports appeared in 15 volumes which were published between 1956 and 1960.

INSTITUTE FOR LABOR-MANAGEMENT RELATIONS.

This group is the successor of the Institute for Labor Disputes headed by Dr. Ichiro Nakayama. It soon embarked upon a research enterprise (a three-year project under the financial aid of the Asia Foundation) aimed at a comprehensive analytical study of labor-management relations in Japan. Here, special emphasis was placed on seeking out such stabilizing factors or expedients as are calculated to contribute to industrial peace. This group was divided into subgroups, each to conduct fact-finding research in major industries. Also, a special group for the international comparison of labor-management relations was formed to analyze the characteristics of industrial relations in Japan. This project is now successfully under way, and some reports will be published in due course.

COMMISSION FOR COMPILING THE DOCUMENTARY HISTORY OF THE JAPANESE LABOR MOVEMENT.

As research in industrial relations, particularly trade-unionism in postwar Japan, developed, it was recognized that the features and characteristics of Japanese industrial relations as they were then should be traced back to their formative stages in the prewar days. With this consideration in mind, a commission was founded in 1956, with a generous grant from the Ford Foundation. Specialists in the history of the labor movement in several leading universities (Tokyo, Keio, Hosei, St. Paul, Kyoto, and Doshisha) participated, with Professor Kazuo Okochi as their head. This commission is now about to complete its work, which will be published in 11 volumes under the title of *Historical Documents of the Japanese Labor Movement.*

As industrialism in Japan entered a new phase, there emerged a new need for research in this field. Favored by the prosperity that has continued for nearly a decade since 1955, the economic development of Japan has been spectacular, and, one could say, without counterpart in any country other than West Germany. New technology, innovation, and automation have had an impact which is now being acutely felt in almost every aspect of industrial relations. There is, on the one hand, a continuing substantial shortage of the younger workers and technically skilled workers required by new technology. On the other hand, it is becoming increasingly difficult for the middle-aged or older workers, whose skills have become obsolete, to meet the requirements of the new technology. The industrial pattern, traditionally based on the system of permanent attachment to a particular enterprise, has been faced with the necessity for drastic changes. The practices of hiring, promotion, wage determination, personnel administration, collective bargaining, and grievance procedures all must be re-examined and readjusted.

Research projects studying the impact of the new technology of industrial relations are now in progress. The Tokyo University Trade Union Research Center is conducting research on technical innovation and its impact on labor administration, taking as a model enterprises in the coal, steel, and shipbuilding industries. An interim report on this project was published in 1961.

The Japan Institute of Labor has also organized a research group which has been joined by many specialists from the universities of Tokyo. This is a three-year project, headed by Dr. Okochi, and aimed at the analysis of the effect of collective bargaining upon wage determination in some key industries.

The Institute of Industrial Relations, which was recently founded at Keio University, is engaged in research on the impact of technical innovations on industrial relations in Japan, taking the automobile and petrochemical industries as examples.

Another big problem which has emerged in the process of rapid industrial growth in recent years is labor relations in small or medium-sized industries. This sector of industry includes almost 90 per cent of all establishments and approximately 70 per cent of all employees. The workers have long been poorly organized—a circumstance which has enabled management to retain autocratic and patriarchal power over the employees. In general, the working conditions for these workers have long been far worse than those for employees in the big industries. Moreover, labor relations in the small and medium-sized establishments form a pattern quite different from that of big industry. This condition has persisted because of the large number of underemployed people. However, the situation has begun to change as a result of recent economic growth in Japan. Management in this sector has begun to suffer from a shortage of younger, skilled workers, and it has been forced to improve working conditions; this has brought about a narrowing of wage differentials between the big industries and the smaller ones. The organization drive, pushed by the national centers of labor unions, has showed considerable success. It seems clear that a fundamental change in labor relations in the small and medium-sized industries is now taking place. However, this process of modernization has been inevitably accompanied by trouble. In recent years there have been many labor disputes in this area involving bitter struggle and violence. This provides another challenging reason for research in labor relations. These research studies have been conducted at the local level, dealing with trade-union organizations; with wages and hours, particularly of the minimum wage system; with welfare programs; and with labor disputes.

IV. Conclusion

In concluding, I should like to attempt some assessment of the research that has been conducted in the past, pointing out some of the failures or shortcomings which prevented our research activities from developing in a more satisfactory way.

1) As a matter of fact, industrial relations in Japan has been changing so rapidly that research activities have not been able to keep pace with the requirements of developing situations. As mentioned above, there are several lines of approach in research on industrial relations. It must be admitted that we have failed to establish between the different lines of approach co-operation and co-ordination adequate to make the research activity efficient and comprehensive. Many of the research studies have been conducted on an individual basis; this has sometimes resulted in waste and overlapping.

2) Co-operation between the research organizations, particularly between academic circles and management, cannot be said to be satisfactorily established. It is regrettable that in the majority of cases management in Japan does not permit outside researchers free access to their establishments.

3) We have failed to develop comparative research in industrial relations on an international basis; however, considerable effort is being exerted in Japan to promote inquiry into industrial relations in other countries, particularly Great Britain and the United States. This is necessary if we are to benefit from the more modern patterns developed in the advanced

Western countries. However, it cannot truly be called a comparative study, but, rather, a simple introduction into Japan, a translation, of the systems or practices used in foreign countries. Research in the labor relations of foreign countries has not been adjusted or co-ordinated to the research in our own country. Moreover, we have been perhaps too hasty in taking for granted that the systems or practices in Western countries were more advanced than ours, and in taking them as examples. We have failed to conduct a study of systems in the underdeveloped countries, and our study of foreign countries is therefore one-sided.

If we are favored with the opportunity and measures to develop international co-operation in this field of research, through effective exchange of information and scholars, the research activity in our country will become more advanced and fruitful, and we will then be able to make an appropriate contribution toward peace and social welfare in Japan and in the world at large.

RESEARCH IN INDUSTRIAL RELATIONS IN CANADA

CHAPTER 3

by A. W. R. Carrothers

The major centers for research in labor relations in Canada are the educational institutions (particularly colleges and universities), the employers' associations, the trade-unions, and the government. Undoubtedly, the most significant of these are the universities and the government. It probably can be said that, in general, the research being done by industry and labor is self-serving and *ad hoc,* inasmuch as most of it is concerned with preparation for negotiations over the bargain-issues involved in making new agreements or renewing old ones. At any rate, little if any of it has proved to be of fundamental importance.

There is just now emerging in Canada a "labor college." It is the fruit of the co-operative efforts of the Canadian Labour Congress and the universities of McGill and

Montreal. It seems not to be laid out for research enterprises; it may become, however, an outlet for research findings. Its first educational program, for staff employees of the trade-unions, is to begin next year. It will take the form of a lecture course, to run for two or three sessions, for about seventy students each session. The program will probably start with senior staff personnel of the unions and, as it gets underway, it may be expanded for a wider audience. It appears that it is not at present designed for union members as such.

The two major sources of research in Canada at present are the government and the universities. Canada is a federal state. The provincial governments produce what are largely compilations of statistics—by-products of their activities in administering statutes which fall within their jurisdictions. However, the Federal Department of Labour does have a research program. It has published a monthly journal, the *Labour Gazette,* since 1900. This is a vehicle for the publication of statistical information collected by both the Department and the Bureau of Statistics and for summaries of research projects. It also publishes the results of some of the government's own research enterprises. After the war, the Department established the Labour Department–University Research Program, which has had a remarkable impact on research activities in the universities. The Program distributes funds to encourage research, either for the support of junior faculty members during summer vacations or for help in defraying expenses incident to research. It is vicarious research so far as the Department of Labour is concerned, but, without this financial support, I doubt if a fraction of that research would be undertaken. The Department itself has its legislative branch and its economics and research branches, all of which produce useful information.

In describing research in industrial relations carried out in the universities across Canada, I shall begin with the East Coast because that will lead me in the end to my own university, which I can tell you more about.

Dalhousie University in Halifax has had an Institute of Public Affairs for a good many years. At one time, it worked actively in the field of industrial relations, but its recent activities have been in other areas of public affairs. St. Francis Xavier University at Antigonish, Nova Scotia, has done pioneering work in the field of co-operatives, particularly in the fishing industry, but it has not been concerned directly with industrial relations research as we use the term.

We then come to an interesting and unique aspect of activities in Canada—the work in French-speaking Canada in the universities of Laval and Montreal. The Roman Catholic Church has played a unique role in industrial relations on the North American continent. Until recently, Quebec had an ultraconservative government. Segments of the Church, both at Laval and at Montreal, tended to take a much more liberal position in respect to industrial problems than did the government of the day. Laval survived the resulting pressures, but the Montreal program was attenuated. As a result, the Montreal program had to be recast; the Laval program persisted with a fair measure of continuity.

The University of McGill has had an Industrial Relations Center for a number of years. It has been active mainly in the postwar period. Its directing head, Professor H. D. Woods, built up a useful library and working collection of documentary information for management interests, has been active in organizing seminar programs for labor and management, and has published the proceedings of these seminars. Proof of the high regard in which the Center is held is shown by the fact that the new Labour College organized by the Canadian Labour Congress is under the joint auspices of the universities of McGill and Montreal.

Queens University at Kingston, Ontario, is developing a program of faculty research and graduate education. At the moment it is consolidating its program.

The University of Toronto started a program in the postwar period of popularity for centers or institutes of industrial relations. The program at Toronto was established on a five-year grant of money from industry. The program finally was relocated in the school of business administration.

Although the program at the University of British Columbia is in its infancy, I think it, too, is unique. We have attempted to learn from the experience of other groups in Canada and have set up an organization which we hope will grow as money and personnel become available. The standing committee on industrial relations at the University was dormant for a number of years because the labor situation in British Columbia made it extremely difficult for the University to determine its proper role in the field of industrial relations research. The general level of sophistication in the province was such that it was difficult, if not impossible, to determine what could be done responsibly and effectively.

The difficulties faced are highlighted by the embarrassing fact that the five basic industries of British Columbia are all within the category of highly strike-prone industries. These five industries are shipping and longshoring, logging, fishing, mining, and construction. Significantly, a recent important study by Clark Kerr and Abraham Siegel, about the interindustry propensity to strike, comes up with this list of the most strike-prone industries: shipping and longshoring, logging, fishing, mining, and textiles![1] When the hypotheses of Kerr and Siegel explaining the high propensity to strike are applied to the construction industry of British Columbia, it is apparent that it also rates among the top five.

Thus it is apparent that British Columbia has a sensitive problem so far as industrial relations are concerned. About three years ago, the board of governors of the University decided that something should be done. The committee on industrial relations organized a conference, to which Dr. Arthur M. Ross, of the Institute of Industrial Relations at Berkeley, California, was invited as speaker and adviser. Subsequently the committee recommended that there be an institute of industrial relations, to be oriented primarily to research. The board of governors accepted the recommendations, and the Institute of Industrial Relations was established.

The policies and programs of the Institute are relevant to the theme of this paper. The policies are five in number. First, a broad meaning is to be given to the term industrial relations, so that it will include not only the institutional aspects of industrial conflict, collective bargaining and negotiation, but, also, "human relations in industry." It is to be concerned with psychological problems on the shop floor, sociological aspects of the subject, and so on.

The second policy is that the Institute shall belong to no single faculty of the University, but shall be structured in such a way that it will be able to develop a truly inter-disciplinary program. We do have a program that involves a large number of disciplines, but I do not think the program will become truly inter-disciplinary until two things happen. First, we need to build up a body of basic data and a team skilled in industrial relations research on which to build the program. And second, we must break down the psychological barrier against inter-disciplinary research.

The third policy is that the Institute program shall be carried out by individuals who hold their primary appointments in an existing department or faculty of the University and who will be on loan to the Institute for a portion of their time during the academic year. The formula that we have worked out provides that the individual be on loan a third of his time. His teaching load will be cut by one third, and that third is to be spent on research in the institute. There are three reasons for this policy. First, it safeguards the quality of the work, inasmuch as the person is a teacher as well as a research man and is under the eyes of his own department. Second, it avoids setting up the Institute as a competitive organization and creating jealousies between the academic members of the faculty and persons engaged solely in research. Third, we see it as a device for strengthening existing departments in the field of industrial relations, since departments would be encouraged to bring men onto their faculties partly in order that they might lend them to the Institute and share in the research program of the Institute. This arrangement has indeed been successful. Four faculties have strengthened their departments in this field in order that they might share in our program.

The fourth policy is that the budget for the Institute shall be rooted in the general university budget and that funds will not be accepted from outside the university. This may sound strange, but we had seen what happened at the University of Toronto, had observed the difficulties that others were having at various places in Canada, and had heard about failures in other parts of North America. In each of those instances, funds had come mainly from industry; programs had been terminal, and, when the funds had been spent, the universities had staffs which they were unable to keep. In addition, the programs were suspect, on the theory that money talks, that he who pays the piper has a right to call the tune. So far we have been successful in keeping our souls out of hock!

The fifth policy is that the community program (which will be referred to later) shall be limited to the dissemination of the results of the research program.

The program of the Institute itself is divided into three branches—the faculty program, the graduate student educational program, and the community program. The faculty research program, resting in the loan of faculty members to the Institute for research purposes, is going ahead satisfactorily. The graduate student program is designed to attract high-quality students at the M.A. and Ph.D. levels. We provide $1500 research fellowships in order to insure that students will not have to work during the summer. Students work on their own projects, but with the full co-operation and support of the Institute.

The Institute itself does no teaching and carries out no institutional research program. It administers a program which is carried on through the co-operation of certain departments and faculty members in the rest of the University. The time may come when we will establish our own program, but we are not anxious to do so at the moment, because we are not satisfied that we are doing the student a favor by giving him, say, an M.A. in industrial relations as distinct from an M.A. in labor economics. We think it is better that the student have a degree in economics with emphasis on industrial relations (or in psychology with a similar emphasis) than that he appear to be an expert in industrial relations as such. We are satisfied, from the advice we have received and from our observations of other universities, that our policy in this area is a wise one, at least for the present.

The third branch of the program is the community program, divided into two parts—the general program and the university labor-education program. The community program is organized for labor, industry, and the general public. It consists of night lectures and courses on the published results of the research of faculty members and students. The only course presented so far was a ten-week course last winter, for labor and industry, on grievance arbitration. The textbook used was one by the present writer—a research study of grievance arbitration.[2] We hope next winter to have more of our research projects published, and we will then have a special community program for those who may be interested in the results of that research. This is a strictly limited program for the reason that we have seen how teachers elsewhere are being burned out by having to conduct seminars and courses at nights and during weekends.

There was established four or five years ago a university labor education committee to assist organized labor in developing its own programs. This plan was started all across Canada and has culminated in the establishment, in Montreal, of the Labour College, to which we have referred. We do not think that this will come about in British Columbia for some time since there are not the numbers in British Columbia to support such a program. Two years ago we organized and helped to administer a weekend seminar for the labor movement on problems of automation, and we assisted the labor movement in 1962 in a program centered on the administration of the collective agreement.

The policies of the Institute are shaped at the top by two important committees. One is the Faculty Advisory Committee, consisting of the deans and heads of departments of the cooperating faculties and departments and of others who are interested or knowledgeable in this field, including the president of the University and a member of its board of governors. The committee is responsible for determination of policy, and as its director [1960–1962], the present writer is under its instructions.

The other committee is the Community Advisory Committee. It is composed of five members from industry, five from labor, five public members, and five from the University, with the director of the Institute as chairman. The members are selected by invitation from the Faculty Advisory Committee and serve as individuals, not as representatives of the industry or labor organization from which they are drawn. The Community Advisory Committee has pledged itself to assist the Institute in its research program by making information available to the Institute, and thus, by providing ready access to organized labor and industry, is breaking down one of the barriers to field research. This arrangement has proved useful.

Within the Community Advisory Committee, the labor and faculty representatives also form a kind of subcommittee, called the University-Labor Education Committee. The public members of the main committee at the moment include three civil servants, and two members of the legal profession who are currently active in the settlement of industrial disputes. They are not identified with the interests of either labor or industry.

The research carried through or supported by the Institute so far may be divided into three areas: the area of settlement of industrial conflict, the area of human relations in industry, and the area of fiscal and monetary policies as they affect industrial relations.

As an illustration of studies in the area of settlement of industrial disputes, there is the study, just completed by Dr. S. M. Jamieson, of ten years of conflict in the construction industry in British Columbia. This work is scheduled for early publication. When it is published, we hope that it will provide a basic text for a course for management in the construction industry and for the building trade-unions. The publication should be useful to them in the handling of their affairs. Moreover, it should be of general interest to all those concerned with the settlement of industrial problems. Dr. Jamieson is now working on a comparative study of theories of industrial conflict. His point of departure is his study on the construction industry, but on a much broader base. My book, *Grievance Arbitration,* has been mentioned, and I have another study under way (scheduled for publication in 1964) on the Canadian law of collective bargaining. A student in the department of anthropology has just completed an M.A. thesis on wildcat strikes. He is concentrating on a logging community on Vancouver Island, British Columbia, and his study, in part, is an effort to determine whether the hypotheses of Kerr and Siegel, already referred to, conform to his findings for the logging industry. He seeks to demonstrate that some of the Kerr-Siegel hypotheses are less relevant—or less generally applicable— than they appear to be, and he is at the same time developing hypotheses of his own. It may well be that Kerr and Siegel are completely accurate in respect of the industries they studied. This student, on his part, may be discovering something new about British Columbian problems. In any event, it is a most exciting development, and it is particularly so to see this quality of work being done by someone still at the M.A. level. Another study in this field is one being conducted by a student in the department of sociology. It involves examination of the operations of conciliation boards by using the technique of the observation room and role playing.

The second field is in the area commonly referred to as "human relations in industry." Dr. N. A. Hall in the faculty of commerce has just completed an interesting study, "Roles of Union Leadership." He Boswellized half a dozen union officials for some months, watched what they did, how they behaved, and what their functions were within their respective unions. He followed that by a study of the union constitutions and has produced a very interesting report on how union officials behave and why. The report, when published, could very well constitute a text for a community program. Two men in sociology, Dr. Kaspar Naegele and Dr. R. A. H. Robson, are working in the field of determinants of occupational choice, i.e., why certain persons enter certain professions. The techniques these investigators are developing should be usable in determining why people choose the avocations they do, and in a country whose economy is causing such an alteration in manpower demands, it seems possible that what they discover may teach us how to insure that certain vocations or trades are sufficiently manned for the needs of our economy and how to avoid surpluses in crafts and vocations that are subject to obsolescence. In psychology, Dr. William Read is working in the field of communication and morale. He is on the threshold of this work at the moment. This summer the Institute is financing the cost of research assistants who will go out into the field, into plants and industries, making observations, taping answers to questionnaires and so on, with the co-operation of industry secured through the Community Advisory Committee.

The department of social work of the University has been making a study of the attitude of organized labor toward social welfare agencies in order to determine why organized labor is or is not interested in maximizing available social services. This inquiry seems likely to become a part of a broader study on the current and future objectives of organized labor in Canada. It is on this front that a study (now completed) by a German student is going to be most interesting. He is endeavoring to compare the Canadian movement with the American and the German, in which latter he has had some experience. He is formulating some interesting theories about the characteristics of organized labor in Canada. Mr. D. C. Aird in the faculty of commerce is working in the field of efficiency in the construction industry and has concluded that the labor force in the construction industry in British Columbia is idle 50 per cent of the time, most of which idleness is due to bad programing by management. This last winter he worked out of Queens University making a comparative examination in Ontario. This work now is completed.

In the field of fiscal and monetary problems, we have three studies going forward. One is by Professor Milton Moore, of the department of economics, on the relation between wage and price increases in British Columbia and Canada.

Another student is writing an M.A. thesis on "Causes of Changes in the Percentage Share of Labor in the National

Income." He is reviewing the statistical record for a period of fifty years and has found a variation of about 20 per cent in labor's share of the national income. He indicated in his most recent report that he had been isolating the actual differences and was about to try to determine why there should be such a variation. Still another student is writing an M.A. thesis on "Changes in Wage Rates and Productivity in the Mining Industry of British Columbia."

These are the research projects that are under way or completed at the present time.

Next year's research program will be participated in by at least four university departments: There will be one professor with research assistants and three graduate students in anthropology and sociology, two professors in commerce, a professor working during the summer with two research assistants in psychology and one professor and five graduate students in economics.

The program is deficient in four areas. The department of history, it is hoped, will play a part in the industrial relations program. The faculty of medicine should be interested in the program, particularly in the area of communication and morale, in questions of an aging working force, in aspects of geriatrics, and in problems of retraining. It is hoped that it will be possible to implicate the faculties of engineering and forestry.

Something should be said about research needs. Money, of course, is always needed. The whole program is going forward on a comparatively small budget. The first year's budget was $25,000; the second was $35,000; and the third was $40,000. The sum of $40,000 a year is not very much money for such an operation as this. Yet by distributing the money as we have done, we have supported some sixteen research projects. Two or three, very possibly, will fail. This year, fourteen more projects are being supported. Evidently good use is being made of the funds available. However, even if twice as much money were available, it is doubtful whether it would be possible to do twice as much work. The personnel are simply not available. There is in Canada a shortage of people qualified to do research in this field. We must move slowly and carefully in the hope that some of these young people who are doing M.A. and Ph.D. work will be induced to remain in the field of industrial relations.

There is difficulty in getting raw data. Probably there is not as much difficulty at the moment in getting access to information from industry and labor as there is in developing techniques for getting that information quickly, accurately, and inexpensively. Publication, probably, will be the next difficulty as far as money is concerned. No doubt, when the manuscripts become available, the money will be found. Finally, the findings and results must be circulated within the community. Research that is shelved is ineffective research.

I hope to find out how we can co-operate with the countries represented at this conference and how we can take advantage of their special offerings.

INDUSTRIAL RELATIONS RESEARCH IN AUSTRALIA

CHAPTER 4

by Edward I. Sykes

We have in Australia almost nothing in the way of organized group- or institution-inspired research. In this respect, Australian arrangements are in sharp contrast to those in Japan and, apparently, to those in Canada. Superficially, this may appear surprising, since our Australian system has been developing for a fairly long time, and it appears that we have developed, at the least, something which, from the viewpoint of other countries, is regarded as somewhat controversial. This lack of group-managed research activity is probably also responsible for another feature, namely, the very diverse interpretations given to our system of industrial relations by our own commentators. The lawyer, looking at the statutory arrangements, will in all likelihood arrive at one conclusion. Followers of another discipline, looking at what the system does, how it works, and what it accomplishes, are likely to draw other inferences. One consequence of this situation is the somewhat dismaying circumstance that has arisen in other countries—what I regard as a considerable misunderstanding of the basic aspects of our system and certain of its phases. For example, Australians are rather disposed to challenge the appropriateness of the word "authoritarian" as it is often applied to our system by foreign commentators.

I propose to divide what we have in Australia in the way of research in accordance with the source from which its inspiration comes. Perhaps I should preface this remark by saying that the lack of organized research as a branch of university activity, to which I shall later draw attention, can well be understood by reason of the obvious fact that even teaching in the category of industrial relations—in fact even the teaching of industrial law—is of comparatively recent origin. We feel that from an increase in teaching we are going to become more aware of what is meaningful in the way of research activity. At the moment, the universities lack money to expand what already is being done, let alone to push forward inquiries of an inter-disciplinary character.

Although this is only a short survey, perhaps I should say something of general application. The Australian system, as originally introduced, looked as if it were something that belonged to the lawyers. The result was rather to repel inquiries from other disciplines. This condition is still with us to some extent. As far as the lawyers themselves are concerned, they are still somewhat doubtful about the claims of the subject to be called "law." Industrial arbitration, forsooth, is neither law nor economics.

Among the sources from which research activities have emanated, let me first refer to the government. Note should be made of the activities of the Commonwealth Government statistician, who compiles statistical data relating to such matters as employment and unemployment figures, the number of industrial disputes, loss of manpower hours due to such disputes, and so on. He also records the number of trade-union registra-

tions, compiles figures relating to trade-union membership, and
the like. This is not really regarded as research. The Commonwealth statistician also produced an *Annual Labour Report*
which, I believe, is now two years behind time, but which,
nevertheless, contains valuable, even if belated, source materials for research workers. There is also a *Monthly Bulletin of
Employment Statistics.* As mentioned before, these publications amount to little more than repositories of statistical
data.

The Commonwealth Department of Labour and National
Service (a federal government instrumentality) is in a rather
different category. Although interested in the employment situation and the labor market, it does, through its personnel
practice branch, conduct active research in the field of personnel management. Current studies include the effect of earnings
and conditions of work, the effect of mechanization upon operators, the organizational structure of Australian employing
units, induction practices for new employees, and suggestion
schemes.

The Department publishes the *Industrial Information Bulletin,* which is for the most part a record of legal decisions
by the arbitration tribunals; in some instances it presents
merely condensed summaries of cases, but for important cases
it sets out in fairly full form the reasons for judgment and the
terms of the order made. These case records constitute important research sources for investigators who are interested in
the pattern, direction, and implications of the decisions. For
legal scholars this journal would seem to be of considerable
value. And the data included under the heading "General Industrial Information," perhaps especially the information set
out there on basic wage rates, would seem useful to the economic investigator. Such work is hardly research activity; but
another publication of the Department, the *Personnel Practices Bulletin,* is in a somewhat different class and does contain
the results of certain activities which we can well term "research."

The second category has to do with research activity emanat-
ing from management and labor. I do not need to spend much

time on this. The Australian Council of Trade Unions, usually called the ACTU, which is our most important and significant association of Australian trade-unions, does maintain a research officer, who currently, however, is almost entirely engaged in arbitration cases before the tribunals. Some of the state trades and labor councils maintain research officers. Some of the employer organizations publish journals and maintain what they call research departments. I think that this is all mainly self-serving—in the sense of providing fodder either for the preparation of cases currently proceeding in the arbitration tribunals or for propaganda purposes. The same might be said of what the trade-unions do.

Now we come to the universities, the third source. The only work which in any way could be described as having a group or co-operative character, is the study currently being undertaken by Professor R. Davis, now at Monash University, Victoria, and Dr. J. E. Isaac of the University of Melbourne. This project is a study of Australian trade-unions. The first part, by Professor Davis, is more broadly factual and institutional, a day-by-day account of what trade-unions do and the part they play; the second, by Dr. Isaac, is from an economic viewpoint. When I last heard from Professor Davis in 1961, he was undertaking a very painstaking examination of the various trade-unions in Victoria, going through all their internal records of proceedings back for many years. This all sounds very "long term" to me; also, Davis has since accepted the post at Monash University and possibly is busy with other activities.

As indicated in the beginning, there is a lack in Australia of what might be called group research. In view of this, I may be pardoned perhaps, particularly now that we have got to the universities, for spending a little time on individual research activities, and for coupling that with merely an outline of what is being done in the way of teaching. As mentioned once before, I think that only out of teaching will we in Australia eventually get to see what we want in the way of research and where we are lacking. As regards particular pieces of research in industrial relations, there are, first, in point of time of course (perhaps I should say, in all modesty, not necessarily first in dignity), the lawyers. We might say that up to World War II, studies of the arbitral systems emanated almost entirely from legal scholars. It is well known that Dr. Orwell Foenander of the University of Melbourne has written a number of books. He has been very prolific, though many people have been disposed to criticize his general approach.[1] There is a very good study of Australian trade-unions, not only from the aspect of the legal rules, but also from the viewpoint of the link-up between English historical development and Australian conditions, by Mr. J. H. Portus, a (federal) conciliation commissioner.[2] I have published two recent works, one of them being an examination of just how far strikes are in fact made unlawful in Australia.[3] Mr. D. C. Thomson, of the Sydney Law School, has written widely, though mainly in legal periodicals; a good deal of his material goes to the journal which Kingsley Laffer will be mentioning in his presentation.

So much for the lawyers. The second stream has consisted of writings by or from the standpoint of economists; I cannot think of any one big substantial contribution, but perhaps George Anderson's *Fixation of Wages in Australia*,[4] though by no means new, should be mentioned. There are contributions in economic journals; there have been considerable spirited discussions among economists as to the theoretical economic basis for the fixation by the Commonwealth Arbitration Court of the national "basic" wage and "margins" ("differentials" to people from collective bargaining countries). There are examinations of the economic basis on which the Court either proceeds or should proceed. Kingsley Laffer, of the University of Sydney, of course, is an economist, but he favors an interdisciplinary approach, and his studies of various industries have been made on that basis.

Third, there are surveys of particular industries which offer a measure of unified treatment. There is a study of industrial techniques in the schoolteaching service of the State of Western Australia that has just been completed. There should also be mentioned a study of the Western Australian building industry by R. Flecker and K. F. Walker, the latter a professor of psychology at the University of Western Australia. I should mention that Walker has contributed a good deal to this kind of study. The work entitled *Judges in Industry,* written by Dr. Mark Perlman,[5] an American economist, embodies the results of research done by him on his visit to Australia a few years ago, and comprises carefully conducted surveys of the shearing, metal trades, and waterfront industries in Australia.

Social and psychological studies, studies in human relations or behaviorism, have been late in getting under way in Australia. The most outstanding contributor in this field has been Professor K. F. Walker, to whom I have just referred. He has published a work on industrial relations [6] and is currently active in examining industrial relations in its socio-psychological aspects, and investigating current worker and management attitudes. "Worker" attitudes, be it noted, rather than trade-union attitudes.

At this stage, I would like to indicate briefly what is being actually taught. This is what we are perhaps more concerned about in Australia at the moment. As I have suggested, out of our teaching activities will probably grow the possibility that more will be done in the way of research. The subject of industrial relations is not really treated as a discipline in its own right in our universities. To be sure, there are courses in industrial law in at least four law schools. Yet, even here they are not regarded as necessary parts of the curricula; as a matter of fact, in some cases they are optional. In Sydney, until a year or so ago industrial law was not even an examination subject, though offered for lecture purposes. In Queensland, it is an optional item. The courses in industrial law are not bad; one defect is an undue concentration on English legal history in industrial matters up to about 1870. Such courses place emphasis on the *legal* rather than *sociological* aspects of the Australian compulsory arbitration system. However, I am not convinced that this is a fault. Lawyers in Australia, in general, may not be aware of the social undercurrents or backgrounds to the legal structure, but I do not think that can be said of legal thinking on industrial law. The lawyers, I think, are aware of the social and economic background.

Industrial relations, as distinct from industrial law, is

mainly taught as a division of the work of the faculties of economics in the various universities. This may be too much of a generalization. There is a separate subject called "industrial relations" in some universities, mainly taught as part of the curricula of the faculty of commerce or of economics. In my own university in Queensland, we have a subject called "labour economics," one half of which is very uneasily occupied by industrial relations. The nearest approach to something of an inter-disciplinary character is what Kingsley Laffer is doing, but even he is still functioning within the department of economics. There are some strange mixtures; for instance, in the University of New South Wales, students take as part of their commerce course a little economics, a little psychology, a little law, with nothing under the heading of "industrial relations."

I think I am warranted in saying that a fourth contributor to industrial relations research in Australia is the judiciary. In my judgment, this contribution of the "industrial" judges is significantly distinguishable from the (largely statistical) contributions of government departments. Reference here is to the grist of the Commonwealth and state industrial courts: their awards, orders, decisions, judgments, and "reasons for judgment." These constitute a body of source material for the exploration of Australian industrial relations more formidable —certainly more voluminous—than any other. The judgments in many cases comprise detailed histories of the industries involved and insights into their labor problems. In some cases there may be no more than the citation, seriatim, of earlier awards, that is to say, merely a history of the various awards which have come and gone, but in many cases the judgments involve the compilation of highly informative material as to the attitudes of labor and management in the industries dealt with. I do not hesitate to say that these cases involve a good deal of research and exploratory activity. The material is difficult to collect and can be quite illuminating. I think it is fair to say that these judicial activities are in the nature of research, although it is not research for the sake of research, but for a collateral purpose.

One of the most helpful developments, from our point of view, is the formation of the Industrial Relations Society and the publication of its journal. In Australia, the *Journal of Industrial Relations* is considered a very useful medium for the expression of views and a source of inspiration for continued research activity. The Society itself is a New South Wales product, but similar societies have now been formed in South Australia, Queensland, and Victoria. A distinctive feature is that membership is drawn from both management and the unions, as well as from the government, the legal profession, and the universities.

The field of labor relations research in Australia is far from fully cultivated. We desire, and need, more exchange of information with the specialists in other countries. We do not know exactly what we can give them; we need to analyze further what we ourselves have. Perhaps more information is needed in Australia about what its system really does. There is, perhaps, too much concentration on statutes, awards, and the like. All this may paint an unreal picture. It is not the peripheral emergency situation from which our system can be truly gauged, but from its day-to-day working.

Perhaps one may appropriately conclude with a quotation from Professor K. F. Walker: "It seems likely that our knowledge of Australian industrial relations will be much more adequate in another ten years, but it is likely to be far from complete because Australia reflects at present a particularly instructive type of cross current involving research of particular interest in view of the strength and maturity of its labour movement, its experiment with compulsory arbitration, and the fact noted by Ross and Hartman that it does not conform to the general pattern of development of industrial relations." [7]

Professor Walker concludes with the hope that scholars from other countries will participate fully in the research that is necessary to enhance such knowledge. This writer is happy to echo this hope.

DISPUTE PREVENTION AND SETTLEMENT

THE WORKING OF AUSTRALIAN COMPULSORY ARBITRATION

CHAPTER 5

by Kingsley M. Laffer

It is proposed herein to deal with our system in broad perspective as a set of arrangements for the settlement of industrial disputes.[1] One would like to think of it more broadly than that, as a set of arrangements designed to bring about "good" industrial relations, but this would be going beyond the current Australian conception of arbitration. The Australian system is a pluralistic one. We have a Commonwealth system, six state systems, and a number of special tribunals such as the Coal Industry Tribunal and the Commonwealth Public Service Arbitrator. There are many similarities among these bodies, also important differences.[2] I cannot discuss these here and shall refer mainly to the Commonwealth and New South Wales systems. From the standpoint of comparison with collective bargaining countries, all our systems are very much alike, and the differences are of relatively minor importance.[3] It will also be convenient in a general survey of this kind to avoid reference to changes in name, e.g., from "Court" to "Commission," or in powers, e.g., in respect to conciliative or judicial functions, that affect some of our arbitration tribunals from time to time. It may be noted, however, that in 1954 approximately 44.3 per cent of employed males and 37.2 per cent of employed females (excluding rural and domestic employees in both cases) were covered by Commonwealth awards, while 44.3 per cent of males and 54.9 per cent of females came under the various state awards. Only 11.4 per cent of males and 7.9 per cent of females did not come under any award and even these undoubtedly would be greatly affected indirectly. The Commonwealth system, covering as it does nearly half of all Australian employees under awards,[4] is of dominant importance, not only in its own right, but also because of its influence on many state awards. The state systems, however, do not slavishly follow the Commonwealth; they occasionally take initiatives which may be followed later by Commonwealth tribunals.

I. The Background

How did Australia come to develop this distinctive approach to the settlement of industrial disputes? The answer is complex, but part of it is to be found in the important role played by the state in Australia's early development and the attitudes toward state activity that were then built up. Australia began her history as a convict settlement and, as Marjorie Barnard says, "the habit of looking to the Government for everything, whilst adopting an attitude of critical hostility, began then."[5] At a later stage, railway and much other development had to be undertaken by governments because of the large amount of capital required and the uncertainty of profit prospects. Land legislation enacted by governments in an attempt to redistribute some of the land that had been pre-empted by the pastoralists is another example of resort to the state as an instrument of social reform. These are just a few examples from the nineteenth century of our readiness to accept a major role for the state in our affairs.

So, when serious maritime, shearing, and other strikes occurred in the 1890s, causing severe hardship to the community as well as to the parties directly concerned, with one of the parties usually reluctant to meet and negotiate a settlement, a movement for compulsory arbitration gained ground rapidly. New Zealand had introduced compulsory arbitration in 1894, and many people were impressed with the record of industrial peace in that country around the turn of the century, in comparison with the epidemics of disputes in Australia and Great Britain under collective bargaining. Wages boards established in Victoria in 1896 to deal with problems of "sweated labour" in certain industries did good work and helped to make trade-unions feel that arbitration could to some extent promote their interests. Largely through the efforts of Henry Bournes Higgins, who later became president of the Commonwealth Arbitration Court, at the constitutional convention preceding the adoption of federation in 1901, arbitral powers were provided in the Constitution of the new Commonwealth. Most of the states also adopted some form of compulsory arbitration or wages-board systems around this time or within a few years thereafter.

Another important aspect of the background to compulsory arbitration in Australia is the link between wages and the tariff. In effect, manufacturers said to the trade-unions, "We will support wage arbitration for you if you will support tariffs for us." [6] This link between wages and tariffs has been a major factor in the stability of our system. Many times, when arbitration tribunals have awarded wage increases, tariffs subsequently have been raised to enable manufacturers to pay them. The burden has fallen largely on the farm export industries. A very perceptive inquirer from the British Government, Ernest Aves, saw this as long ago as 1908. [7] He said Australia had been able to develop its distinctive system because the prosperity of her agricultural industry was such that she could afford it. Even today the conflict between employers and wage earners in Australia is to some extent a sham battle. The question is largely whether or not the workers will get something at the expense of the farmers. No doubt this is an over-simplification. Import-competing industries may fail to get the tariffs they desire, and in any case will have to wait for them. The export of manufactured goods is showing signs of becoming more important in our economy, and this will modify the working of the wage system. Historically, however, the link between wages and the tariff has been of fundamental importance.

II. Early Results

Compulsory arbitration achieved some early results which were valuable in an undeveloped economy such as Australia's was at the time. The system provided machinery, of which there was virtually none at the time of the maritime and shearing strikes, which compelled employers and trade-unions to get together. Collective-bargaining countries have developed their machinery differently; we provide it through government initiative. Very early our system provided two layers, so to speak, of minimum wages, on a largely uniform basis, made up of a basic wage, which is the minimum wage for an unskilled worker, and a margin (i.e., differential) based on the degree of skill, training, responsibility, unpleasantness of work, and the like. This system has proved to be of great assistance to weaker groups of workers, who have had their wages determined on the same principles as those of stronger groups. To an increasing extent, also, the conditions of work have been regulated by compulsory arbitration, and the legal sanction behind such regulation is valued highly by weak and strong unions alike.

Another early development, and perhaps the most important of all, is the legal recognition afforded to the trade-unions, who appeared before arbitration tribunals on a basis of legal equality with employers. The trade-unions were given a legally recognized status at a time when many of them were weak and insecure. Many employers did not like this at first, but in the course of time became used to dealing with unions, extended recognition to them, and in most cases established satisfactory relations with them. Instead of employers thinking of trade-unions as outside the pale, as they did in the 1890s, they came to accept them. This gradually led to modification of employer-employee conflicts. One of the major claims that can be made for our arbitration system is that it provided this foundation for workable employer-employee relations very early in Australian industrial development.[8]

III. *Characteristics of Australian Compulsory Arbitration Today*

INTEREST DISPUTES AND RIGHTS DISPUTES.

Turning now to the characteristics of the Australian system, it is important to realize, first, that it deals with conflicts over interests as well as with conflicts over rights, and a major part of its activity is concerned with conflicts over interests. In American terms, our arbitrators are likely to write the whole contract, thus determining the substantive issues between the parties, and not merely the grievances. If you look at one of our arbitration awards you will see that it looks very much like an American collective-bargaining contract, at least as far as subject-matter is concerned. The differences are mainly in detail, e.g., we have not given nearly as much attention to seniority problems as has been given them in the United States.

DIRECT NEGOTIATION WITHIN THE ARBITRATION FRAMEWORK.

Although our arbitration system deals with interest conflicts as well as with grievances, I hasten to add that our system is not an all-embracing one that excludes all direct negotiation and bargaining. Nothing could be further from the truth. First, as to grievances at the plant level, I suppose 99 per cent of these are dealt with on the spot without arbitration tribunals ever hearing of them. When the parties directly concerned cannot solve their problems, employer association and trade-union officials are often brought in from outside to help in effecting a settlement. Much is done in this way. Though we lack the formal grievance machinery of the United States, we have these informal procedures which do not work so badly. Some issues, however, are not thus settled, and the arbitration machinery is brought into play. There is much variety in this machinery in the different systems, but, to take an example, we have under the Commonwealth system officials called "commissioners." These commissioners are often quite remarkable for the lengths to which they will go to conciliate and persuade the parties to reach agreement. If, however, conciliation fails, the commissioner will arbitrate. It will be seen that there is a great deal of direct negotiation and conciliation in the settlement of grievances. It is a weakness of our system, however, that the commissioner who conciliates becomes the arbitrator if conciliation fails.[9] The commissioner in conciliation realizes that he may ultimately have to arbitrate and this will affect his suggestions to some extent. The attitudes of the parties might also be affected, as it might seem unwise in conciliation to make a concession that might tilt a subsequent arbitration decision against one. The pattern is somewhat complex, since under the Commonwealth system the interpretation of awards is now regarded as a judicial matter and is supposed to be handled by a special body, the Commonwealth Industrial Court. In fact, however, not a little implicit interpreting is done by the Commonwealth Conciliation and Arbitration Commission. For one thing, we do not normally make a sharp distinction between interest disputes and rights disputes; indeed this distinction is largely unknown in Australia. Arbitrators commonly go ahead and settle disputes of all kinds, in some cases even to the extent of varying the awards, if this seems expedient, unless some legal question of jurisdiction is brought up.

We come now more specifically to the making of new awards. After an award has run for, say, five years, a new award may be in order, i.e., a new contract in American terms. Now, even the drawing up of new awards is done in many industries very largely, and sometimes even completely, by the trade-unions and employers themselves. Even in industries where there are very militant unions, such as the seamen's union—a very left-wing union, with tough employers on the opposite side—the parties may work out much of the award themselves. As might be expected, there are usually some issues on which the parties cannot agree, and these will go to the arbitrator, though there are cases where agreement is complete. It should be noted, however, that when the parties are working out awards this way, they generally show much more flexibility when it comes to special conditions pertaining to their industry than over general matters, such as differentials, overtime rates, or the length of the working week. Employers will seldom, if ever, yield on these major matters for fear that it will create a precedent in other industries. They will say, "You'll have to go to arbitration on this." So, in fact, when parties are working out an award, in effect what they are often largely doing is trying to apply to their industry something which has been determined by arbitration elsewhere. Ultimately, everything that is done is done under the shadow of the arbitration system. Thus, negotiation and agreement do not have quite the same meaning under compulsory arbitration as under collective bargaining. Everything tends to be related to the standards set by arbitration.

It is important not to overlook our "industrial agreements," of which large numbers are in existence. They may be made between trade-unions and employers in single firms, or they may be broader than that; they may even cover a whole industry. They are usually reached without any assistance from arbitrators, and they frequently provide for wages and conditions above those of comparable awards. They are commonly registered with the arbitration authorities and when so registered have the legal force of awards and are no less binding on the parties than actual awards. Here one has an interesting combination of the legal sanctions of an award with the industrial relations aspects of direct negotiation.

Furthermore, arbitration awards provide only for minimum wages and conditions of work. There is nothing to prevent any employer from paying more than the minimum. So we have in Australia what we call "over-award payments," similar to what economists often describe as "wage-drift." A good engineering fitter, for example, might insist on and get, say, four pounds above the award rate. Under full employment, over-award payments have tended to grow, and they now amount to about 10 per cent of the total wage bill. Thus, in addition to the bargaining preliminary to arbitration, discussed above, we have on the periphery of our system a feature of growing importance, namely, bargaining about over-award payments on top of arbitration. Much of this is of an informal character, between the individual insisting on the going rate and the employer, but severe trade-union pressure and strike activity are often involved. There are also incentive systems, overtime arrangements, and the like, which result in rates above the arbitration minima. Over-award payments are becoming increasingly important and a great deal of direct negotiation is necessarily involved. It must be reiterated, however, that everything is done under the shadow of arbitration, and employers are very resistant to anything new that departs significantly from arbitration standards.

LEGALISM UNDER COMPULSORY ARBITRATION.

Next, it is necessary to deal with the question of "legalism." To begin with, Australia has a federal system, and this itself almost necessarily gives rise to a good deal of legalism. For example, the Commonwealth arbitration system is empowered under the Constitution to deal only with *industrial disputes,* so questions may arise as to whether there is a dispute and as to whether, if there is a dispute, it is *industrial.* The Commonwealth tribunals may deal only with interstate disputes, so it may have to be decided in the courts whether a particular dispute is an interstate one. With the passage of time, the decisions of our Courts have clarified the law concerning many of these matters, but new issues are continually arising. Sometimes, however, there are ways of getting around constitutional problems, and some of the judges have been extremely ingenious in finding ways of doing things that legally they could not do. For example, I know of one judge who would sometimes say, "Well, I can't legally deal with this matter under the Act, but if you will appoint me as your voluntary arbitrator and agree to accept my award I will arbitrate." This judge was very successful in his use of this approach. When, however, the industrial relations situation is such that people want to fight every inch of the way, our Constitution often affords wonderful opportunities.

The position of the trade-unions is of considerable interest. A trade-union may have some of its members working under Commonwealth awards and others under a state, say, a New South Wales award. In this case, it will be registered with both Commonwealth and New South Wales arbitration authorities. Confusion may follow. The union will be a corporate body under the Commonwealth Arbitration Act but not under that of New South Wales. The requirements as to the rules that have to be followed as a condition of registration are likely to differ in the two cases. The trade-union rules that will satisfy Commonwealth requirements may fail to satisfy state requirements, or vice versa, and it may be necessary to construct two sets of rules. One set of rules might be forgotten for a long time and then be brought to light by a dissident group wishing to make difficulties for those in control of the union, e.g., by claiming that they do not lawfully hold office. The legal problems that can arise are extremely complex.[10]

Legalism, however, may mean a number of different things. The above difficulties arise largely from the characteristics of the Australian federal system rather than from compulsory arbitration as such. Problems of a different kind arise from the virtual necessity for arbitration tribunals to deal with particular issues in the light of previously established principles. Such principles may need to be modified or adapted in the light of changing circumstances or to meet the special requirements of a particular situation, but such modification and adaption might not easily occur, especially if the arbitrator has a high regard for legal precedent. It has not always been recognized that much of the work of arbitration tribunals is of a legislative character [11] and that there may sometimes be considerable value, from an industrial relations standpoint, in flexibility of approach. For example, as we have seen, our Commonwealth arbitration tribunals determine a basic wage, and on top of that, a structure of margins (i.e., differentials) for skill and the like. During the postwar period, the real value of differentials, both absolute and relative to the basic wage, tended to be eroded as a result of the inflation which over the years 1947–1954 had led to large basic wage increases while margins remained relatively static. The Commonwealth arbitration tribunals persistently said, however, during this period, that it would be against their established principles [12] to adjust margins in the light of the changes in their purchasing power. Here one seems to have a legalistic application of principles to a new type of situation. We are paying the price today in the shortage of skilled labor.

A fascinating story is that of the professional engineers, who, over many years, failed to obtain salary increases which they claimed were necessary in order to attract people into the profession and help overcome the shortage that existed during a large part of the postwar period. When the engineers submitted their claims to the Commonwealth arbitration tribunal, the tribunal pointed out that it was against its established principles to award "attraction" wages, that wages were arbitrally determined on principles of comparative justice, rather than on the basis of what was deemed necessary to attract the labor. The engineers then shifted their ground and based their claim on their qualifications, responsibilities, and their need to maintain a professional status. On this footing they succeeded magnificently in their claim.[13] Such happenings are of course only to be expected where principles have to be laid down and followed and there is nothing inherently unreasonable about them. They do illustrate, however, a certain rigidity in our system. Parties have to lean over backwards to accord with the principles likely to be followed by tribunals, however artificial this might be in a particular situation and however far removed from the "real" issues the case put up might have to be.

Another point to be noted is that, in a system like ours, there must be some provision for appeals, e.g., to allow fuller account to be taken of broader national considerations or in case one happens to be assigned a conciliation commissioner or a judge who is a little lacking in common sense and does silly things. Rights of appeal have, however, often been used by parties largely to delay decisions, and sometimes cases have gone on

for years because of them. Rights of appeal have therefore
been restricted greatly in recent years. Many appeals must
nevertheless be allowed, and they often cause frustrating delays, especially when in the hands of those who give little
weight to industrial relations as compared to legal considerations.

There is, however, a possible qualification to what has been
said. Some of the examples of "legalism" cited have been taken
from the postwar period of full employment when our arbitration tribunals have been under tremendous pressure to raise
wages and improve conditions. When this is taken into account,
it might be possible to regard at least some of our legalism less
as an unfortunate aspect of Australian compulsory arbitration
than as an integral part of the working of the system, serving
the purpose of imposing delays in a period when tribunals were
under very heavy pressures of the kind indicated. Inconsistent
with this interpretation are the attempts made by legislators
and by the tribunals themselves to speed up procedures; con-
sistent with it are the built-in delays that nevertheless frequently manifest themselves.

It must also be pointed out that arbitration awards are legal
documents and that there is inevitably much controversy about
their provisions. This writer is advised, however, that under
American collective bargaining there are many disputes over
contracts and their interpretation that could come under the
heading of "legalism," and there is perhaps nothing especially
noteworthy about our arbitration system in this respect. There
is, however, a question of the procedures themselves. Much has
certainly been done to make our arbitration procedures more
informal, to recognize more explicitly the legislative nature of
much of the work of the tribunals, and to make arbitrators
more accessible to the parties in dispute. In some jurisdictions
the tribunals make much less use of legal phraseology and
precedent than formerly. Nevertheless, I am sure that any
visitor from overseas would say that by and large our procedures are still largely legal and judicial in content and in
appearance. Recent discussion has suggested that the conven-
tional legal process of cross-examination leaves something to

be desired as a means of enabling the members of the tribunals to get the evidence they want from expert witnesses.[14] Many arbitration procedures utilize the services of lawyers, and costs are sometimes very high. For example, it took the professional engineers several years to get their award; the various employers used every legal device available to them in their efforts to obstruct proceedings. The cost to the engineers was approximately £70,000.

Another legal aspect has to do with the penalties against strikes. They exist in the Commonwealth and in some state systems,[15] and arise from the conception of our system widely held in Australia that it is an application of the "rule of law" to industrial relations. It is held that people who benefit from arbitration awards should not be able to have it both ways by going on strike for something more. A variant is that those who do not abide by the umpire's decision should be penalized. This is the way our system has developed, and penalties against strikes have tended to increase in recent years. However, one might have developed instead the alternative concept that the wages and conditions awarded were welfare minima, similar for example to minimum safety conditions in factories. The parties might then be completely free in their bargaining concerning wages and conditions above the minima, instead of this freedom being qualified, as at present, by limitations on the right to strike. A system which placed more emphasis on the positive aspects of the development of "good" industrial relations and less emphasis on the mere settlement of disputes, would also have less regard for penalties. This is the approach I myself would prefer.

In fact, however, our system does make use of penalties, and two further comments may be made about them. First, penalties are not applied very often compared with the number of disputes,[16] and it is probably still true to say that they are a weapon of last resort in difficult cases rather than a routine characteristic of the system. There must be qualification here with respect to the growing tactical use by some employer organizations of applications both for "bans" clauses in awards forbidding strikes and for penalties. There is great danger that penalties may become an accepted everyday aspect of the working of the system. Second, in most industrial relations systems, ways have been devised to put pressure on people to go back to work, and the threat of penalties to some extent performs this function. A good example of this is to be found in Judge A. W. Foster's arbitration in the maritime industry.[17] The Judge hated to apply penalties and never did apply them in that industry, but he frequently threatened to do so, and with effect, when things seemed to be getting out of hand. It is difficult, however, when there are penalties, not to use them more than is desirable from an industrial relations standpoint, and this seems to be what is happening at present. Many employers readily choose the easy way of getting penalties applied rather than the hard way of improving their industrial relations procedures.

RECOGNITION AND REGULATION OF TRADE-UNIONS.

As the respresentatives of employees, trade-unions and other employee organizations must necessarily have certain rights before arbitration tribunals, and, in fact, they appear to be substantially on a basis of equality with employers and their associations. In the earlier days of trade-unionism, when the unions were struggling for acceptance by employers, recognition of them by the arbitration tribunals was of very great value to them and greatly assisted their development. However, the employers, although very reluctantly in some cases, became used to dealing with the unions and learned by experience the advantages of viable union-management relations. In more recent times, the organization of white-collar workers has been greatly assisted by the recognition of them under compulsory arbitration. From this standpoint, compulsory arbitration has contributed greatly to the development of a modern industrial relations system.

An interesting by-product of the Australian system is that a number of the important issues dealt with by arbitration are matters of common interest to both manual and white-collar workers. Thus, both groups are interested, not only in higher incomes, but also in the extension of annual leave, long-service leave, and the shortening of the working week. Attention to these common interests, assisted by a good deal of organizational astuteness on both sides, has helped the trade-union and white-collar organizations to maintain fairly close relations with each other.[18]

As a corollary of recognition has come regulation. The arbitral tribunals considered that they must satisfy themselves that the trade-unions recognized by them as representing certain groups of employees actually did so represent them, that their officials were properly elected, that their powers were appropriate and properly delimited, that their rules were reasonable, and that the rights of their individual members were respected. Thus compulsory arbitration has provided a comprehensive basis for the regulation of trade-union affairs.[19]

ECONOMIC ASPECTS.

Australian arbitration tribunals attempt to determine general wage levels according to the capacity of the economy to pay and differentials ("margins") in accordance with the principle of "comparative justice." This, perhaps, looks a little like the formulation and administration of a national wage policy, but any such impression would be a mistaken one. First, the arbitration tribunals determine minimum wages only; there is nothing to prevent employers from paying above the minima and they frequently do so. Second, the Commonwealth Government, which is responsible for monetary and tariff policies and the critical elements of fiscal policy, has no control over the wage determinations of arbitration tribunals. The arbitration tribunals, for their part, have to adapt themselves to governmental monetary, fiscal, and tariff policies as best they can, even if these happen to be inconsistent with the wage policies the tribunals would like to follow. Third, state governments can and sometimes do legislate so as to affect the discretion of state arbitration tribunals, e.g., in New South Wales, by requiring them to adjust the basic wage to changes in the cost of living. Finally, at any particular time the Commonwealth and the various state tribunals may not follow precisely the same principles or make similar determinations. The significance of these points should not be exaggerated. In fact, there is usually a high degree of uniformity and a good deal of implicit co-ordination. It would, however, be incorrect to call what emerges a national wage policy.

It will be convenient to focus attention on the Commonwealth arbitration tribunals as those of the states do not differ sufficiently in their determinations to materially affect the discussion. The general wage levels determined by the Commonwealth tribunals comprise a basic wage, together with a structure of margins (i.e., differentials) ; the latter are based very largely on a key determination of margins in the metal trades.[20] The main criterion in such general wage determination is the capacity of the economy to pay, though, in the important metal-trades-margins-determination, additional factors may be taken into account. In assessing capacity to pay, the Commonwealth Arbitration Commission strikes one as being rather opportunist, i.e., giving most weight to what seems important in the Australian economy at the time of the particular determination. If one may venture a generalization, it might be said with some warrant that over the years most weight has been given to the prosperity of the export industries and of the import-competing industries, both of which are largely indirect ways of looking at the balance of payments, the critical economic factor in an open economy like Australia's. As the Commonwealth Government's monetary and fiscal policies are also heavily influenced by balance-of-payments considerations, a certain amount of rough implicit co-ordination with government policy is achieved. However, special considerations are stressed from time to time in the Commission's determinations.

The economists' problem of shaping wage policy so as to achieve price stability under full employment has not been an overriding concern of the Commission, though there are signs that it is developing a more sophisticated awareness of this issue. When the results of loose monetary and fiscal policies of government or of administered price policies by industry are such that "wage justice" appears to require an increase in wages, the Commission grants the increase if it believes that the economy can afford it, even if it knows that some price increases will follow. Some leading Australian economists have been severely critical of these policies and of the procedures associated with them.[21] However, the writer does not propose to discuss these controversies now, but merely to make the point that the Australian system has not yet solved the wage-price problems involved. Probably, the situation requires a combination of further development of economic analysis, appropriate government monetary and fiscal policies, and improvements in industrial relations at the firm level in order to increase productivity, and the like. One may doubt whether compulsory arbitration as such has much to contribute to a solution.

Margins (i.e., differentials) are determined on principles of "comparative justice," which take into account such factors as differences in skill, responsibility, and unpleasantness of work. There are three problems here. First, the principle of comparative justice has been very favorable to weaker groups of workers, because they have been able to get their wages determined according to the skill, etc., involved in their work rather than according to their bargaining power. The practice of granting general basic wage and margins increases to almost all workers also helps them. Under full employment, however, stronger groups of workers often have been able to secure through direct bargaining "over-award" wages in excess of those prescribed by the tribunals. Differentials in favor of stronger groups are thus very slowly being established. Stronger groups, indeed, seem to some extent to get their wage increases "twice" when a general wage increase is superimposed on the over-award wages they have obtained for themselves.[22] Probably the only solution, if the Commission wishes to continue its traditional help to weaker groups, is for it to allow the wages of the stronger groups to be determined by collective bargaining and to concentrate on determining the wages of weaker groups in some appropriate relation to the bargained wages of stronger groups.

Second, there is the problem of "wage-drift" incident to the growth of over-award payments. Many Australian economists are greatly concerned about this, but it has been discussed sufficiently for our purpose under the previous heading.

Third, in following the principle of comparative justice, arbitrators largely ignore economic considerations of demand and supply and firmly set their faces against what are called "attraction wages," for fear of possible repercussions on other awards. This means that there is no easy mechanism for overcoming shortages, e.g., of some types of skilled tradesmen at present, by granting appropriate wage increases to stimulate supply. Resistance by employers to over-award wages makes these a slow and uncertain method of achieving the required wage incentive. Strangely enough, however, our relatively rigid system of wage determination does not appear to have unduly impeded mobility of labor. Opportunities for advancement arising from rapid industrial development and the flexibility arising from over-award payments, housing provisions, and the like seem to have taken care of this problem.

THE PUBLIC INTEREST.

It is a very strongly held tenet of supporters of compulsory arbitration in Australia that this system has special regard for the "public interest," since arbitrators in making decisions not only are concerned about the interests of the parties immediately before them but are also sensitive to the broader interests of the community at large. It is very difficult, however, to determine what this regard for the public interest amounts to in practice.

To take some examples, general wage levels, as we have seen, are determined according to the capacity of the economy to pay, not merely according to the interests of the parties, and the public interest is thus said to be taken into account. One must surely judge a system of wage determination, however, not by what is said about it, but by its results, and if one looks at such results as the amount of inflation or the level of strike activity in Australia, compared with conditions in other countries, it becomes very difficult to argue that our system works more in the public interest than the systems of other countries. Certainly in one respect, i.e., assistance to weaker groups of workers, our system probably achieves more than that of any other country, and, if one approves such a result, one may no

doubt say, if one wishes, that in this respect the system operates in the public interest. However, there does not seem to be
any advantage, other than a possible propagandist one, in
using such language. A better case for use of the term "public
interest" perhaps arises in the case of collusive efforts of
groups of employers and employees to raise both wages and
prices. In such situations, the arbitral tribunals understandably refuse, in the public interest, to sanction wage increases.
Cases of this kind, however, have not been numerous and do
not seem important enough to serve as a basis for attributing
any special "public interest" character to our system, especially as the Australian tribunals determine *minimum* wages
and cannot prevent collusion outside of their determinations.

As our arbitration system developed, it no doubt seemed
reasonable to envisage the development of machinery to settle
disputes as being in the public interest. What has been lost
sight of in Australia, however, is that collective bargaining
countries have developed their own distinctive types of procedures for settling disputes and that these developments could
in the same way, perhaps, be said to be in the "public interest."
In this respect, what is common between the two different
types of system seems much more significant than what is
different. There is the further point that one is always seeking
to improve one's dispute settlement procedures in one way or
another. Thus, the United States at present appears to be
seeking ways of putting more pressure on parties to effect
speedy settlements. Descriptions of any particular proposal as
being in the public interest seems more useful as propaganda
than as candid analysis of the workings of the system.

A CHANNEL FOR THE APPLICATION OF LEGISLATION.

The arbitration system is a very convenient channel for the
introduction of improvements (in working conditions) authorized by legislation. This is highly significant from a trade-
union and labor standpoint. Suppose, for example, the trade-
union movement wants to obtain more annual leave or
long-service leave for employees but has difficulty in getting
employers to agree. A common way of achieving the objective

is to persuade a Labour government in one of the states to introduce the desired change by legislation. Thus the New South Wales government in the last few years has introduced both long-service leave and increased annual leave. Subsequently, long-service leave has spread to other states,[23] and three-weeks annual leave is virtually certain to do so before very long. This is a way in which trade-unions achieve what may be regarded as "social reform." You obtain parliamentary legislation and the arbitration tribunals give effect to it in their awards. This cannot happen, however, in the Commonwealth sphere, because the Commonwealth Government lacks power under the Constitution to enact such legislation.

IV. Assessment

DEVELOPMENT.

There is a good deal of evaluation implied in what already has been said, and the points made need not be repeated in detail. It can be said broadly that compulsory arbitration provides useful machinery for dealing with industrial disputes, it assists the weaker groups of workers, and it recognizes the trade-unions and helps to give them a secure status in the community. This writer believes that, in undeveloped countries, there is much to be said for this kind of system. When, for example, you have employers very reluctant to recognize the trade-unions, there can be little doubt that a compulsory-arbitration system helps. We have today in Australia a vastly wider recognition of trade-unions than exists in the United States, and the Australian system undoubtedly has helped to achieve this prerequisite for the satisfactory operation of an industrial relations system.

The assistance rendered to weaker groups has, moreover, been of great help in our economic development. Australia's flow of immigrants averages about 100,000 a year, compared with a total population of just over 10 million. When added to natural increase this gives us a very high rate of population increase. Now one would expect that this rapid rate of immigration, with many newcomers incompletely unionized, looking for jobs and unacquainted with Australian notions of worker solidarity, would lead to a good deal of industrial friction. But, in fact, these newcomers have been protected completely by arbitration awards, and employers have had to pay them the award minima, so there has been little scope for the undercutting of wages and conditions. The Australian trade-unions have had little to fear. It seems unlikely that our immigration program could have been carried out nearly as smoothly in the absence of the arbitration system.

WAGES UNDER FULL EMPLOYMENT.

A second comment is that there is no evidence so far that compulsory arbitration can resolve the wage problems of a full-employment economy. The discussion of the problems of wage determination has suggested that the problem of checking inflation could well force the tribunals to choose between, on the one hand, allowing the wages of stronger groups of workers to be determined by collective bargaining and, on the other, largely abandoning their concern for the weaker groups of workers. In any case, the pressures of the market in recent years have produced in Australia a substantial increase in direct bargaining, e.g., concerning over-award payments, and while full employment continues, this trend seems likely to continue. My view is that, while a strong case can be made for compulsory arbitration in a developing economy with a labor surplus, the case is much weaker in a well-developed economy with full employment.

POLITICAL.

A third comment relates to the significance of compulsory arbitration from the standpoint of political theory. Pluralist political theories, with which this writer is in sympathy, would lead one to prefer collective bargaining. It would seem better for people to solve their own problems as far as possible rather than to have them solved by arbitral tribunals. Also, it seems desirable to have a number of centers of power in the community. A few years ago, however, I heard a very distinguished British economist, reasoning from a pluralist standpoint, describe the Australian system as "totalitarian." To be fair to our system, this seems just plain ridiculous.

Certainly, there is in the Australian system an authoritarian element, e.g., penalties against strikes, which does not normally obtain in collective-bargaining countries. The potentialities are no doubt there for judges or governments to exercise controls that could seriously weaken the trade-union movement. This writer would prefer a system in which these potentialities do not exist. In appropriate circumstances, however, such things could happen anywhere. What prevents them from happening are the political values and sanctions of the community. Australian arbitration is not imposed by a dictator. The system has been built upon statutes enacted by legislators elected by the people. It has the support of virtually all sections of the community, including employers, trade-unions, governments, and the major political parties. The arbitrators must act in accordance with the democratic political values of the community. Both they and the legislatures which frame the statutes under which they operate are subject to political and public criticism. Trade-union and employer organizations are strong and well organized. In economic matters, arbitrators are pretty much bound by market conditions which limit severely the area in which they can exercise discretion. If a tribunal were to act irresponsibly, e.g., by determining wages in such a way as to place an intolerable burden on export industries, it would probably find itself legislated out of existence. This is not to say that wages in Australia are exactly the same as they would be under collective bargaining. Unquestionably, arbitration has made differences, some of which have been alluded to. What is argued is that the political and economic framework within which the Australian system operates makes ridiculous the use of the term "totalitarian" in relation to it.

INDUSTRIAL RELATIONS.

In theory, collective bargaining, by bringing the parties face to face and forcing on them the need to reach a solution and take responsibility for it, should develop better industrial relations than does compulsory arbitration.[24] The differences in this respect between the two types of system do not seem, however, to be in any way spectacular, to say the least. Although this writer still is willing to argue that collective bargaining has a slight advantage, he doubts whether the controversy over compulsory arbitration *versus* collective bargaining is worth pursuing. What we must all try to do is to improve the effectiveness of the systems we have.

The true position seems to be that both compulsory arbitration and collective bargaining represent stages in the development of industrial relations systems in which great emphasis is placed on the development of procedures and machinery to help achieve peaceful settlement of industrial disputes. Historically, these have been valuable, indeed essential, developments. But it is a stage in which managements typically regard industrial relations as rather remote from their organizations' main interests, as very much of a nuisance, and as something to be hived off as much as possible to an industrial relations or personnel department or to an arbitration system and thought about as little as possible. Both collective bargaining and compulsory arbitration procedures suffer at present from being useful but ultimately very limited approaches to industrial relations problems.

Under both systems it seems necessary now to aim at a further stage in industrial relations development, giving more thought to the application of the large amount of industrial relations research that is being done, e.g., concerning the effects of organizational structure and of technology on industrial relations, and to the possibility of making fuller use of the decision-making and problem-solving capacities of employees.[25] Procedures for settling disputes must, of course, remain available in this next stage, but, instead of being regarded as all-important in themselves, they will become an adjunct to a broader and more fundamental approach to industrial relations.

STATUTORY DISPUTE SETTLEMENT IN INDIA

CHAPTER 6

by A. S. Mathur

Statutory measures for settlement of industrial disputes have developed in India mostly in the post-independence period since 1947. It had been the policy of the British Government not to intervene in the regulation of labor-management relations in private industries. Hence, during British rule, state intervention in the form of compulsory arbitration was confined mostly to the war period under the Defence of India Rules, 1942. The government of India has now evolved an industrial relations policy in consultation with the trade-unions and employers' associations, which finds expression in India's three Five-Year Plans. Lack of experience and a changing concept of state responsibility towards the working classes have necessitated frequent amendments in the statutory provisions to meet the growing and varying needs of both labor and industry.

The industrial relations policy of the government has been to encourage mutual settlement through collective bargaining and voluntary arbitration and thereby to reduce to a minimum any occasions for state intervention. If parties are unable to reconcile their differences through voluntary methods, state intervention through compulsory conciliation and compulsory arbitration is deemed necessary for industrial peace. The industrial disputes legislation of the country gives much discretion to the government, and this discretion has generally been used to settle disputes through compulsory conciliation and compulsory arbitration.

Systems of industrial relations machinery developed in various countries have to be viewed against the social, economic, and political conditions prevailing in those countries. International comparisons are difficult. Methods developed for settlement of industrial disputes in India should be studied in the light of her social and economic environment, the labor policy of the government, and the state of organization of workers and employers.

In India, labor is a subject on which both the Union [1] and state governments may concurrently legislate. We find, therefore, both central and state laws on industrial relations. The industrial relations legislation now in effect under the Union Government consists of three acts, viz., the Indian Trade Unions Act 1926, the Industrial Employment (Standing Orders) Act 1946, and the Industrial Disputes Act 1947; the first two were enacted during British rule. Separate industrial disputes laws have also been passed in Bombay, Uttar Pradesh, and Madhya Pradesh. Compulsory arbitration [2] through courts and tribunals is the key feature of the Indian system of industrial relations.

We take up first the Indian Trade Unions Act 1926. This Act was passed because of certain disabilities faced by the trade-union movement. There was a major dispute in Madras State, in 1920, involving the Buckingham Mills and the Madras Labor Union. The Mills sued the union for civil damages in the amount of $15,000 and applied for an injunction, which the court was pleased to grant. The court decision came as a great surprise to trade-unionists in India and in England. The British Trade Union Congress approached the Secretary of State and impressed upon him the necessity for legislation for the protection of the trade-union movement. The matter was also taken up by our trade-union leaders, and Mr. N. M. Joshi moved a resolution to this effect in the Legislative Assembly in 1921, requesting the government of India to pass trade-union legislation. This legislation (the Indian Trade Unions Act) was passed in the year 1926.

There are two aspects of the problem—one, registration, and two, recognition. The Trade Unions Act provides only for registration of unions. Registration is voluntary. It permits even employers' organizations to register under it. Some of the big employers' associations are listed as "trade-unions" under our Trade Union law. Any seven or more persons can get a union registered by the Registrar of Trade-Unions. Of course, they have to meet certain requirements stipulated in the Act. The general funds of a union cannot be utilized for political purposes. There is provision for cancellation of registration and also for appeal in case unions are aggrieved by the decisions of the registrar.

The question of recognition has been a somewhat controversial one in India. It was examined in 1931 by the Royal Commission on Labor. The Royal Commission recommended voluntary recognition. It did not favor compulsory recognition. The government took the view that employers should of their own volition recognize trade-unions. But it found that recognition by employers was not forthcoming, and, therefore, the Trade Unions Act was amended in 1946 to provide for compulsory recognition of unions fulfilling prescribed statutory conditions. One of the important conditions is that a union, to be recognized, should be representative of the employees. Where application for recognition is made by more than one union, the trade-union having the largest membership is to be given preference by the labour court. It may be noted that the Amendment Act, though it was passed in 1946, has not been enforced as yet, and at present unions cannot ask for statutory recognition. Under the Amendment Act of 1946 two types of recognition were provided. The first type was recognition by agreement, and the second was recognition by the order of the labour court, in case the employers did not recognize unions. The labour court was to consist of judicial officers of the rank of a high court or district judge. A registered trade-union which failed to get recognition from an employer could approach the labour court, and in case the labour court was satisfied that the union fulfilled requirements of the law, it was to make an order directing the employer to recognize the union. The present policy of the state seems to be not to have compulsory recognition. Some of the state governments have, however, gone ahead and made provision for compulsory recognition in their industrial disputes legislation.

To illustrate, we refer to the Bombay Industrial Relations Act, which is a state Act. The Bombay Industrial Relations Act provides for registration of four types of unions—representative union, qualified union, primary union, and approved union. In any local area, there cannot at any time be more than one registered union representing an industry.

In recent years, government has been using persuasion to get recognition for trade-unions. Some of these measures are reflected in the *Code of Discipline*. This Code was evolved through tripartite deliberations in 1957. Its objective is to maintain discipline in industry. It has been ratified by central organizations of employers and workers, and became effective as of June 1, 1958. This Code is a voluntary measure, and there is no compulsion of law behind it. One of the recommendations of the Code is that employers recognize those unions which satisfy the Code's criterion for the recognition of the unions. This criterion says that only one union will be recognized; the union which is to be recognized should have as its members at least 15 per cent of the workers in the establishment concerned. The union may be recognized as a representative union for an industry in a local area if it has a membership of at least 25 per cent of workers of that industry in that area.

The second statute is the Industrial Employment (Standing Orders) Act 1946. The purpose of this act is to require employers to define conditions of employment with regard to certain industrial matters which are laid down in it. Before 1946, employers were under no obligation to define the conditions of employment of workmen. Under this Act, the government has imposed an obligation on them to define service conditions for workmen regarding certain matters given in the schedule appended to the Act. This schedule is fairly comprehensive and covers many important industrial matters. These standing orders [3] are to be attested by the certifying officer under the Industrial Employment (Standing Orders) Act; and then they are to be posted in the places where workmen are employed, so that they may know what their conditions of employment are. By 1959, nearly 14,000 establishments, employing 4 million workers, had come under this law. Of these 14,000 establishments, 8,000 establishments employing 3.3 million workers had certified standing orders.

Before 1956, workers could not ask for a change in standing orders; this right was granted only to employers. Obviously, this was unfair to workmen. Subsequently, the 1956 Industrial Disputes (Amendment) Act modified certain provisions of the Industrial Employment (Standing Orders) Act and permitted both employers and workers to ask for a change in the standing orders. The second important modification has to do with certifying standing orders. Before 1956 certifying officers were not required to go into the fairness of the standing orders. If they covered specified matters and were in conformity with the provisions of the law, the certifying officer had to certify them. These provisions have now been amended, and the certifying officer can also look into the fairness of the standing orders. Parties aggrieved by the orders of the certifying officer have the right of appeal.

Some of the industrially advanced states felt that the Industrial Disputes Act 1947 of the Union Government did not meet their requirements fully, so they went ahead and passed their own industrial disputes laws. There are 15 states and 8 Union (or federal) territories in India. Three of the states, viz., Bombay, Uttar Pradesh, and Madhya Pradesh, have separate acts with jurisdiction confined to their respective areas. Bombay has been the pioneer state and so far has maintained her lead. In fact, sometimes central (or federal) law has been changed along the lines of the Bombay Act. Provisions of state legislation vary from state to state, but the laws of each of the three states provide for compulsory conciliation and compulsory arbitration for the settlement of industrial disputes.

Section 3 of the Uttar Pradesh Industrial Disputes Act will give some idea of the working of the conciliative and arbitral machinery in that state. It reads as follows: "If in the opinion of the state government it is necessary or expedient so to do for securing the public safety or convenience or the maintenance of public order or supplies and services essential to the life of the community or for maintaining employment, it may, by general or special order, make provision (a) for prohibiting, subject to the provision of the order, strikes or lockouts generally, or a strike or lockout in connection with any industrial dispute; (b) for requiring employers, workmen, or both, to observe for such period as may be specified in the order, such terms and conditions of employment as may be determined in accordance with the order." There is also a provision for appointment by the government of an authorized controller to carry on the trade or business or any public utility service if it is satisfied that it is necessary for the maintenance of supplies and services essential to the life of the community or the maintenance of employment. This can, however, be done only in the case of a public utility service.

We will confine ourselves to the Industrial Disputes Act of the Union Government, under which statutory machinery for settlement of industrial disputes has been established throughout the country, except in the above-mentioned three states. Growth and development of Industrial Disputes Legislation in India can be divided into four periods: First is the pre-independence period; second, the period between 1947 and mid-1950; third, the period from mid-1950 to 1956; and fourth, the period from August, 1956, to date. If we exclude wartime legislation, we have had only 16 years of experience with compulsory arbitration. Conciliation came much earlier, but extensive use of conciliation has also been resorted to only during the last sixteen years. Each of the afore-mentioned four periods discloses certain distinctive features of our system of conciliation and arbitration. The machinery is in the process of evolution. There has been no finality about it. The machinery has been changed from time to time to remove some of the difficulties experienced in the administration of the Act and to meet new situations.

The first legislation in the field of industrial relations was the Trade Disputes Act 1929. There were some important strikes in the winter of 1918–1919, and, by the winter of 1920–1921, industrial strife had become almost general in organized industry. Industrial Disputes Committees were appointed in March, 1921, in Bengal and in November, 1921, in Bombay, to go into this question and consider the possibility of alleviating industrial unrest. The Bengal Committee was opposed to state intervention except when both parties desired it. The Bombay Committee advocated the establishment of industrial courts under statutes. With the decrease of strikes in 1922–1923, both public and official interest in the matter tended to languish. The second wave of strikes came in 1928, and the question of settlement of industrial disputes once again engaged the serious attention of the government. Arbitration did not find favor with the government at that time, and only conciliation and investigation were provided for in the first statutes enacted in this field. There was no provision for settlement of disputes by arbitration in the first industrial disputes legislation passed, as noted above, in 1929.

The Trade Disputes Act was an experimental measure for five years, the legislature being uncertain as to what form permanent legislation should take. It was modeled to a large extent on the British Industrial Courts Act, but it did not provide for any standing industrial court or any other arbitral authority. It created only two authorities, viz., a court of enquiry and a board of conciliation. It made lightning strikes in public utilities punishable offenses. Fourteen days' notice for strikes and lockouts was required. The statute also contained provisions, along the lines of the clauses of the British Trade Disputes and Trade Unions Act, aimed at the prevention of general and political strikes. The Trade Disputes Act was made permanent in 1934.

Wartime legislation marks an emergency period. World War II broke out in 1939, and the ineffectiveness of the Trade Disputes Act in dealing with the emergent situation soon became apparent. It was therefore supplemented by Rule 81A of Defence of India Rules in January, 1942. This legislation gave the government powers (1) to make general or special orders to prohibit strikes or lockouts in connection with any trade dispute unless reasonable notice was given; (2) to refer any dispute to conciliation or adjudication (i.e., compulsory arbitration); (3) to require employers to observe such terms and conditions as might be specified; and (4) to enforce the decision of the adjudicators. It prohibited strikes and lockouts without 14 days' previous notice and during the pendency of conciliation and adjudication proceedings. Mahatma Gandhi launched the "Quit India" Movement in 1942 in the struggle for independence, asking the British Government to withdraw from India. The government wanted to prevent the workers from striking for the promotion of Indian independence. The Defence of India Rules were therefore amended in April, 1943, to prohibit concerted action in establishments employing one hundred or more persons, unless it was in furtherance of a genuine trade dispute.

With the cessation of hostilities in 1945, the period of war emergency came to an end. Popular governments were formed in April, 1946, and their assumption of office coincided with a spate of industrial disputes. For some time the machinery set up under Rule 81A of the Defence of India Rules, read with the Emergency Provisions (Continuation) Ordinance, was utilized. The Defence of India Rules were essentially wartime statutes; they expired, therefore, on September 30, 1946. The situation had deteriorated because of large-scale industrialization during the war period and the change-over from wartime to peacetime economy. The government of India, having had the experience of wartime operation of conciliation and arbitration, decided to retain both of these devices in the proposed industrial disputes legislation, which was designed for permanent postwar use. The new measure, the Industrial Disputes Act 1947, incorporating the provisions of both the Trade Disputes Act and the Defence of India Rules, was passed by the national legislature in March, effective as of April 1, 1947. It applies to the whole of India, except Jammu and Kashmir.

The Industrial Disputes Act 1947 has been frequently amended, but it continues to be the base on which the Indian system of conciliation and arbitration rests. Changes in the adjudicatory machinery have been frequent, whereas provisions regarding the conciliation services have remained very much the same. Amendments to the adjudicatory or arbitral provisions have been necessitated, both because of changes in the industrial relations policy of the government and because the courts have found legal or constitutional defects in the statutes.

The Industrial Disputes Act is a national (or federal) statute, but it is administered by the "appropriate government." This term means the central government in relation to any industrial dispute concerning any industry carried on by or under that government's authority; or by a railway company; or by any centrally controlled industry specified in the statute; or in relation to any industrial dispute concerning a banking or insurance company, mine, or oil field; or involving a major port. In relation to all other industrial disputes, "appropriate government" means the state government.

Authorities constituted under this act were conciliation officers and boards of conciliation for conciliation, industrial tribunals for adjudication, courts of enquiry for investigation, and works committees for negotiation. The act contains provisions for the modification or setting aside of the awards of the tribunals. It was felt when the legislation was enacted that the tribunals might not be in a position to assess properly the effects of the enforcement of their awards on the national economy. Discretion to decline to enforce awards opposed to public interests might become necessary. The power to reject or modify awards was vested solely in the legislature. If the government felt that it would be inexpedient, on the ground of public policy, to give effect to an award, it was required to refer the award to the legislature, which by a resolution could confirm, modify, or reject it. There was only one arbitral authority, viz., the industrial tribunal, and the parties had no right of appeal against its awards. Whatever was decided by the industrial tribunal was final and binding, subject to appeal on matters of law to the appropriate court, and subject also, as noted, to modification or rejection by the legislature.

The third period dates from mid-1950, with the enactment of the Industrial Disputes (Appellate Tribunal) Act in May of that year. The 1950 statute established the Labour Appellate Tribunal, to which parties were given the right of appeal from the awards of industrial tribunals on specified matters. The Appellate Tribunal functioned until 1956, when it was abolished under the Industrial Disputes (Amendment and Miscellaneous Provisions) Act. Two tribunals, therefore, functioned between 1950 and 1956. Industrial tribunals had original jurisdiction over industrial matters, and the Appellate Tribunal had appellate jurisdiction over their awards. Soon after the coming into effect of the Industrial Disputes Act 1947 the government recognized the necessity for a Central, All-India Tribunal to hear appeals from the decisions of industrial tribunals and other adjudicating authorities constituted under both federal and state laws. Industrial tribunals had now and again made conflicting awards. It seemed desirable, therefore, to have an "all-India" appeals tribunal for the sake of uniformity throughout India. It was also felt that there should be a court of appeal in industrial as in civil and criminal cases, so that aggrieved parties might have access to a higher court in industrial cases also. Difficulties were also being experienced by employers having branches in more than one state, since their employees might find themselves under the jurisdiction of more than one tribunal. Hence the Industrial Disputes (Appellate Tribunal) Act of 1950.

This measure necessitated changes in the Industrial Disputes Act 1947, and some of the provisions of the 1947 law consequently were amended by Appellate Statute of 1950. Authorities constituted under the original Industrial Disputes Act 1947 continued to function, but provisions regarding the modification and rejection of awards were considerably modified. Formerly the power to modify or reject awards was given only to the legislature. Under the 1950 statute, this power was vested in the government. Awards can now be rejected or modified by executive action by the government, but it is required as soon as possible thereafter to seek the approval of the legislature.

During this period, the government contemplated enactment of more comprehensive legislation on industrial relations, and to that end the Labour Relations Bill was introduced in 1950. It was framed at a time when the labor policy of the state had taken a definite shape and the First Five-Year Plan was under preparation. It sought to break new ground. It was to supersede the Industrial Disputes Act 1947 and similar legislation in the states, with a view to uniformity in the basic law governing industrial relations in India. This bill failed of enactment because of the strong opposition of labor. The bill lapsed after the dissolution of the Parliament on the eve of fresh elections. The government did not introduce the bill again, but some of its important provisions have been subsequently adopted piecemeal in suitably modified form through amendment acts.

Mention may be made of the two important new provisions for the settlement of disputes which the government sought to have introduced in 1950. They rejected the federal policy then prevailing. The government believed that negotiations should be attempted at every stage and not only after a strike had taken place or after a conciliation officer had been brought into the dispute. The Labour Relations Bill, therefore, contained provisions for compulsory collective bargaining. The government desired that there be no strikes or lockouts until the parties had come together and negotiated their differences. These provisions were to be tried as experimental measures in certain industries and in selected areas. The bill did not specify that negotiations should be successful or that collective bargaining should lead to an agreement. All that was intended was that the parties should come together for the purpose of negotiation or collective bargaining. Unless that was done, no strike or lockout could be legally undertaken. Compulsion was to be used indirectly to bring the parties together. They were to be completely free to act during negotiations. It was hoped that compulsory negotiation and compulsory collective bargaining would promote better understanding between the parties and lead to more amicable settlement of differences. These provisions have not been enacted as yet, and, at present, there is no statutory obligation on the parties to enter into negotiations or collective bargaining before declaring strikes or lockouts.

Another important development in this period was the application of the "Giri" approach to industrial relations. Mr. V. V. Giri, formerly federal Labour Minister, when he was in office in 1952–1953, wanted to encourage collective bargining. The controversy over compulsory arbitration and collective bargaining came into the limelight during his tenure of office and was discussed in various conferences. He wanted to delete the provisions regarding compulsory arbitration from the statute book. He thought that collective bargaining would be successful and that trade-unionism would not thrive in an atmosphere in which the law provided for settlement of disputes through compulsory arbitration. Mr. Giri subsequently modified his position. Existing conditions in the country convinced him that the statutory provisions regarding compulsory arbitration should be retained. The trade-unions were opposed to the removal of compulsory arbitration, as they felt that they were weak and would not be able to obtain the necessary benefits and concessions from employers without the help of the adjudicating machinery. The state governments also favoured the retention of industrial tribunals. They believed that unresolved differences should be settled, in the last resort, through compulsory arbitration and not through a trial of strength between the parties. State intervention was considered necessary in a planned economy where the state is committed to redress the balance in favor of the weaker segments of the society. Neither the state governments nor the trade-unions seem to have changed their attitudes towards compulsory arbitration during the last ten years.

The proposals made in 1950 were not shelved. They were simply postponed. Speedy justice is the keynote of the industrial relations policy of the government. Experience with the operations of the industrial tribunals had been gained during the last decade, and it was felt that certain amendments should be effected to remove certain shortcomings. The work of adjudication by the tribunals was increasing year by year, and in the absence of any other adjudicating machinery they were handling all types of labor disputes. Some difficulties were experienced in finding the right type of personnel for them. Parties were frequently exercising their rights of appeal to the Appellate Tribunal. All this was leading to inordinate delays and labor was clamoring for a change.

The government of India, therefore, amended the Industrial Disputes Act 1947 by enacting the Industrial Disputes (Amendment and Miscellaneous Provisions) Act 1956. Provisions regarding works committees, courts of enquiry, conciliation officers, and boards of conciliation remained more or less the same, but substantial changes were made in the machinery providing for the arbitration of disputes. New provisions regarding notice of change and voluntary arbitration were enacted. Formerly the employer was under no obligation to give notice of change, but the 1956 Act specifically provides that notice of change of at least three weeks is to be given in respect of specified matters. It is really surprising that, though the government had laid very great emphasis on settlement of disputes through voluntary arbitration, the Industrial Disputes Act 1947 did not contain any provisions regarding voluntary arbitration; these were finally incorporated by amendment in 1956. Now employers and workmen can enter into written agreements to refer their existing or apprehended disputes to the arbitrators mentioned in the agreement. Awards of the (voluntary) arbitrators are treated like the awards of the (compulsory) tribunals. Bipartite agreements are legally binding on the parties, as are settlements reached in conciliation.

Changes made in the statute of 1956 in the system of tribunals may be summarized as follows: The industrial tribunals and labor appellate tribunals have been replaced by a three-tier system consisting of a labor court, an industrial tribunal, and a national tribunal. Right of appeal (to the courts) has been withdrawn. Decisions of these three authorities are not subject to appeal to any higher tribunal. The Labour Appellate Tribunal was abolished because it did not make for the creation of a climate conducive to industrial peace. Litigation had increased and the policy of the state to encourage mutual settlement of differences had received a setback. Apprehensions of labor that there would be inordinate delays in arbitral proceedings were justified.

During this period, the federal government has twice been faced with the threat of a general strike by its own employees—once in 1957 and again in 1960. The federal government was of the opinion that the Industrial Disputes Act 1947 was not sufficient to meet the strike threat. Promulgation of essential services maintenance ordinances had to be resorted to on both occasions to prevent strikes and lockouts in essential services. An important feature of the ordinances was that the police were given the right to arrest without warrant any person who was suspected of having committed an offense under them. A number of union leaders were arrested and put behind bars under the ordinances.

The Constitution and functions of the various authorities created under the Industrial Disputes Act 1947 as in force today (under the 1956 amendments) may now be described:

Works committees had been recommended as early as in 1921. They were again recommended in 1931 by the Royal Commission on Labour, but statutory provision for their constitution was not made until 1947. Now all establishments which employ one hundred or more workers are required to set up works committees consisting of equal numbers of representatives of employers and employees. The function of these committees is to promote measures for the preservation of amicable relations between employers and workmen. India now has nearly 2,000 works committees. It is uncertain how far they have been successful. Some of the important factors which stand in the way of their successful functioning are multiplicity of trade-unions, rivalry in trade-union leadership, lack of satisfactory relationships between trade-unions and works committees, the illiteracy of workers, the hostile attitudes of employers, and delay in the implementation of decisions made by employers.

The function of the courts of enquiry is to investigate industrial matters and to submit reports thereon within six months. The courts consist of independent persons; little use has been made of them and very few have been established in the past.

Conciliation services are provided through conciliation officers and boards of conciliation. They are charged with the duty of mediating the settlement of disputes. Conciliation officers are government servants. They may be appointed for industries or regions. Boards of conciliation are constituted by the government. They are made up of a chairman and two or four other members. The chairman is an independent person and the other members are appointed on the recommendation of the parties to the dispute. Parties to the dispute are given equal representation on the boards. Conciliation officers must hold conciliation proceedings in public utility disputes when a notice of strike or lockout has been given. They are required to submit their reports within 14 days of the commencement of proceedings. Boards of conciliation are given two months to complete their proceedings. This period may be extended by agreement of the parties.

Compulsory arbitration is effectuated through three authorities, viz., the labor court, the industrial tribunal, and the national tribunal. No time limit is set for them to complete their proceedings. An important change made in 1956 is that each court and tribunal is to consist of only one person. Formerly they could be made up of more than one person. There will now be no more dissenting votes, as there is only one member. Industrial discontent will not be simmering beneath the observance of the majority judgment. This change will make for a more wholesome influence on the parties. The second important change is that now assessors can be appointed to help the courts and tribunals. Adjudicating authorities may require the help of persons from management or from the unions who possess special knowledge of the issues in dispute. Presiding officers of courts and tribunals may lack this knowledge.

Expert assistance is all the more necessary, as these awards and decisions are likely to have a profound influence on the economy of the country. Moreover, utilization of assessors appointed in consultation with the parties is likely to bring about a more acceptable award or agreement which parties may observe more readily. The government, under the amended Act, also may appoint two persons as assessors to advise the tribunals in proceedings before them. The Act further authorizes a court, industrial tribunal, or national tribunal, if it so thinks fit, to appoint one or more persons, having special knowledge of the matter in dispute, to serve as assessors. They may be additional to government-appointed assessors. The advice of assessors is not binding. It is hoped that this system will avoid the risk of unsound judgments and ill-conceived awards, and will ensure more speedy and informed decisions.

Labor courts, tribunals, and national tribunals are made up of judicial persons. The labor court consists of a person who has held judicial office in India for not less than seven years or who has been the presiding officer of a labor court constituted under any provincial or state act for not less than five years. The presiding officer of a tribunal or national tribunal is a person who is or who has been a judge of a high court or who has been chairman or a member of the Labour Appellate Tribunal, or of any other tribunal, for not less than two years. The presiding officer—who, under the 1956 statute, is the only officer—should be an independent person who is not connected with the industrial disputes referred to him or with the industry directly affected by such dispute. A person does not cease to be independent by reason only of the fact that he is a shareholder in a company affected or likely to be affected by the dispute. He is, however, required to disclose this information to the government. A presiding officer should be less than 65 years of age.

Labor courts and industrial tribunals are constituted by the appropriate government, which may be either the Union Government or a state government. A national tribunal can be set up only by the federal government. National tribunals are constituted for the adjudication of industrial disputes involv-

ing questions of national importance or affecting establishments in more than one state. This is the difference between the
industrial tribunal and the national tribunal. Labor courts and
industrial tribunals have no jurisdiction to adjudicate upon
any matter which is under adjudication before the national
tribunal. If a matter referred to a national tribunal for adjudication is pending before another court or tribunal, the proceedings related to that matter which are pending will be deemed to
have been quashed, and the matter will be decided by the
national tribunal only. The federal government has constituted
national tribunals on very few occasions.

Industrial matters have been classified in the statutes under
two schedules (Schedule 2 and Schedule 3), and the work of
adjudication has been divided between courts and tribunals on
the basis of this classification. The labor court is the competent
authority for adjudicating on industrial matters contained in
Schedule 2. These matters are the following: (1) the propriety
or legality of an order made by an employer and designed to be
a standing order in his establishment; (2) application and
interpretation of standing orders; (3) discharge or dismissal
of workmen; (4) withdrawal of any customary concession or
privilege; (5) illegality or otherwise of a strike or lockout; (6)
all matters other than those specified in the third schedule.

Industrial tribunals may adjudicate on any industrial matter
whether specified in Schedule 2 or Schedule 3. The following
matters are contained in Schedule 3: (1) wages; (2) compen-
satory and other allowances; (3) hours of work and rest inter-
vals; (4) leave with wages and holidays; (5) bonus, provident
fund, and gratuity; (6) shift arrangements; (7) classification
by grades; (8) disciplinary rules; (9) rationalization; (10)
retrenchment; (11) other matters that may be specified.

Labor courts are presided over by persons with lesser judicial experience and deal with industrial matters of a routine
type and of minor importance. They do not, unless the industrial dispute affects less than 100 workers, deal with matters
contained in Schedule 3. Since presiding officers of tribunals
are persons with greater judicial experience, they generally
deal only with industrial matters of major importance. Divi-

sion of work between courts and tribunals will lighten the work of both and ensure speedy disposal of disputes.

For the purposes of the industrial disputes legislation, industries have been broadly classified into two categories—public utility services and all other industry. Public utility services are also of two types. In the first category are those services in which government has no discretion and which must be treated as public utility services. In the second type are included those services in which government has discretion. If the government is satisfied that the emergency or the public interest so requires, it may declare any industries to be public utility services for specified periods. There is a tendency to bring more and more industries within the purview of public utility services so that conciliation and adjudication can be made obligatory for them.

In public utility services, at least 14 days' notice of strike or lockout must be given. After the notice has been received the conciliation officer must begin conciliation proceedings. No notice is prescribed in industries other than public utility services. The conciliation officer has discretion to hold conciliation proceedings even when notice of strike has not been given in public utility services or when the dispute does not concern public utilities. The government can refer any dispute to a board. If the dispute is settled during conciliation proceedings, a memorandum of the agreement is signed by the parties. If no settlement is reached, a full report is sent to the government, together with a statement of reasons why settlement could not be reached. The report of the conciliation proceedings will be considered by the government, and, if the government is satisfied, it will refer the industrial dispute to the labor court or tribunal for adjudication. In case the government decides not to make such a reference, parties to the dispute will be informed accordingly.

Government has discretion to refer at all times any disputes which exist or which are apprehended, together with related matters, to the appropriate adjudicating authority for decision. If the dispute relates to "a public utility service" and a notice of strike or lockout has been given, it becomes obligatory upon the government to refer the dispute to arbitration, even though other proceedings under the legislation in respect of the dispute may have commenced. The government is authorized, however, to use its discretion and to make no such reference if it considers "that the notice has been frivolously or vexatiously given or that it would be inexpedient so to do." Where the parties to an industrial dispute, whether jointly or separately, request that the dispute be referred to the labor court, tribunal, or national tribunal, the government must make the reference if it is satisfied that the persons applying represent the majority of their respective parties. These provisions reflect official policy towards settlement of disputes through adjudication. Differences in public utilities are to be settled through compulsory arbitration, as dislocation in their activities would seriously inconvenience the public. The government may refer an award for interpretation to a court or a tribunal.

The important difference between industrial law and civil and criminal law is that proceedings in industrial disputes before a labor tribunal cannot start until the government makes a reference to it. Parties cannot on their own approach it as in the case of civil and criminal courts. The government is the prime mover and must set in motion the machinery for adjudication.

It is specifically stated that no party can be represented by legal practitioners in conciliation proceedings. They may, however, be represented through lawyers in the arbitral proceedings before courts and tribunals with the consent of the other parties and permission of the presiding officers. At present, both labor and management prefer to represent their cases through legal practitioners.

A settlement remains in operation for such period as is agreed upon. When no period of effective operation is mentioned, an agreement remains in effect for six months. Ordinarily, an award of a court or tribunal remains in operation for one year, but the period of its operation may be extended or shortened by the government.

The Act contains specific provisions for limiting strikes and lockouts in public utility services and general provisions for regulating strikes and lockouts, which apply both to public utility and nonpublic utility services. A strike without notice or a lockout in public utility services is illegal. Strikes and lockouts are also prohibited in public utilities during the pendency of proceedings before a conciliation officer and for another seven days after the proceedings have concluded. General provisions which cover both public utility and nonpublic utility services prohibit strikes and lockouts during the pendency of proceedings before boards of conciliation, labor courts, and tribunals, and during any period a settlement or award is in operation in respect to the matters covered by the settlement or award. Strikes and lockouts are also illegal if undertaken in contravention of government orders prohibiting strikes and lockouts at the time of reference of disputes to boards, courts, or tribunals. Financial aid to illegal strikes and lockouts also is prohibited.

The Act contains provisions which curtail employers' rights to change conditions of service of workmen during pendency of conciliation and adjudication proceedings. There has been a fair amount of controversy over these provisions. Before 1956, the provision was that conditions of service regarding any industrial matters could not be changed during the pendency of proceedings. Employers felt that their rights had been unduly restricted. On their representation, the Act was amended in 1956, and a distinction has now been made between conditions of service regarding industrial matters connected with the dispute and which are pending before conciliation and arbitration authorities and those industrial matters which are not connected with the dispute. Conditions of service regarding the first type of matters cannot be changed without the permission of the authority before which the proceedings are pending. Conditions of service in respect of those matters which are not connected with the dispute can be changed according to the Standing Orders in effect in the particular establishment. Workers were afraid that this change might lead to victimization of trade-union officers. The government met their demands half-way by creating a class of "protected workmen" and giving them full protection. It has been specifically provided that their conditions of service, whether or not connected with the dispute, cannot be changed without permission from the authority before which proceedings are pending.

Protected workmen are those who, being officers of a registered trade-union connected with the establishment, are recognized as such in accordance with the rules. Their number should be one per cent of the total number of workmen employed, subject to a minimum of five and maximum of one hundred. Trade-union officers are given special protection, but it is for the government to decide as to which of the officers will be considered protected workmen for the purpose of the Act.

Conciliation and adjudication machinery in India is still in the process of evolution. New developments in the future may be expected in light of the fresh experience gained in the field of regulation of labor-management relations, the changing character of labor organizations and employers' associations, and the labor policy of the government in the framework of the Indian Constitution. Very often the approach of the government in a period has been affected by the personality of the man in charge at the time of the labor portfolio in the federal Cabinet.

There has been a growing realization that compulsory arbitration has not been an unmixed blessing. Large-scale industrial strife has been avoided, but at the same time a measure of aloofness and tension has developed between employers and workers. Serious and persistent attempts have therefore been made by the state in recent years, more especially since 1957, to counteract this unhealthy tendency and to regulate labor-management relations through voluntarily accepted codes and conventions developed in consultation with the central organizations of employers and workers. These codes and conventions are neither superimposed from above nor outlined by any statute. They are voluntary in character, and the parties accepting them are honor bound and under moral obligation to abide by their provisions. They symbolize the new policy of the state to build up industrial democracy and to preserve industrial peace with the help and co-operation of the parties.

THE NONSTATUTORY APPROACH TO THE SETTLEMENT OF INDUSTRIAL DISPUTES IN INDIA

CHAPTER 7

by Asoka Mehta

In attempting to describe the machinery and procedure for the settlement of industrial disputes in India, one must keep in mind the ideological and political framework of the country. Under British rule, the motive in introducing labor legislation seems to have been strictly selfish; thus, protective legislation was extended first to the cotton textile industry, where there was a distinct possibility of conflict arising between British and Indian commercial interests, but not to the coal mines or the plantation industry, where the threat did not appear so imminent. At that stage in industrial development, the cotton textile industry had the largest amount of capital investment and was the major industrial employer. As a result of this early bias, Indian opinion came to consider labor legislation as the tool of an alien government, directed primarily toward crippling indigenous industrial development. This controversy vitiated, for quite some time, the entire approach to labor problems and labor-management relations.

In 1918, Mahatma Gandhi entered the political scene and inspired a national awakening; the impact of his personality can also be found in the labor field. His basic approach was that of a philosophical anarchist who distrusted the entire machinery of the state, particularly in the case of a state controlled by an alien ruler. He favored voluntary arbitration, and made it the basis of his theory of the labor movement. He felt that it was not civilized behavior on the part of workers to strike or of employers to declare a lockout. In the major textile center of Ahmedabad, he developed a system of voluntary arbitration that rigorously excluded any attempt at state intervention. Even today, a succession of labor ministers at the Centre (federal level) and in the states (provincial level) preserve the Gandhian tradition in labor relations and display an evident bias against compulsory arbitration.

Turning now to the facts of the situation, one must accept the fact that the Indian Trade Union movement is weak and fragmented. Data available for the period 1951–1960 indicate that, while the number of registered trade-unions has more than doubled (from about 4,600 to 10,800 unions), the total membership has not increased proportionately (from 2 million to 4 million members). Average membership during the period has decreased from 780 to 600 members per union. Further scrutiny of these data shows that about 40 per cent of all unions have less than 100 members each, and together account for about 3 per cent of the total membership; at the other extreme, 1 per cent of the unions have a membership of over 10,000 each and account for about 40 per cent of total membership. Most of these large unions are concentrated in the railways, posts, and telegraphs (nationalized undertakings) and in the mines and plantation industries. Most of the smaller unions are listed under the classification "manufacturing and allied industries," which covers more than 40 per cent of all trade-unions, but a little less than 40 per cent of total membership.

It is part of a vicious circle that, because most unions are weak, their membership small, and their resources limited, employers are reluctant to recognize unions as effective bargaining agents. The result is that the smaller unions tend to seek the protection of the industrial courts, where they can expect some implicit recognition of their status and, more important, some relief in respect to the claims which they put forward on behalf of their members. When an earlier federal labor minister, Mr. V. V. Giri, tried to dismantle the existing machinery of compulsory arbitration and move directly towards collective bargaining, he found that the unions were not ready for such a step. They felt that they would be at a considerable disadvantage vis-à-vis industrial employers, and, therefore, it would be better to retain the existing machinery of adjudication.

The traditional machinery for joint consultation at the national level is the Indian Labour Conference, which was set up in 1942 on the model of the International Labour Conference. It is tripartite in character and brings together representatives of the workers, employers, and government in a discussion of labor issues. The Conference meets once a year, and, although the decisions arrived at are not legally binding, the consensus acquires the strength and character of a national labor policy, operating on a voluntary basis. This tripartite opinion is directly reflected in the legislative and administrative action taken by the government and in the standards set by the workers and employers in the conduct of their day-to-day affairs.

While the attention of the Indian Labour Conference is directed mainly towards a broad analysis of labor policy and the underlying principles involved, matters of detail are dealt with by supporting machinery, such as, the Labour Ministers' Conference, the Standing Labour Committee, and the various industrial committees that have been set up to examine the specific labor problems of individual industries, such as plantations, coal mines, cotton textiles, and cement.

To cite an instance where the Indian Labour Conference gave a specific direction to thinking on labor matters, there is the Fair Wages Committee which was set up by government in

1948 at the instance of the Conference. A little earlier, in 1947, the Conference had accepted the terms of an Industrial Truce Resolution, and it felt that the determination of a fair wage for workers would be a logical follow-through, especially as the entire wage system seemed to lack rationale.

Under British rule, the country was divided into two distinct factions: British India with a democratic pattern of elected legislatures, on the one hand, and, on the other, over 500 princely states with an autocratic internal administration, quite free from troublesome details such as income tax or factory legislation. Naturally, entrepreneurs were encouraged to set up industrial units in these states where, from their point of view, conditions were favorable.

The reports of the Fair Wages Committee helped to arrive at some measure of agreement on wage fixation in what, till then, was a chaotic field. It recommended, with a sense of realism, that the fair wage should be set somewhere between the lower limit of a minimum wage and the upper limit of the capacity of the industry to pay a living wage. For the first time, the Committee prescribed definite criteria for determining the actual wage in terms of (a) the productivity of labor; (b) the prevailing rates of wages; (c) the level of the national income and its distribution; and (d) the place of the industry in the economy of the country. These criteria have been used in later years by pay commissions, wage boards, and industrial courts in translating the remuneration paid to a worker in more concrete terms, such as food, clothing, and housing.

The scope of these tripartite committees is as wide as the labor field itself. Their particular contribution is to focus public attention on current problems and to help evolve acceptable solutions. For example, during the depression years of the 1930s, and later during World War II, many Indian industries were allowed to run down, very little money was ploughed back, and few of the machines were replaced. On achieving independence, the new government found it necessary to set up rationalization committees to recommend a phased program for the replacement and modernization of machinery and also to suggest a basis for sharing the resultant benefits and bur-

dens among the workers, employers, and the consuming public.
Thus, it was possible to arrive at a formula for sharing the
gains achieved through higher productivity and to work out a
plan for retraining and absorbing in employment the workers
who were declared surplus.

Up to now, we have been dealing with a rather traditional
approach to labor relations. In the context of planned development, it was felt that, while government intervention could
help keep work stoppages to the minimum, a radical change
would be necessary if production targets were to be achieved in
full and on schedule. In 1958, a *Code of Discipline in Industry* [1]
was evolved with the intention of giving a more positive orien-
tation to industrial relations, based on moral rather than on
legal sanctions. This is an extra-legal code; it is not supported
by any legal sanctions and has been accepted on a voluntary
basis by the Central organizations of workers and employers
and, also, by government. The Code enumerates specific responsibilities for management, unions, and the government;
the entire effort is aimed at securing maximum production and
raising productivity standards. The Code does not play favor-
ites; it covers industrial units in both the public and private
sectors. It tries to anticipate the type of problem that occurs
most often, prescribes a basis for the recognition of unions, and
suggests a model grievance procedure for adoption in industry.
It has been said that the Code is rather amorphous, and yet it
fits perfectly into the Indian scene and, most important of all, it
works.

At about the same time, a *Code of Conduct* was drafted for
trade-unions. In India, as in most other countries, union leaders are faced by problems that are very similar: how to get
workers to join the unions and pay their dues, and how to keep
them from switching loyalties to a rival union. The Indian
situation has its strengths and weaknesses. The movement is
not organized on the basis of craft unions, but on the basis of
industry. There is, however, a considerable amount of trade-
union rivalry based not on jurisdictional issues but on political
affiliation. As a matter of historical tradition, Indian trade-
unions owe much to the inspired leadership provided by "out-

siders" drawn from among social workers and politicians, persons who were affected by the conditions that prevailed in the early stages of industrial development. Today, every important political party has its own trade-union wing, and most major trade-unions are affiliated in some way with a particular political party. The *Code of Conduct* is intended to permit the worker to select the union of his choice and to check attempts at intimidation and violence.

The codes are supported in a practical manner by a system designed to keep frivolous disputes to a minimum and to ensure that awards and agreements, once arrived at, are implemented correctly. Screening committees have been set up by employers' and workers' organizations to check on the validity of disputes and to see that there is some basic justification for filing an appeal from the decision of a lower court. Implementation and evaluation divisions have been set up by government at the Centre and in the states to keep track of any violations of the codes mentioned above, and to follow up failures to implement industrial awards or collective bargaining agreements. The whole emphasis is on building up a body of public opinion that will have an inhibiting influence on potential violators of the codes and agreements.

A tripartite body has also drawn up a *Code of Efficiency and Welfare*, with a view to defining for the worker his place in the framework of industry and to arrive at an agreed basis for sharing the gains of productivity. The question of implementing this code has been deferred for the present.

With the successful working of the codes, it has been considered logical to extend the tripartite approach to the vexed subject of wage determination. In the past, wage disputes at the level of an individual unit or a group of units in a local area were usually referred to the industrial court for decision. These awards have given rise to numerous local variations in wage determination. In recent years, there has been a trend towards reference of wage disputes in an entire industry to a wage board set up at the national level. These wage boards are usually tripartite in character, i.e., they include representatives of employers, workers, and "independent" persons,

with the chairman drawn from among the "independents."
(This category of "independents" is usually drawn from
among economists or members of Parliament with the reputation for being well informed and impartial.) The terms of
reference to the boards are drawn up in advance by agreement,
and it has been traditional that all unanimous recommendations by the boards are accepted and implemented by both
parties. These recommendations do not have a legal basis, but it
has been found through the process of getting the parties to
state their cases in writing, or orally, that most of the unreasonable claims tend to get watered down or completely removed. Another welcome feature of the wage board recommendations is that they are essentially long-term in character, say
three to five years, and it would require a major shift in conditions before either of the parties would be in a position to
suggest the need for review. Such wage boards have been set up
in a number of major industries with nationwide implications,
e.g., cotton and jute textiles, cement, sugar, plantations, iron
and steel, and coal.

This tripartite basis has also been extended to the Bonus
Commission whose report is currently awaited. In this way an
effort has been made for the first time to establish a direct link
between wages and productivity.

In this context, it is also necessary to draw attention to the
Industrial Truce Resolution of November, 1962, which was
evolved in the wake of the national emergency declared under
the threat of external aggression. The resolution embodied
unanimous agreement to the sinking of all partisan differences
and the firm determination to mobilize all resources as a ges-
ture of national unity.

One must draw attention to a special section of the labor
force, i.e., the government servants, whose service conditions
are regulated by special machinery. Workers in state-owned
industrial units are covered by the usual factory laws, but these
laws do not extend to non-industrial workers in government
offices, the railways, the post and telegraphs operations, and
so forth. About once every ten years, a Central Pay Commission is appointed by the government to examine the entire

wage structure, starting from the top civil servants and going down to the lowest paid messenger. They usually take into account any changes that have taken place in the pattern and content of administration and try to make up any differences that may have arisen since the last report. The Commission is usually headed by a senior judge, who is assisted by some eminent persons, including an economist or an experienced administrator.

The recommendations of the Commission are not binding on the government, but are discussed in Parliament and are usually accepted without any major modification. There was an unfortunate exception when the last Commission recommended that the wage should be linked directly to increases in the cost-of-living index. Government countered by abolishing the All-India cost-of-living index. This caused much resentment, culminating in 1960 in a general strike of government servants that tied up the entire country. Firm action was taken by the government, and the strike was broken in a very short time. One does have a certain amount of sympathy for the woes of the educated middle-class government employee or the factory worker in the urban areas, struggling with a strict budget and rising prices. But he is lucky to be a wage earner with a secure job and as such he is much better off than his brother in the village. As a result, it was not very difficult to make invidious comparisons and to build up a considerable amount of public pressure against strike action taken by government servants. The strike was broken, certain concessions have since been made, and there is a suggestion that Whitley Councils, on the British model, be set up.

One would also like to draw attention to certain new programs that have been undertaken on an experimental basis. A program of workers' education has been organized with the intention of building up well-informed and articulate union members drawn from the ranks of workers, who would be capable of running their own unions and negotiating with management on matters that affect them. The workers' education program envisages the setting up of a network of training classes that will reach right down to the plant level and provide for the training of a cadre of worker-teachers and worker-administrators.

The other scheme refers to workers' participation in the management of industry and is considered to be a logical outcome of the legitimate aspirations of labor and the declared objective of a socialist pattern of society, that has been accepted by the country as one of the major national goals. After the expert study of foreign experience, it was agreed in a tripartite meeting that a start should be made with the scheme on a strictly voluntary basis. Joint management councils have been set up so far in a number of units, and, apart from consulting the workers on matters that directly affect them, they have been entrusted with executive responsibility for certain matters, such as training, welfare, and safety.

In conclusion, one can say that in this sensitive area of labor-management relations, the area of agreement is steadily increasing. The tripartite approach is being utilized with a considerable measure of success to evolve a consensus on vital labor issues. The success of these experiments has been guaranteed in a very substantial way by the agreement of all sections of the community—the workers, the employers, and the general public—that nothing must interfere with planned development. If these development programs are to be completed according to schedule, it will be necessary to enforce a certain measure of economic discipline. The encouraging feature of the industrial relations scene in India today is that this discipline is being enforced on a voluntary basis by the various parties, with an understanding of mutual problems. It is evident that when faced by the challenge of economic growth, the various interests involved are prepared to transcend political and industrial controversies.

SETTLEMENT OF INDUSTRIAL DISPUTES IN NEW ZEALAND

CHAPTER 8

by Arthur Tyndall

New Zealand has an area of 103,000 square miles and a population of 2½ million persons, of which 175,000 are Maoris. It is predominantly a pastoral country and derives its economic advantage from its ability to grow grass. It supports 6½ million cattle (of which nearly 2 million are dairy cows in milk) and about 50 million sheep, equivalent to 20 per head of population. Ninety-four per cent of its exports are pastoral products, the main items being wool, meat, and dairy produce, together with associated by-products such as skins, hides, tallow, etc. The total labor force is estimated to be 917,000, of which 16 per cent is engaged in primary production, 25 per cent in manufacturing, 9 per cent in construction, and 50 per cent in the provision of services.

The settlement of industrial disputes in New Zealand is governed mainly by the Industrial Conciliation and Arbitration Act 1954 and its amendments (referred to for convenience hereinafter as the I.C. & A. Act). There are also a number of other statutes which have a bearing on industrial relations and on terms and conditions of employment; notably, the Labour Disputes Investigation Act 1913, Minimum Wage Act 1945, Factories Act 1946, Shops and Offices Act 1955, Annual Holidays Act 1944, Industrial Relations Act 1949, Apprentices Act 1948, Agricultural Workers Act 1936, Waterfront Industry Act 1953, Government Service Tribunal Act 1948, and Government Railways Act 1949. The original I.C. & A. Act was placed on the New Zealand Statute Books in 1894. Its object was to encourage the formation of industrial unions and associations of both workers and employers and to facilitate the settlement of industrial disputes by conciliation and arbitration. The system is based on the voluntary registration of industrial unions and associations. Industrial unions must be registered before the machinery of the Act can be invoked. Industrial associations representing any number of affiliated industrial unions in the same or in related industries may also be registered. The following statistics disclose the extent to which industrial unions and associations have been formed since the original Act was passed.

In the year 1900, there were about 200 registered industrial unions of workers with a total membership of approximately 18,000. By December 31, 1962, the total number of registered industrial unions of workers was 391, with a membership of 332,695, representing about 45 per cent of the total number of salary and wage earners in the country. At the same date there were 41 industrial associations of workers comprising 220 affiliated unions.

Likewise, there has been considerable growth in the membership of employers' unions. In 1914, there were 149 registered unions of employers with a total membership of 5,819. By December 31, 1962, there were 254 unions, with a membership of 22,308. At the same date, there were 17 industrial associations of employers, representing 130 affiliated unions.

The greater proportion of workers' unions rests on the basis of the occupation of the workers; there are, for example, unions of bakers, bricklayers, butchers, carpenters, clerical workers, coal miners, drivers, dairy factory managers, engineers, journalists, laborers, painters, airline pilots, plumbers, and so forth. Other unions rest on an industry basis or on the basis of the individual commercial or other activity of the employer or group of employers, such as unions of employees of freezing companies, of woollen mills, and of harbor boards.

The original I.C. & A. Act has been amended, consolidated, and re-enacted on a number of occasions. The present statute is the result of 70 years of experiment, expediency, and experience. It is designed to encourage conciliation in the settlement of industrial disputes, but if no settlement can be reached, a dispute must be referred to the Court of Arbitration for decision.

The Court is established and holds office under the authority of the statute. It is a Court of record and consists of three members, one of whom is designated as the Judge of the Court. To be eligible for appointment as the Judge, a person must be a barrister or solicitor of the Supreme Court of not less than seven years standing. The other two members are lay persons known as nominated members, one of whom is appointed on the recommendation of the industrial unions of employers and the other on the recommendation of the industrial unions of workers.

The recommendations are reached by the process of a ballot conducted in accordance with the requirements of the statute. The actual appointments are made by the Governor-General. There are statutory bars as to persons who have been convicted of indictable offenses or who are bankrupts, but outside of those restrictions, any person may be appointed.

The appointment of the Judge continues in full force during good behavior until he resigns or reaches the age of 72 years. The nominated members hold office for three years or until the appointment of their successors. Except in the case of one particular jurisdiction, which will be mentioned below, the presence of the Judge and at least one other member is necessary to constitute a sitting of the Court, and the decision of a majority of the members present at the sitting of the Court or, if the members present (including the Judge) are equally divided in opinion, the decision of the Judge becomes the decision of the Court. The Court is peripatetic and sits in all the principal cities and towns of the country as the exigencies of the work demand. The proceedings of the Court are almost invariably conducted in public. It has full and exclusive jurisdiction to determine all matters coming properly before it in such manner in all respects as in equity and good conscience it thinks fit. There is no right of appeal against its decisions, provided it does not act in excess of its jurisdiction. The statute declares that proceedings in the Court shall not be impeached or held bad for want of form, nor shall they be removable to any court by certiorari or otherwise; and no award, order, or proceeding of the Court shall be liable to be challenged, appealed against, reviewed, quashed, or called into question by any court on any account whatsoever.

The Court of Arbitration has a number of powers and functions under the I.C. & A. Act, some of which are legislative in character and others judicial.

a) The principal function of the Court is to settle any matters which are outstanding after the representatives of workers' unions and employers in any industry have failed under the procedure laid down in the Act to reach complete agreement in conciliation upon the minimum rates of wages and conditions of work which are to govern employment in the industry for a limited future period. This function of the Court is really legislative in character, for the legislature in effect has delegated to the Court authority to make law in a restricted field, but its awards must not be inconsistent with any statute. The Court does not settle strikes or lockouts which constitute offenses under the statute. If there is a strike or lockout in an industry, access to the Court is not usually available to the parties unless and until work is resumed.

b) The provisions of awards and industrial agreements are

enforced through the ordinary magistrates' courts and the Court of Arbitration. There are limited rights of appeal against the judgments of magistrates to the Court of Arbitration, the determination of which is final. Inspectors of awards (who are officers of the Department of Labour) may proceed directly in the Court of Arbitration for recovery of penalties. In the magistrate's court, actions for penalties may be brought at the suit of an inspector of awards or at the suit of any party to the award or industrial agreement.

c) The Court has power to impose penalties for a number of offenses against special provisions of the I.C. & A. Act; for example, being a party to a strike or lockout when bound by an award or industrial agreement, combining to defeat an award, contempt of Court, obstruction of a conciliation council or the Court, failure to comply with a summons to give evidence, victimization, and so forth.

d) Actions to recover moneys, including holiday pay, due to workers under awards and industrial agreements may be brought by inspectors of awards in the Court of Arbitration or the magistrate's court.

e) The Court of Arbitration, upon application of inspectors of awards or upon applications of parties joint or otherwise, may give its opinion upon any question connected with the construction of any award or industrial agreement or upon any particular determination or direction of the Court or upon the construction of any statute relating to matters within the jurisdiction of the Court. This function is largely availed of and enables many legal disputes to be settled with a minimum of friction and at a minimum cost.

f) The Court of Arbitration is vested with jurisdiction to hear applications from decisions of disputes committees set up to consider differences arising between parties to awards and industrial agreements, as to any matter arising out of or connected with an award or agreement but not specifically dealt with therein.

g) The Court has a special jurisdiction to conduct enquiries into allegations of irregularities in connection with the election of the officers of any industrial union and to make and enforce orders relating to such matters. This jurisdiction is exercisable by the Judge of the Court alone.

An "industrial dispute" is defined in the I.C. & A. Act as any dispute arising between one or more employers or industrial unions or associations of employers and one or more industrial unions or associations of workers, in relation to "industrial matters," a term which is broadly defined. There is no compulsion on any organized group of workers to submit to the provisions of the Act unless it is registered, and, as noted above, registration is entirely voluntary. Once a group of workers has registered as an industrial union, it may compel the employers of its members to accept action under the Act, but, broadly, employers cannot compel their workers to come under it unless the latter are members of a registered union. Mere registration, however, does not of itself carry with it any obligation to take a dispute to conciliation or arbitration, but once the processes under the Act are embarked upon, there is no longer any legal right to strike.

Workers' unions registered under the I.C. & A. Act must follow a definite procedure for the settlement of claims relating to wages and conditions of employment. The first step is to establish that there is a dispute in existence, and the usual practice is for a workers' union to forward a set of claims for improvements in wages and/or working conditions to a union of employers or a group of employers. If and when the employers decline to accede to the claims, and notify the workers' union accordingly, or if within some specified period they fail to indicate their attitude, an industrial dispute is deemed to be in existence. Similarly, a union of employers, a group of employers, or a single employer may initiate a dispute by asking a union of workers to agree to a change in rates of wages or to some modification in working conditions. A dispute having been "created," any union or employer party to it may make application asking that the dispute be heard by a council of conciliation. A council is then set up by a conciliation commissioner, a statutory officer, who appoints an equal number of assessors from both sides, after recommendations of qualified persons have been received from the parties, now termed, respectively, applicants and respondents. The respondents are required to lodge a statement with the commissioner admitting such of the claims of the applicants as they accept, or making counterproposals to the claims. The council then meets on a date fixed by the conciliation commissioner who presides over its activities. The statute directs that the council shall expeditiously and carefully inquire into the dispute and all matters affecting the merits and the right settlement thereof.

The council has considerable latitude in its procedure, but no barrister or solicitor is allowed to appear or be heard. The council may hear any evidence that it thinks fit to hear, whether or not that evidence would be legally admissible in a court of law.

If a complete settlement of the dispute is arrived at in council, the terms of settlement may be set forth as an industrial agreement, or, alternatively, the terms may be reduced to writing and forwarded to the Court of Arbitration to be made into an award without a hearing. The latter course is the one more usually adopted, because of the general binding effect of an award upon all persons or firms and upon all workers engaged in the industry covered by the award, whether or not they or their unions were original parties to the proceedings. An industrial agreement binds only the parties to the agreement, including the members of any industrial union or association which is a party.

Even if councils of conciliation cannot arrive at complete settlements, they are usually able to settle some of the matters in dispute, and the Act therefore provides for the preparation and execution of partial settlements, which ultimately reach the Court of Arbitration. No memorandum of partial settlement has in itself any binding force or effect, but, when making its award, the Court has the discretionary power to incorporate any of the terms of partial settlement without making enquiry into the matters concerned. If a council of conciliation has failed to settle the dispute, the latter is referred to the Court of Arbitration. If the Court deems it advisable to alter any provision that has been agreed upon in the partial settlement, it is required by the statute to consult the parties before making any such variation.

The currency of an award must not exceed three years from the date on which it is to come into force, or, if it fixes different dates on which different provisions are to come into force, then from the earlier or earliest of those dates. In practice, many awards are made for periods varying from one to two years, but the statute directs that they continue in force until they are replaced by a new award or industrial agreement.

At the present time, there are approximately 400 awards and 200 industrial agreements in operation, all of which have been made under the provisions of the I.C. & A. Act 1954. In addition, there are about a dozen agreements of relatively minor importance made and filed pursuant to the provisions of the Labour Disputes Investigation Act 1913. Of the 400 awards in operation, about 80 per cent have resulted from the incorporation of the terms of complete settlement reached by the parties in conciliation. In the case of the other 20 per cent of existing awards, many of the provisions have been agreed upon by the assessors representing the parties in councils of conciliation, and have been incorporated in the awards, together with provisions dealing with the matters which the Court was called upon to decide. An analysis of the 2,000 awards made during the last 13 years shows that 75 per cent represent complete settlements by the parties. In addition, during the same period 1,005 industrial agreements were made, so that, out of more than 3,000 enforceable documents, in only 486 did the Court have a direct hand in settling some of the terms.

While conciliation is compulsory once the provisions of the I.C. & A. Act are invoked, there is no doubt that the proceedings in conciliation councils to a major extent involve bargaining between the representatives of management and labor. It is probably true that such bargaining is often circumscribed by the knowledge of the parties about recent decisions of the Court when disposing of disputes in comparable industries, but in some important cases the nature of the terms of settlement indicates that the parties have not felt themselves so circumscribed. In the interests of maintaining a reasonably balanced wage structure the Court has not been disposed to ignore such developments.

The Court itself encourages the settlement of disputes by conciliation. The conciliation councils have a statutory duty to endeavor to bring about settlements. If in any particular case the parties show a disinclination to make a genuine attempt to settle a dispute and it is referred to the Court with an unduly large number of matters left unsettled, the Court does not hesitate to refer the dispute back to the parties. This procedure, in effect, provides a cooling-off period in those cases where some animosity may have risen, and, in practically all such cases, is followed by beneficial results. From the foregoing the reader will be able to assess for himself the major degree to which negotiations between the parties determine the minimum rates of wages and terms and conditions of employment which operate throughout New Zealand industry.

A factor which has probably contributed to the preponderant degree of settlement in conciliation is the power of the Court to order retroactive variations in wages. The I.C. & A. Act provides that in making its award the Court shall, unless the parties agree otherwise, direct that any provision relating to the rate of wages to be paid shall come into force (a) in the case of an award for one industrial district, as from the expiration of two months; and (b) in the case of an award relating to two or more industrial districts, as from the expiration of four months from the date first appointed for the hearing by a conciliation commissioner, or from the date on which the award was made, whichever is the earlier, unless the Court in its discretion and after taking all relevant matters into consideration decides to fix some other date. The object of this provision is to discourage undue delay or obstructive tactics by any of the parties during conciliation proceedings.

The Act provides that awards shall not contain any provision that is inconsistent with any Act that makes special provision for any of the matters before the Court. Since 1936 the Court has been required in every award to fix at not more than 40 the maximum number of hours (exclusive of overtime) to be worked by any worker bound by the award, unless the Court considers that it would be impracticable to carry on the industry efficiently if the working hours were so limited. The Court originally exercised its discretion in a number of cases, but in 1945 the Legislature decreed that the ordinary working hours in all factories and shops should not exceed 40. As a consequence, the application of the 40-hour week has become almost universal. This does not mean that workers work 40 hours per week only. Many workers exceed this period, particularly under conditions of full employment, but any excess over 40 hours must be paid for at overtime rates.

From 1936 to 1962 the statute contained a further mandatory direction to the Court relating to what is commonly referred to as "compulsory unionism." The Court was directed to insert in every award a provision to the effect that while the award continued in force it would not be lawful for any employer to employ in the industry concerned any adult person who was not for the time being a member of an industrial union of workers bound by the award. The enforcement of the provision was in the hands of the Department of Labour.

Since March, 1962, this mandatory direction has no longer remained in force. In its place, the statute provides for the insertion of "unqualified" or "qualified" preference provisions, which are defined in the statute. An unqualified preference provision differs very little in effect from the requirement of compulsory unionism, but it is now left to the parties to have it inserted by agreement in an award and to enforce it. All awards that have been made since the amendment to the statute came into force have included, as a result of agreement of the parties, an unqualified preference provision.

In addition to its jurisdiction to settle industrial disputes, the Court of Arbitration is vested with a number of other powers and functions. By far the most important of these is the power to make general wage orders from time to time that have the effect of simultaneously increasing or reducing the rates of remuneration prescribed in all awards and industrial agreements for the time being in operation. The authority to make general orders is not derived from the I.C. & A. Act but from regulations made under the Economic Stabilization Act 1948. The present jurisdiction to make general orders was introduced in 1940 as a war measure. The legislation has been varied on numerous occasions in the intervening years, but the basic power of the Court still endures. General orders may be made by the Court of its own accord or on the application of any industrial union or industrial association of employers or workers. This special jurisdiction is not really arbitration in the ordinary sense, for the reason that it is not preceded by any attempt through conciliation to arrive at a settlement. The incidence of the Court's decisions upon applications for general orders is extremely wide, and its judgments have considerable effect upon all industrial activity and upon the general economy of the country, including the national budget.

In making a general order, the Court is directed by the current regulations to take into account (a) any rise or fall in retail prices as indicated by any index published by the government statistician; (b) the economic conditions affecting finance, trade, and industry in New Zealand; (c) any increase or decrease in productivity and in the volume and value of production in primary and secondary industries of New Zealand; (d) relative movements in the incomes of different sections of the community; (e) all other considerations that the Court deems relevant. Since 1940, 14 such major cases have been heard, and, as a result, nine general orders have been issued.

In dealing with such applications, the Court is required to afford such opportunity to be heard as it thinks proper to representatives appointed by the parties bound by awards and industrial agreements or by orders of certain tribunals. In practice, the major burden of conducting the cases has been accepted by the New Zealand Federation of Labour and the New Zealand Employers' Federation.

In the general-wage-order proceedings all the main aspects of the economy of the country are examined in considerable detail, and expert evidence usually is called in support of the submissions or to assist the Court in its task. For example, such prominent persons as the governor of the Reserve Bank, the secretary to the treasury, and the government statistician have frequently given evidence. It should be noted that the Court itself has no research staff. For basic information it relies for the most part on the comprehensive statistics published by the government statistician, the reports of the Reserve Bank of New Zealand, official economic and other surveys, and reports of government departments such as the Treasury, Department of Labour, Department of Agriculture, and the Department of Industries and Commerce. The advocates for the parties are invariably persons with long experience in the industrial arena. No professional lawyer has ever been engaged on the hearing of an application for a general order. The applications have varied in nature and magnitude from time to time and have involved claims for annual increases in wages and salaries up to as much as 17 per cent of the gross national product. In the last application made on behalf of the workers of the country, a general order was requested which would have increased by 10.4 per cent the minimum rates of remuneration fixed by all awards and industrial agreements. Concurrently, an application was made by an industrial union of employers that all minimum prescribed rates of remuneration should be amended to provide for a decrease of 10 per cent or such other percentage as the Court might think just and equitable on the basis the evidence produced. After an extended hearing, the Court decided to increase all minimum rates of remuneration by an amount equal to 2½ per cent. It should be mentioned that the continuation of these extraordinary powers vested in the Court have been the subject of many representations to successive governments. The employers have submitted on numerous occasions that the powers should be withdrawn, but without success. The workers' organizations have consistently advocated the retention of the powers in some form or other.

To make clear how the New Zealand system operates, it is necessary to describe the methods by which illegal stoppages of work or threatened stoppages are dealt with. When an award or industrial agreement is made for an industry, strikes and lockouts in that industry are prohibited by the I.C. & A. Act, and any breach of the prohibition is punishable by heavy penal-

ties. Illegal stoppages of work do occur, of course, but the puni-
tive provisions of the Act are seldom invoked. The policy has
been to deal with work stoppages by administrative methods
rather than by juridical process, and, consequently, the Court,
in practice, has not been directly involved in dealing with such
stoppages. The usual procedure is for some interested party to
invoke the good offices of the Department of Labour with a
view to obtaining a resumption of normal work. Most awards
and agreements provide for the setting up of disputes committees to deal with certain classes of minor disputes or differences
that may arise, usually with a right of appeal to the Court of
Arbitration, but in the event of stoppages such committees are
not, as a general rule, set up unless and until normal work is
resumed.

Another procedure which is available in certain circumstances is prescribed in the Industrial Relations Act 1948. A
conciliation commissioner at any time, if he thinks fit, whenever he has reasonable grounds for believing that a strike or
lockout exists or is threatened in any district in which he
exercises jurisdiction in respect of any matter which in his
opinion is not specifically provided for in any award or industrial agreement, may call a compulsory conference of the parties in an endeavor to effect a settlement of the dispute. Any
person other than a conciliation commissioner may also be
nominated by the Minister of Labour and vested with similar
powers.

There is a further provision in the I.C. & A. Act which in
extreme circumstance may be invoked as a disciplinary measure and which has proved effective on several occasions during
the postwar years. The Act provides that if, in respect of any
discontinuance of employment, the Minister of Labour is satisfied that it has caused or is likely to cause serious loss or
inconvenience and that it has been brought about wholly or
partly by any union of employers or workers or by any member
or members of such union, the Minister may cancel the registration of the union or cancel any award or industrial agreement so far as it relates to that union.

LABOR DISPUTE SETTLEMENT IN JAPAN

CHAPTER 9

by Iwao Ayusawa

It seems appropriate to begin with the Meiji Restoration of 1867—called a "restoration" because at that time the shogunate, or military dictatorship which had usurped the powers of government some 700 years earlier, was abolished and the powers of government restored to the Emperor of Japan. The Emperor who ascended the throne in 1868, at the age of sixteen, came to be known posthumously as Emperor Meiji. He was a very brilliant person. Almost immediately after ascending the throne, he issued what is known in Western history as the Charter Oath of the Emperor, consisting of five articles which laid down the guiding principles of government for the new regime in Japan. Their importance seems to warrant setting them out at length: "(1) Assemblies widely convoked shall be held and all important decisions shall be made only after public discussion. (2) The welfare of the whole nation shall be promoted by the combined efforts of the government and the governed. (3) All subjects shall do their best and never grow weary of accomplishing their legitimate purposes. (4) All absurd usages of the past shall be abandoned; justice and righteousness shall regulate all actions. (5) Knowledge shall be sought all over the world and thus shall the foundation of the Imperial polity be strengthened."

Considering that Japan had been ruled under a feudalistic regime for well over seven centuries, the principles enunciated by the young emperor, only sixteen years of age, were obviously revolutionary. All important functions of the state were to be decided only after public discussion. This is the essence of democracy, though it will be noticed that the fifth article of the Emperor's oath stated that knowledge was to be sought all over the world for the strengthening of the foundations of the empire.

The Labor Disputes Mediation Law was enacted in 1926. This was also the year when Japan put into force the first National Health Insurance Law. In this same year the Factories Act was revised and became more widely applied than in the past. The year 1926 was a year of great significance in Japan—if for no other reason than for the passage of the Labor Disputes Mediation Law. The new statute provided for the tripartite handling of labor disputes, by the use of *ad hoc* committees.

The MacArthur Revolution, which commenced in 1945, was a phenomenal historical event, and came as a consequence of Japan's acceptance of the Potsdam Declaration of July, 1945. When General Douglas MacArthur, Supreme Commander for the Allied Powers, landed in Japan in September, 1945, he came with a complex mission under the Potsdam Declaration, which had laid down the terms of surrender. MacArthur had, first, to punish the Japanese war criminals and, second, to limit Japan's industrial power so that Japan could not rise again as a military power and menace the rest of the world. Third, MacArthur had to further the movement toward democracy in

Japan. He did these things with great competence and authority, and in the latter task, that is, in his effort to democratize the nation, he gained the respect of the whole country. He carried out these responsibilities with enthusiasm and with a sense of dedication. He issued a series of important directives in his attempt to reform Japan. In America, critics ridiculed his "democracy by directives," asking if such a thing were possible. But Japan had to adopt democratic institutions and enact democratic laws under the directives, because this was a condition laid down in the Potsdam Declaration. In these circumstances, naturally, some people in Japan thought that it was as punishment for Japan's defeat that she had to adopt democracy.

Three basic labor laws were adopted in the course of the democratic reforms which came to be known collectively as the "MacArthur Revolution." They were the Trade Union Law 1945, the Labor Relations Adjustment Law 1946, and the Labor Standards Law 1947. Incidentally, the present writer was a member of a small committee, the Rōmu Hōsei Shingi Kai (Labor Legislation Council), which drafted these laws. Fortunately, thanks to the liberal inclinations of Baron Okura, who was chairman of the drafting committee, the proposals made by the committee concerning the basic rights of workers to organize and to bargain collectively, and also to set up tripartite labor boards to safeguard those rights, were adopted by the committee and finally incorporated in the Trade Union Law. That law brought about great changes in the methods of dealing with labor disputes in Japan. The Trade Union Law and the Labor Relations Adjustment Law are directly concerned with the prevention and settlement of labor disputes. The Labor Standards Law must not be equated with the Fair Labor Standards Act of America, which is a relatively simple statute dealing with wages and hours. Japan's Labor Standards Law sets up a much wider range of standards. It is a comprehensive law for the protection of workers. But it is the Trade Union Law and the Labor Relations Adjustment Law which are of prime concern to anyone who is interested in methods of settlement of labor disputes.

The Trade Union Law created two kinds of tribunals for dealing with labor disputes: (1) the central and local labor relations commissions and (2) the Maritime Labor Relations Commission. Later the government created (3) the Public Corporations Labor Relations Commission, under a new law for dealing with the disputes of workers employed by public corporations or government enterprises. The first-mentioned commissions, the central and local labor relations commissions, are in a sense the capstone of the system. Supplementing the central labor relations commission are the 46 local or prefectural labor relations commissions, which correspond roughly to the state labor relations boards in the United States. However, in Japan, there is a prefectural commission in each of the 46 prefectures, whereas, as I understand it, in America by no means do all of the 50 states have state labor relations boards. All of the labor relations commissions in Japan are tripartite in pattern. They have equal numbers of representatives of employers, of workers, and the public interest. For judicial or semijudicial functions, such as union certification, handling of unfair labor practices, decisions in arbitration of labor disputes, etc., only the public members are called upon to participate.

All of these commissions are appointed by the government, but they enjoy administrative independence. By this it is meant that the decisions of the commissions are independently reached without reference to the government. The Prime Minister, Minister of Labor, Minister of Finance, etc., may—indeed, they do—find it very embarrassing when the awards of the commissions are beyond the financial capacity of the government, but the members of the commissions need not worry about that. When a dispute over wages is submitted to a labor relations commission for arbitration, both parties to the dispute, i.e., the employers and the workers, must abide by the award of the commission. When the government is the employer, as is quite often the case, the government must abide by the award of the commission. For this reason, there is a provision in the law to protect the government. According to this provision, if there is no budgetary allowance or source of funds to enable the government to pay the full amount indicated by the award, then and only then is the government exempted from the obligation to pay the full amount.

The commissions also have judicial power. Perhaps it should be called "semijudicial." At any rate, these commissions do deal with unfair labor practice cases. Of course, there are ways open for appeals to the courts of justice, but the courts have only the authority to review, and very seldom have there been any cases of court reversal. The courts, as a rule, have endorsed the decisions of these commissions, hence I do not hesitate to describe the power wielded by the commissions as "judicial power."

Certification of unions is next. It is very much as in other countries, so I will not go into the details. Our labor relations commissions have the function of certifying the unions and thus are empowered to deal with cases of unfair labor practices. What is unfair labor practice under Japanese law? It is much the same as under the Wagner law in the United States. The practice called "yellow-dog contract" in America is also banned in Japan. So is discriminatory treatment of a worker for his trade-union activities. Also, it is construed as an "unfair labor practice" if the employer discriminates against a worker whose testimony before the court or before one of the labor relations commissions has included statements unfavorable to the employer. It is also unfair labor practice for an employer to refuse to engage in collective bargaining. Finally, it is unfair labor practice for the employer to contribute financial support to a union. These actions all constitute "unfair labor practices." However, in Japan, we have not extended unfair labor practices to cover the acts of trade-unions, as has been done in America under the provisions of the Taft-Hartley law.

Furthermore, in Japan the functions of the labor relations commissions include conciliation, mediation, and arbitration. In this respect the Japanese law differs from the American. In America, the National Labor Relations Board (with one exception) does not directly engage in settlement of labor disputes. There was some controversy in Japan as to the wisdom

of having the labor relations commissions engage in conciliation, mediation, and arbitration, but we are convinced that it is
desirable to have our tripartite tribunals engage in these activities. As noted, arbitration is handled by the public members
only and not by the entire tripartite bodies. We have to depend
on the accumulated wisdom of the intellectuals, men in the
legal profession, university professors, etc., and we are satisfied with our experience with the system.

As regards the effect of settlement of labor disputes, of the
three methods of adjustment provided by law, namely, conciliation, mediation and arbitration, mediation happens to be the
method most widely utilized. In 95 out of 100 cases, mediation
has been the effective means of settlement. The process of
mediation is like that of a court, with sessions open to the
public as a rule, though this was not the original intention of
those who drafted the law. Both parties to the dispute are
brought in for the mediation sessions, which are public. The
radio helps by giving publicity to the work of mediation. In the
case of labor disputes in which big industries and unions are
involved, there is tremendous public interest in the work of the
commissions. Newspapermen and partisans on both sides are
likely to be present and to be listening in at the sessions. Very
often the hall of the central labor relations commission is
surrounded by throngs of people (union members and others)
who come out for demonstrations, waving union flags, and so
forth.

In private industries, it is almost always voluntary arbitration that is resorted to and only seldom compulsory arbitration.
Arbitration in private industries is resorted to only when the
two parties apply for it or agree to it in advance by collective
agreement. In only a very few cases has arbitration been resorted to in the past.

The situation is different in public corporations or in government enterprises. In cases involving public corporations, the
disputes may be dealt with by compulsory arbitration proceedings in any one of three circumstances: (1) when either party
applies for it after the expiry of two months, during which
time the commission will have tried without success, to concili-

ate or mediate; (2) when the commission decides on its own
authority to arbitrate; and (3) when the competent minister of
the government requests the commission so to arbitrate.

In 1949, four years after the Trade Union Law went into
effect, the Public Corporations and Labor Relations Law was
enacted and the Public Corporations Labor Relations Commission was appointed. It has jurisdiction over industrial disputes
on state railways, in the telegraph and telephone industry, the
Japan Monopoly Corporation, and in the various enterprises of
the government. The compulsory arbitration outlined above is
applied in these industries. The Public Corporations Labor
Relations Law prohibits the unions, whose members are employed by the corporations, from having as members or officers
people who are not actually employed in these corporations. In
other words, the unions in the public corporations can have as
their representatives for collective bargaining purposes only
persons employed by the corporations. This is inconsistent
with the provisions of Convention 87 of the International
Labour Organization, according to which workers may engage
in collective bargaining "through representatives of their own
choosing."

Under our Constitution, in a number of cases, the freedoms
generally guaranteed to the people are subjected to limitations
in order to protect the "public welfare." What is meant by
"public welfare"? As this term is not defined anywhere, we
have to define it through the accumulation of awards by the
various commissions and through the interpretations given by
the courts. For instance, in Article 28 of the Constitution, "the
right of workers to organize and to bargain and act collectively
is guaranteed." But public servants, who are mostly "workers" under the definition given in the Trade Union Law, have
been deprived of the right to engage in labor dispute activities.
Workers employed by public corporations or government enterprises have also lost the right to engage in collective stoppages of work (or strikes). Because of these conditions, the
workers of Japan have much to learn from the experience of
other countries in asserting the rights which are guaranteed by
the Constitution.

May I add a few casual remarks, before concluding, about the place of the government in industrial relations, in connection with "tripartitism." Frankly, I was a little disappointed when I went to the United States in 1955 to find that tripartitism in the handling of labor problems in wartime, notably in the case of the National War Labor Board, was adopted more or less casually without very much thought or discussion. Of course, America had many years of experience in these matters previous to World War II, but in Japan we believe that tripartitism is of crucial importance because it protects the public. I hold that, in industrial relations, there are not just two parties, employers and workers, but three parties at least, the employers, the workers, and the public. The general public, i.e., the consumers and those who receive the services, should be in the picture when it comes to the settlement of labor disputes.

In this connection, you may remember Barbara Wooton, the British writer, who is very active in the field of labor relations. She has written a helpful book entitled *The Social Foundations of Wage Policy*. In it she said that in Britain people *"took pride in the impotence of the government in matters of industrial relations."* I was very much interested in it; so in a book review, which I wrote for an English journal, I quoted these words of hers. But the typesetter, knowing a little English, apparently thought that I, a university professor, had misspelled a word, and corrected it to read: *In Great Britain people take pride in the importance of the government in industrial relations."* Of course, this was exactly the reverse of what she had said! But are we doing the right thing by giving, as is done in England and in other countries, less authority to the government, less and less room for guidance or planning for the future of industry? That is a question I would like to have discussed and on which I crave more light. Am I right in assuming that the government is playing a role of importance in many countries? Do we not need to adopt a new concept of the role of the government or of the public in industrial relations?

SETTLEMENT OF LABOR DISPUTES IN AUSTRALIA, NEW ZEALAND, AND THE UNITED STATES *

CHAPTER 10

by Paul F. Brissenden

It is proposed, in this paper, to attempt a comparison of the principal labor-dispute-settlement processes used in Australia and New Zealand with those used in the United States. The procedures examined are (1) industrial or direct action, especially by way of a strike; (2) collective bargaining; (3) conciliation; and (4) arbitration.

Australia and New Zealand, like the United States, are "mixed" capitalistic democracies, with most economic activities carried on more or less competitively, under law, by private businessmen and corporations seeking to make money. Each of the three countries has systems of courts and popu-

* This chapter appeared initially in substantially its present form as a publication of the University of Hawaii Industrial Relations Center, Honolulu.

larly elected legislatures substantially similar to those of the other two. An exception pertinent here is that the United States does not have the specialized "compulsory industrial arbitration" courts which exist in the Commonwealth and the Dominion, although the legislature of the State of Kansas did enact in 1920 a statute establishing a "Court of Industrial Relations"—an act in due course invalidated as unconstitutional by the United States Supreme Court.[1]

Australia has, as we have, a written federal (or Commonwealth) Constitution, modeled, in no small measure as it happens, upon the Constitution of the United States. New Zealand, on the other hand, has no states and no written Constitution, its fundamental law being comparable, rather, to the English Constitution. Consequently, the New Zealand Parliament—the only legislature in the country—is a law-making body exercising plenary authority, while the Commonwealth Parliament of Australia, like the Congress of the United States, is a legislature possessed only of the powers enumerated in the Constitution.

Although the three countries are capitalistic democracies, their capitalism is "welfare capitalism." Each of the three countries, in considerable measure, is a "welfare state"—the Anzac countries more so than the United States. Thus, the railway transportation systems are owned and operated by the government in New Zealand and mostly by the states in Australia, whereas in this country the railroads are owned and operated by private corporations under pervasive state and federal regulations. Our own emergence as a "welfare state" is more recent than it has been in Australasia. In all three countries the extent of welfare capitalism is on the increase.

Partly as a result of the wide extent of public ownership and partly because of government "welfare" services, the proportions of gainfully employed persons who are in government service are higher in Australasia than in America. Both here, and there, the economies are characterized by formidable labor movements and well-established employers' associations. The growth of both forms of organization was greatly accelerated Down Under, at about the turn of the century, as a result of the creation, beginning in New Zealand in 1894, of industrial arbitration courts, not only in the Dominion, but also in four of the six Australian states, and federally for the Commonwealth. Typically, access to these tribunals can be had only by organizations of workers and employers which are registered with the "registrars" (provided for in the several statutes) as "industrial unions," of workers or employers as the case may be—groups known to us, respectively, as trade-unions and employers' associations.

Although trade-unions were by no means unknown in Australasia in the nineteenth century, the Commonwealth and the Dominion seem to have been what one may call "trade-union countries" only since the beginning of the industrial arbitration era—from 1894 in New Zealand and from about 1900 in Australia. Our own trade-union movement, on the other hand, was not galvanized into comparable size and prominence until much later, in the New Deal period of the early thirties, when the American statutory galvanizers—the big and little Wagner Acts—were written into the statute books in the federal and in some of the state jurisdictions. These statutes were frankly designed to encourage the organization and growth of labor unions and to promote the rights of workers "to organize and bargain collectively through representatives of their own choosing." The Anzac systems of compulsory arbitration tribunals, understandably, produced, or, at least, helped to produce, more pervasive, if not more powerful, labor movements in Australasia than have, so far, been created by, or in the wake of, our New Deal legislation, which nevertheless did much to stimulate labor oganization and collective bargaining here.

In the nineteenth century, in all three countries, the working rules by which going concerns carried on operations were devised and administered almost wholly by employers, subject only to such statutory limitations (respecting, e.g., safety and health standards) as may have been imposed by law.

Both in Australasia at the turn of the century and in America about three decades later, profound changes began to occur in the patterns of controls over the making of industrial working rules. The Australasian "New Deals," if they may be so called, largely supplanted employers as industrial rule makers in respect to certain important incidents of the employment relationship—mostly the wages and hours aspects—replacing them with governmental bodies having compulsory jurisdiction (industrial arbitration courts) to take over as rule makers. It will be necessary later to look more narrowly at these tribunals. But, meanwhile, it seems clear that the creation and operation of these bodies (whose general character, despite numerous amendments of most, if not all, of the basic statutes, has not undergone more than superficial change) have had the effect of substituting public for private rule making in the determination of the minimum basic wage and wage "margins" (or differentials for skill), maximum hours of work, and countless other incidents of the employment relation. The resulting Australasian systems of industrial arbitration are almost unique in the world.

To a very limited extent, the making of the working rules of going concerns in Australasia before 1900 was by collective bargaining and, so, bilateral.[2] But in the nineteenth century, both here and Down Under, working rules were made predominantly by the unilateral prescription of employers. In either case the rule making was private. With regard to subject-matter, the public decision making by the tribunals which supervened in Australasia beginning in 1894 was, and is, a process (arbitral in some sense) which concerned itself mostly with wages and hours, although, understandably, there has been some tendency toward subject-matter expansion. Thus, the arbitral invasion of employers' rule-making prerogatives has come to embrace many incidents of the employment relationship other than wages and hours. Important among these miscellaneous subjects are union preference and apprenticeship. Yet it seems that most of the miscellaneous incidents of the employment relationship have been left much more completely in the hands of employers than is true in the United States. Despite the tribunals, employers in the Commonwealth and the Dominion—especially in the former—seem today to be much freer agents in the running of their establishments than are our own employers in organized industries—always ex-

cepting the rules about wages and hours: in this respect employers in the Commonwealth, and perhaps also those in the
Dominion, seem less free than our own. Put in somewhat different terms, the arbitral invasion of the managerial prerogatives of Australasian employers, instigated directly by governmental action, has been, on the whole, much less cramping to
their style than has been the invasion of American employers'
"prerogatives" resulting from expanded unionism and collective bargaining indirectly encouraged, if not directly instigated, by our "New Deal" legislation.[3]

In the United States, the New Deal period marked the beginning of a gradual supplementation or displacement, as industries became organized, of management-made working rules by
collectively bargained rules. Also, since the latter rules more
and more frequently included clauses prescribing grievance
procedures, commonly culminating in "voluntary arbitration"
at the hands of an "impartial" private person of the contract-
ing parties' choice, it followed that working rules, which had
been unilaterally management-made, came more and more to
be made not only bilaterally by the parties but also (when the
parties deadlocked) by strangers to the enterprise. Some of the
rules continued to be made unilaterally by management, some
bilaterally by collective bargaining, and some unilaterally
(where the bargained contract provided for arbitration) by
"rank outsiders."

These American decisions, or awards, made by "strangers"
to the enterprise concerned, now number many thousands, and
constitute a kind of documentary precipitate which fills many
volumes of arbitration awards. More importantly, the processes which have culminated or become "embalmed" in the
arbitration reports represent the essence of the American
"system" of "voluntary arbitration." Some commentators have
referred to this large and rapidly growing system of industrial
arbitration awards as the embodiment of a kind of "industrial
jurisprudence." However labeled, the work done by the
hundreds of private persons appointed in accordance with the
terms of labor contracts, or pursuant to *ad hoc* submissions, *is*
American labor arbitration as we know it today. It is far and

away the most important arbitral work—indeed, almost the only arbitral work—done in the United States, particularly so, if we include the commercial arbitrations, which are kindred determinations, similarly made and motivated.

These voluntary determinations, on the labor side, involve typically the resolution of disputes as to the meaning and application of the terms of labor agreements, either, as noted, under an *ad hoc* submission setting forth an agreed-upon question, or issue, as jointly formulated by the parties, or, more often, under the dispute or grievance-settlement clauses of an agreement, in which the parties agree to submit to arbitration any and all differences as to the meaning or application of any of the terms of their contract (insofar as those differences may remain unresolved as a result of action in accordance with earlier steps in the grievance procedure) and to give effect to any award the arbitrator may issue. This form of arbitration may be said to be voluntary as to submission but compulsory as to award. It seems reasonable to describe it, as it usually is described, as "voluntary arbitration," since the parties are under compulsion to obey awards only to the extent that they previously (in their "submissions" or in their contracts when made) have promised so to obey. Some authorities describe it as "obligatory arbitration."

These private-person arbitrators are considered, and I think properly, to be engaged in processes of adjudication. On theory, at least, the parties, having contracts—or at any rate instruments that are in some sense contractual—with each other, might have taken their troubles to court.[4] Alternatively, of course, they might have resorted to lockout or strike, although this is done less often in these disputes over the *meaning* of the contract than in disputes over its framing. Actually, many of these labor dispute cases (and, more frequently, the commercial cases) do turn up in court. The important thing to note is that, with the important exception of wage-reopenings, it is unusual in this country for either judges or arbitrators to legislate, that is to say, to make rules for the future. The long struggles here over the use of injunctions in labor dispute situations were repeatedly punctuated by taunts from labor partisans about "judge-made law." In our "system," an arbitrator is a kind of private judge. He should, therefore, adjudicate—never legislate. In any event, the voluntary arbitral work done in this country by private persons is, normally, adjudicative rather than legislative. This certainly is true of our *ad hoc* arbitrators (the most numerous class), though the matter is less simple in the case of a "permanent" arbitrator, or "impartial chairman," or "umpire," named to serve steadily, from case to case, through the contract period. As for him and his work, it is often said that his activities constitute a kind of extension of the collective bargaining process, which is legislative, even though the legislation is private. Thus, it may well be argued that the work (or much of the work) of these industrial "czars" is legislative, or quasi-legislative in character. Judgment on this point may well turn on the wishes of the parties as expressed in their agreement, or, more informally, on the personality of the arbitrator, and other special considerations. My own very limited experience as a "permanent" arbitrator left me with the notion that nearly all of what I did in that role was no less adjudicative than it was in the *ad hoc* cases. At any rate, I endeavored not to rewrite the contracts!

But there are more straightforward situations in which an arbitrator seems clearly cast in the role of legislator. For example, the parties (a union and an employer or employers' association) "legislate" an agreement to run for two years. It contains a wage-reopening clause providing that, say at the end of the first year, there will be a reopening of the wage terms of the contract, at which time the union may request a wage increase, or the employer a decrease. The reopening clause may further provide that, if there is no agreement on wages after bipartite discussion, the unresolved dispute will be submitted to arbitration. This "arbitral" determination of a wage-reopening wage dispute is clearly legislative, and the private person who finds himself holding this bag has a legislative job on his hands. He is, in fact, writing a portion of the contract which the parties have not been able to write for themselves. Sometimes parties endeavoring to work out a new contract find themselves hopelessly deadlocked over much of it and turn in desperation to some private "czar" to write substantial parts of their contract for them.

Industrial operations everywhere must be carried on according to rules, by whomever made. At any given time, certain rules are in force, and, while they are in force, questions may arise and disputes develop over what they are or what they mean. They are, of course, constantly subject to change, and the question whether they should be changed and, if so, what the new rules should be, is a problem which must be resolved either unilaterally by the employer, unilaterally by representatives of employees if they are organized (e.g., by successful strike action), by joint determination of employers and employees, or by government or some other third party. Thus, there may be dispute, not only over whether a given rule should be changed (a dispute over interests) and, if so, what the nature of the change should be, but also there may be dispute over what a given rule may mean (a dispute over rights). Moreover, there may be disagreement as to *how* disputes on rights and interests should be determined, i.e., whether changes that may be made should be made bilaterally or unilaterally, and if unilaterally, whether by one of the parties or by government. This last kind of disagreement, about how labor disputes of various kinds may most effectively be resolved, is crucial for the purpose of this discussion. This is so because the purpose is not, e.g., to assess the merits of a union's claim for a ten per cent wage increase or an employer's claim that its own, rather than the union's, position as to the meaning and application of, say, Clause 51 of their contract represents the "true" construction of that clause. The present purpose is, rather, to describe and evaluate the procedures and principles followed here and in the Anzac countries for the resolution of conflicting claims in industrial disputes of any sort.

In order properly to assess the arrangements in effect for the disposition of industrial disputes in the three countries, it seems appropriate to look more closely at such disputes and at the principal forms they assume. As noted, the two most important types of dispute for our present purpose are disputes over rights and disputes over interests, or differences as to what the

existing rule is, or means, and differences as to what change, if
any, should be made in the existing rule. An example of a
"rights" dispute is one over whether an employee (working
under a contract which says that workers transferred to
higher-rated jobs shall get the higher rate), where temporarily
transferred to a higher-rated job, is entitled to the higher rate
on the new job. An example of an "interests" dispute is one
over whether overtime pay for Sundays and holidays should be
changed from time and one-half to double time.

At least two of our federal statutes contain definitions of the
term "labor dispute." That contained in the Norris-LaGuardia
Anti-Injunction Act of 1932 [5] is as follows: "The term 'labor
dispute' includes any controversy concerning terms or conditions of employment, or concerning the association of representation of persons in negotiating, fixing, maintaining, changing, or seeking to arrange terms or conditions of employment,
regardless of whether or not the disputants stand in the proxi-
mate relation of employer and employee." The Taft-Hartley
Act contains a definition following the Norris-LaGuardia
definition almost word for word. These definitions obviously
embrace both disputes on rights and disputes on interests.

In Australia, the Commonwealth Conciliation and Arbitration Act, Section 4, defines an "industrial dispute" as (a) a
dispute (including a threatened, impending, or probable dispute) as to industrial matters which extends beyond the limits
of any one State; and (b) a situation which is likely to give rise
to a dispute as to industrial matters which so extends.

The definition of the term in the Queensland statute [6] is
almost the same as that for the Commonwealth, as is the definition in the Western Australian statute.[7] Naturally the "inter-
stateness" limitation appears only in the Commonwealth
law.

In the New Zealand Act (Sec. 2), the term "industrial dispute" means "any dispute arising between one or more employers or unions or associations of employers and one or more
unions or associations of workers in relation to industrial matters."

Industrial Action

In Australia and New Zealand, strikes, generally speaking, are unlawful, at least in industries covered by arbitral awards. Yet, as will be noted in more detail, they do occur in both countries. In this country, by contrast, strikes and lockouts generally are lawful, although the Taft-Hartley Act has made strikes by government employees illegal. And strikes in the United States are of frequent occurrence. In Australasia, they occur much less frequently, as one would expect, and they are of much shorter duration than they are here. Strike frequency is much lower, apparently, in New Zealand than in Australia. Even in Australia, where strikes and lockouts generally are unlawful, many such stoppages nevertheless occur. In New Zealand, where, as will be noted, strikes are more uncompromisingly outlawed than in most of the Australian jurisdictions, their impact seems to be much less severe than in the Commonwealth. The impact of strikes in the United States, at least in recent years, has been much heavier than in Australia.

In the two Anzac countries, there are eight political jurisdictions: the six Australian state governments and the two national governments: the Commonwealth of Australia and the Dominion of New Zealand. Six of these eight areas (the Dominion, which has no States, the Australian Commonwealth, and the Australian states, except Victoria and Tasmania) are what may be called "arbitration court" jurisdictions, with their systems of labor relations marked by compulsory conciliative and arbitral settlement of industrial disputes and other "industrial matters." [8]

According to an eminent Australian authority ". . . close upon 90 per cent of the labor force in Australia is now subject to awards, determinations or registered industrial agreements." [9] So far as appears from the record, the work stoppages reflected in the figures given have been stoppages—mostly strikes—in establishments covered by registered industrial agreements or by arbitration awards. In other words, there seems to be no specific indication in the record as to the number of strikes and/or lockouts which have occurred—if *any* have occurred—among the ten per cent of Australia's industrial population *not* covered by the arbitration system. Most, if not all, of the stoppages, then, have involved groups of workers covered by "industrial agreements" or awards.

The coverage of the New Zealand arbitration system seems to be no less inclusive than are the Australian systems. Apart from coal mining—whose approximately 6,000 workers, according to Sir Arthur Tyndall, Judge of New Zealand's Court of Arbitration, "for the main part have for many years preferred collective bargaining" and who have, therefore, not registered under the Arbitration Act—it would seem that no less preponderant a proportion of the Dominion's industrial population than of Australia's is covered by its system of compulsory conciliation and arbitration.[10] Moreover, as in the Commonwealth, strikes persist in the Dominion. Judge Tyndall stresses the fact that "most of the strikes during and since the war have occurred in coal mining (in which collective bargaining prevails) and the waterfront industry, which, he points out, "has had a series of separate tribunals of its own." [11]

Speaking of the Australian jurisdictions as a whole, Mr. J. H. Portus (a member of the Commonwealth Conciliation and Arbitration Commission) points out that ". . . the setting up of compulsory arbitration machinery has been accompanied by legislation making strikes illegal." [12] The same is true of New Zealand, where strikes and lockouts on the part of worker or employer unions registered under it are prohibited by the Industrial Conciliation and Arbitration Act. The statute provides that no strike or lockout shall take place until after a secret ballot, and all members of unions of workers or of employers shall be liable to heavy penalties unless they can prove that "a secret ballot was held as required . . . on the question of whether the strike [or lockout] should take place and that a majority of the valid votes cast . . . was in favor of the strike [or lockout] taking place." [13] Moreover, if a strike or lockout takes place in any industry, all members of workers' or employers' unions bound by an award or industrial agreement in that industry are "liable on summary conviction" to heavy penalties.

There is, however, another New Zealand statute, having general nationwide coverage and dealing with labor disputes. That is the Industrial Disputes Investigation Act 1913, modeled upon a Canadian law passed a few years earlier under the same title. Under this statute, whose provisions may be availed of by organizations which choose not to register under the Industrial Conciliation and Arbitration Act, it is permissible to strike [and evidently, to lockout] after notice and prescribed procedure. Provision is made for settlement of the strike dispute by conciliation and investigation, but there is no resort to arbitration. Sir Arthur Tyndall states that this statute "has been used only to a relatively small extent." [14] Mr. James Shaw, an official associate of Conciliation Commissioner C. L. Hunter of Auckland, told this writer that he was unable to recall a single instance of a strike under the Industrial Disputes Investigations Act. Thus, oddly, it appears that there have been no strikes under the Act permitting them, but there were numerous stoppages in each of the three years 1955, 1956, and 1957, under the much more widely used Industrial Conciliation and Arbitration Act, which prohibits strikes and lockouts.

In Australia, partly due to the multiplicity of jurisdictions, there is less uniformity, but, as in the Dominion, the tendency there has been to make strikes illegal. Apparently, under the Commonwealth Act strikes were penalized until 1930 but have not been since that time. Nevertheless, it appears that awards still may be made by the Commonwealth arbitral tribunals prohibiting the persons bound from striking.[15] In Western Australia and South Australia, there evidently is absolute prohibition of all strikes and lockouts. In Queensland and New South Wales, there is qualified prohibition. In Queensland, strikes and lockouts are prohibited unless a majority of the employees or employers (as the case may be) have voted for such strike or lockout.[16]

The qualified limitations on strikes and lockouts in New South Wales are more involved than in any of the other Anzac jurisdictions. In that state, lockouts are illegal "unless the

employees working in the industry concerned are taking part
in an illegal strike," subject to a maximum penalty of one
thousand pounds.[17] Strikes are illegal (1) if by government
employees, and (2) if by other employees when covered by an
award or "industrial agreement," provided: that any union, by
a majority vote of its members, may render no longer binding
any award which has been in operation for one year.[18]

To say that Australia, at least in its federal jurisdiction, no
longer penalizes strikes is by no means to say that strikes (even
in that jurisdiction) are as freely permissible as they are in the
United States, although Commonwealth arbitration law evidently never has restrained an unregistered labor organization
from strike action. As noted, strikes may be prohibited in
Commonwealth awards,[19] and in two Australian state jurisdictions they are prohibited outright. This does not mean that
strikes are necessarily subject to penal sanctions, although
there are such sanctions in some jurisdictions. As one Australian authority puts it, ". . . the arbitration systems of Australia have not been characterized by legislation penalizing all
strikes, or even all strikes which have an industrial purpose.
The prevention of strikes by conciliation and arbitration has
been the aim of all the systems, but their prevention by legal
action has not." [20] There has been and still continues to be a
long controversy in Australia as to the wisdom of penal sanctions against strikes. According to one member of the Commonwealth Conciliation and Arbitration Commission, ". . .
the Australian community has not made up its mind on the
desirability of strike penalties. . . . [In] most cases where
an illegal strike has occurred the penal provisions have not
been enforced." However, the Commissioner adds: ". . . the
fact remains that cases may occur in which a union persists in
a strike which the trade union movement as a whole makes
clear that it does not support. In such a case the institution of
penal proceedings may be an effective means of ensuring the
termination of the strike." [21] A presidential member of the
Commission, after noting that awards are "enforceable by
criminal procedure in certain circumstances" adds: "There is
much criticism of these penal clauses in Trade Union circles

and they would be repealed if labor ever gained the Treasury Benches. My own view is that they are objectionable and unnecessary." [22]

Although the Commonwealth Act no longer directly penalizes strikes or lockouts, the policy of the statute seems still to be that arbitration should be accepted by the parties as a substitute for the lockout and the strike. This is confirmed by the fact, already noted, that awards still can be made by arbitral authorities prohibiting the persons bound from striking.[23] As to Australasia as a whole, it seems fair to say, in the light of the statutory provisions cited above, that the ruling policy is that arbitration should be accepted by the parties in lieu of resort to direct action. Certainly, the theory there is that, where arbitral machinery is provided to compel agreement on unresolved issues, strikes become unnecessary, just as the American theory is that, in the almost complete absence of authoritative, compulsory determination of such issues, direct action becomes necessary, either to resolve them forthwith or to instill in one or both parties the more conciliatory spirit appropriate to such resolution in renewed negotiations.

The rationale of the matter was put quite plainly by William Pember Reeves, who, as Minister of Labour of New Zealand in the early nineties, sponsored the compulsory arbitration bill which was enacted by the Dominion in 1894: "In countries like England and the United States there is an object in a strike or lockout. It is [designed to] . . . starve the opposing side into submission. But there is no object in a strike or lockout in New Zealand, because you cannot starve the Arbitration Court into submission." [24] Judges of the Australian Commonwealth tribunal have echoed Reeves' observations. Many years ago, Mr. Justice H. B. Higgins, often called the "Father of Australian Arbitration," took occasion to say in one of his opinions as Judge on the Commonwealth Court of Conciliation and Arbitration (now the Conciliation and Arbitration Commission): "I have said on several occasions that unions cannot have relief from the Court by way of award if they are trying to get the same relief by way of strike. A union cannot have arbitration and a strike too. . . . The scheme of the Act is to substitute the remedy of arbitration (by reason) for the remedy of strike (by force)." [25]

Much more recently, the late Mr. Justice Foster, of the same tribunal, took occasion, in a deregistration case, to express himself on the same issue: ". . . the road to industrial peace and the orderly settlement of industrial disputes is always available to organizations who desire to use it; it is a good road kept in first class repair and as a result of the most recent amendments, a high speed road. Both the community and the Court are very anxious that it should be used on all occasions by all organizations, but if organizations decide not to use it, that is their concern; there are no powers of compulsion [to register under the Act]; all the Court can do is to record the fact that an organization has decided to take the other highway of direct action (a somewhat difficult and perilous route) and to keep its record and arrangements unencumbered by the continuation in its books of the registration of Unions which have decided to repudiate it." [26]

In the United States, as Pember Reeves suggested, "there is an object in a strike or lockout." In this country, in the absence of an ultimate power above the battle to resolve labor disputes that resist settlement by negotiation, (unilateral) strike or other direct action supplements bargaining where bargaining falters, infusing the "fear of God" where such infusion may stimulate conciliatory states of mind and thus lead to renewal of bargaining and perhaps, negotiations to a settlement. In Australasia, that "ultimate power above the battle" is a central fact of industrial life. Therefore, it would seem, on theory, that there would be no object in a strike or lockout Down Under, since, as Reeves contended, "you cannot starve the Arbitration Court into submission."

Whether this is so or not, trade-unions in New Zealand and Australia have given evidence that they believed that their arbitration tribunals could be influenced, even if they could not be starved "into submission." Thus, one informed Australian authority writes: "A certain amount of direct action, in the unions' opinion, is necessary, to ginger up the arbitrators, and they have steadily resisted the restraints imposed by arbitration. . . . Strong unions always have been prepared to strike against an award if they thought they would gain their objectives by doing so." [27] This position is confirmed in a more recent discussion by another Australian authority who says: "This attitude of [Australian] union officials—the disinclination to part finally and unreservedly with the strike weapon—shows little sign of change or modification." [28]

A pamphlet issued in 1953 by the Metal Trades Federation [an Australian labor association] quotes extracts from the Amalgamated Engineering Union's monthly journals, which include the following statement: "Our campaign and overtime embargo, in addition to the foundry workers' claim for improved wages, the nine day stoppage, etc., have all been instrumental in forcing the [Commonwealth] Arbitration Court [now the Conciliation and Arbitration Commission] to proclaim the 40 hour week principle and agree to an early hearing of the interim basic wage case." [29]

Also relevant to the question of the impact of unilateral "industrial" action centered upon the arbitral process, or upon the tribunals presiding over it, is Foenander's discussion of the Basic Wage Inquiry case of 1950.[30] He says: "There is little in the decision in the *Basic Wage Inquiry Case* of 1950 to warrant commendation as . . . [an] assessment of facts brought to the notice of the Court by the parties and intervenors.[31] . . . A primary justification for [arbitral] regulation in industry is the opportunity that can be provided for the avoidance of employment contracts detrimental to the public interest—a provision far more adequate and effective than is available in conditions of uncontrolled collective bargaining, where the danger of management-union agreements prejudicial to other sections of the community is only too evident and real." [32]

It is clear that in Australasia, despite compulsory arbitration, and although most labor disputes are "settled" by arbitral determination of them without strikes or other forms of direct action or threat thereof, some are determined against a background of "industrial" action or threat of it. It is equally clear that, although most labor disputes in the United States are negotiated out without strikes or other forms of direct action, many are bargained out only in an atmosphere of strike episodes and other forms of direct action. And perhaps, were the truth known, a large proportion of American labor disputes are "settled" only against a background of *potential* direct action.

The foregoing two statements relate primarily to the adjustment of Australasian and American labor disputes over interests. Despite the work of the Australian boards of reference and the New Zealand disputes committees—and despite the disposition of some, at least, of the disputes over rights by those agencies and by the state arbitration courts (or "commissions") and by the Commonwealth Industrial Court—it seems likely that many local disputes over rights Down Under must be marked by strikes or other forms of direct action. In the United States, it seems probable that, thanks to the operative grievance-machinery provisions in collective bargaining contracts, and thanks also to the operations of the American system of voluntary arbitration of grievance and other disputes over rights, there are relatively few invocations of strike (or other forms of direct) action brought about by such disputes.

In the United States, "the agreement to arbitrate grievance [rights] disputes is the *quid pro quo* for an agreement not to strike." [33] But there is no comparable (or, indeed, any) *quid pro quo* for the right of Americans to strike in default of agreement upon the terms of a contract [interest disputes]— apart from a specific agreement (entered into during negotiations) to waive that right—and such agreements are rare.

In Australasia, the availability of compulsory arbitration for contract disputes (with provision in many Australian awards for Board-of-Reference settlement of some classes of rights disputes [34]) seems to be the *quid pro quo* for disallowance of the right to strike over *either* type of dispute. In New Zealand, the tripartite disputes committees, which are analogous to the boards of reference in the Commonwealth and in two State jurisdictions in Australia, and to which may be referred "any dispute or difference between the parties . . . as to any matter arising out of or connected with the award or agreement but not specifically dealt with therein . . ." [35] seem not to be precluded by the Act from *interpreting* award provisions.

Collective Bargaining

Collective bargaining, as a bilateral process of negotiating changes in working rules, is relevant to discussion of the problems of adjustment of labor-management disputes, because at any stage of the negotiations, differences—disputes over interests—may develop over what, if any, change should be made in this rule or that. Such differences may be, and often are, amicably adjusted without abandonment of bargaining, after more or less protracted discussion among the representatives of the parties. Moreover, the bargaining process, over all, must be recognized as an important method of labor dispute settlement: the major method in the United States, and an important minor one Down Under.

To be sure, there will be times when the parties may not be able to reach agreement on the contract clause under consideration. If this happens, one or another method of settlement is likely to be resorted to—or perhaps, simultaneously, more than one of such expedients: the strike, a lockout, picketing, or resort to outside—or third-party—intervention by mediation, fact finding, or arbitration of one sort or another. At some stage, the boycott or the black list also may be utilized. Such expedients, especially the strike and/or picketing, may be resorted to prior to or in the midst of bargaining. A strike or picketing may be resorted to before bargaining on the union theory that this strategy will instill the fear of God in the heart of the employer. The methods of adjustment mentioned may be resorted to in almost any sequence, and there may be repetition of certain expedients—as is especially likely in the case of picketing. Generally speaking, negotiations, or a strike or lockout, are likely to be resorted to at the outset, with the bargaining, especially if it is marked by serious deadlocks, punctuated by strikes and/or picketing and, perhaps, finally abandoned.

Such final, premature abandonment of negotiations is not typical of collective bargaining proceedings in any of the three countries. This is especially true in the United States, since the federal and some state laws make collective bargaining mandatory where a majority of the employees are represented. Although there are many exceptions, the most likely sequence of dispute-adjustment techniques in the United States, if circumstances make it necessary to resort to more than one expedient, is: negotiation, strike, lockout and/or picketing (and, perhaps, the boycott); then, third-party intervention, likely to begin (and, hopefully, to end) with mediation, and, that failing, to culminate, if the parties can agree to it, in arbitration. Failing agreement, the cycle, or a part of it, may be repeated, with resort to such of the expedients mentioned as the parties may, respectively, think best adapted to serve their ends.

The process of collective bargaining is in some measure self-defining. As the phrase implies, it is a process of dealing—or negotiation—and it is a process of negotiation between groups—or collectivities—on each side. The phrase is used practically everywhere in reference to negotiations between employers and employees. It is a phrase-of-art, referring to certain aspects of labor-management relations. Reference to the phrase as having to do with negotiations between groups is, however, subject to some qualification. It is generally not considered collective bargaining if, on the employee side, only one employee is involved. That, as a practical matter, must be called individual bargaining, even though the single employee's employer is a large enterprise. But common-sense usage classifies the process as collective bargaining, even though on the management side there is only one small employer.[36]

It seems unnecessary, in the context of a discussion of collective bargaining as an expedient for adjustment of labor disputes, to discuss, or even to try to list, the proliferation of patterns into which the process, over the years, has come to be cast. Suffice it to say that there are national, district, and local systems and that union parties may be, *inter alia,* the local union, a union department, or the national union; while employer parties may be the individual employer, a division of the individual (corporate) employer, or a regional or national group of employers.

The process is defined in Section 8 (d) of the Labor-Management Relations (Taft-Hartley) Act, as amended, 1959, as, *inter alia:* ". . . the performance of the mutual obligations of the employer and the representative of the employees to meet at reasonable times and confer in good faith with respect to wages, hours and other terms and conditions of employment, or the negotiation of an agreement, or *any question arising thereunder,* and the execution of a written contract incorporating any agreement reached if requested by either party, but such obligation does not compel either party to agree to a proposal or require the making of a concession." This definition would seem faithfully to describe the bargaining process as it goes on in Australasia as well as in the United States, although, of course, it is drawn expressly for the purpose of Section 8 of Taft-Hartley, which section, with certain reservations, makes it an unfair labor practice for employers or labor organizations, in interstate commerce, to refuse to bargain collectively. Thus, while we do not have in this country (except in rare and extraordinary situations) compulsory settlement of labor disputes (by arbitration or otherwise), or, specifically, compulsory agreement in bargaining, we do have conditionally compulsory collective bargaining, as against the less drastic Australasian technique of "compulsory conference." [37] It often is called, with some warrant, "free collective bargaining."

In the United States, controversy has raged over the question of the subject-matter of collective bargaining; that is to say, over the precise range of subject-matter implied in the words "wages, hours and other terms and conditions of employment." That problem has been wrestled with from case to case by the National Labor Relations Board. For present purposes, it may fairly be said that collective bargaining is a process concerned with any or all of the questions which are incident to the employment relationship and which might be the subject of a difference or dispute between the parties. Perhaps it should be thought of as limited to the range of dispute-matters in accordance with which the parties are to carry on in the future (contract clauses in the United States, award clauses Down Under), though it may be that it also should embrace questions about the meaning and application of those clauses (grievance questions in the United States, questions referred to the boards of reference or to the courts, and especially the Commonwealth Industrial Court, in Australia and to labor disputes committees in the Dominion).

Some students of industrial relations regard the negotiatory process as one which comes to an end with the signing of the contract, not to be resumed until negotiations looking to a new contract are in order, say 30 days before expiry of the old one, or unless a wage reopening is provided for, say, at mid-term. Others conceive of the process as a continuing one which goes on through the full term of the contract.

On either view, it is clear that one important category of disputes is the type which may be precipitated during the process of bargaining for a contract, for a renewal of one, or incidental to the negotiations required by a wage-reopening clause. These differences we have called contract disputes, or controversies over interests. In this country, it is only rarely that these disputes fail of settlement by collective bargaining, interrupted perhaps by resort to strike, lockout, picketing, or boycott pressure. But, at times, the parties may agree to submit a clause, or clauses, over which they are deadlocked, to the ministrations of a state or federal mediation agency and perhaps, mediation failing, to final and binding determination by a private arbitrator, by a process we have labeled "contract arbitration," or "arbitration over *interests*," a type of arbitration relatively rare in America, but omnipresent in Australasia. But in this country, the parties are understandably reluctant to surrender in this way the making of any of the rules under which they will be living together during the term of the contract. They normally much prefer to settle their differences as to what working rules shall be written into their contracts by bargaining them out, fortifying such bargaining, if either party considers it expedient, by resort to some form of direct action.

Once the body of rules which constitute the collective agree-

ment is finally agreed upon and in effect, it has to be administered. In the course of its administration there are likely to be
differences of opinion as to how particular clauses should be
construed and applied. It is these differences that are referred
to in the above statutory definition by the words: "any question
arising thereunder." These we have called grievance disputes,
or disputes over rights. In this country most labor contracts
contain clauses outlining step-by-step grievance procedures,
in accordance with which the designated representatives of the
parties to the contract (the union and the employer) meet
together and attempt to reach an accord—that is to say, they
bargain—as to how, in the clause or clauses involved, the contract should be interpreted or applied. Most grievance disputes
are settled in this way, by bilateral negotiations. However, just
as the original bargaining over the making of the contract may
sometimes face deadlock over some provision, so, in the "grievance" bargaining incidental to the administration of the contract, the parties may face deadlock over a grievance or a
question of interpretation. To meet this difficulty, most grievance provisions stipulate, as a final step in the procedure, that
the parties will refer the deadlocked question to a private
arbitrator for final and binding determination, a process which
we have called "grievance arbitration," or "arbitration over
rights." [38]

There is much less collective bargaining (proportionate to
the size of the gainfully employed population) in Australia and
New Zealand than in the United States. Moreover, whereas in
the United States collective bargaining is something in whose
shadow (or along whose fringes) conciliation and arbitration
proceed, in Australasia it is something going on in the shadow
of conciliation and arbitration. The concomitant process Down
Under, in other words, is the conciliative-arbitral process, or,
more accurately, the twin processes of conciliation and arbitration, of which arbitration seems far the more important, although both overshadow collective bargaining.

The latter process, however, does go on in Australia and New
Zealand, and it plays a significant, even if subordinate, role in
those countries. The bargaining process seems to be engaged in

Down Under at several stages of the process of dispute settlement:

1) As in this country, it may go forward (conducted by the parties without outside assistance) as an initial phase of dispute settlement. In Australasia, there seems to be very little of this (the chief American) manifestation of the process. This perhaps is due to the availability—better, perhaps, the inescapability—of conciliation, and also of arbitration, which, together, seem to put a damper upon it in this role, or at this stage. Just as conciliation evidently is to some extent by-passed because compulsory arbitration is around the corner, so collective bargaining over differences about interests may be by-passed because compulsory conciliation (or assisted bargaining) is around a still nearer corner.

2) Bargaining in the assisted form takes place under the auspices of the conciliator. Bargaining of this sort does not, as yet, go on to any appreciable extent in the United States.

3) Bargaining, if thought of as a continuous process, goes on after agreement on the contract has been reached, after an industrial agreement has been reached with or without the aid of the conciliator, or, more typically, after an award has been promulgated. This type of bargaining is called grievance settlement here. It would seem appropriate to call it disputes-committee adjustment in the Dominion and board-of-reference settlement in Australia (in the Commonwealth and some state jurisdictions). In the United States, the cases have to do with the meaning or application of clauses of the bargained contracts, the decisions being called awards. Such settlement may be made by the parties on their own, or assisted by a government conciliator. In either event, the conclusion is a joint agreement by the parties, rather than a decision or award. But if the parties are unable to agree (even with conciliative aid) and an arbitrator is called in, the conclusion is his award. Down Under, the cases are concerned with the application (but not the interpretation—at least not in Australia) of clauses of the arbitral awards or industrial agreements. These determinations are called decisions. Whether here or Down Under, the

adjustments made seem to be made over "rights," not "interests." There is much more of this grievance settlement in the United States than Down Under. In the United States, moreover, it usually culminates (in the absence of bilateral adjustment) in voluntary private arbitration which is final and binding upon the parties. It is not clear to this writer to what extent, if at all, bargaining goes on Down Under before the boards of reference or labor disputes committees.

4) Finally, there is a sort of bargaining over interests which only emerges when a contract is signed or an award promulgated. Both collective bargaining agreements here and awards Down Under are repositories of minimum rules as to pay and conditions and maximums as to hours of work. What in Australia are called "over-award rates" may be fixed by unilateral action of the employer, or they may be individually or collectively bargained. Bargaining of this sort goes on to an indeterminate extent both in the United States and in Australasia.

It is difficult to say how much collective bargaining goes on Down Under. In New Zealand, working rules in the coal-mining industry, with some exceptions, are determined by collective bargaining. In that industry, the organized coal miners have chosen not to register under the (voluntary) registration provisions of the Industrial Conciliation and Arbitration Act. Instead, they negotiate collective agreements with the mine operators, which are strikingly similar to our own American labor agreements.[39]

Apart from coal mining, it would appear that very little collective bargaining goes on in the Dominion except for negotiations that are ancillary to the arbitration system. But, in the shadow of that system, there seems to be a good deal of bargaining, probably more (proportionately to the population) than goes on in Australia. Judge Tyndall notes that the "extent to which voluntary agreement operates in New Zealand is illustrated by the fact that over the past five years [1948 to 1953] sixty-two per cent of all industrial disputes handled under the I.C. & A. [Arbitration] Act have been completely settled in conciliation, while the Court has had some part in settling the remainder." [40] And the Secretary of Labour, Mr. H. L. Bockett, advised this writer that 75 per cent of the awards in November, 1958, were consent decrees—industrial agreements "made into awards" by the Court, which appends at the foot of the decrees the memorandum: "The award embodies the terms of settlement arrived at by the assessors in Conciliation Council."

This means that the bargaining, which culminates in a "consent award," is assisted bargaining, which proceeds in a conciliation council (made up of assessors more or less directly representing the parties to the dispute) under the chairmanship of a conciliation commissioner appointed by the Governor General. While bargaining in the United States is something less than "free," in the sense that the parties are compelled to engage in it in good faith if the "majority rule" applies, the New Zealand bargaining which culminates (to the extent that agreement is reached) in "industrial agreements" is something less than free in the different sense that, if the parties have failed to reach full accord before a conciliation council is convened, it must be carried on in the presence (and with the assistance) of a conciliation commissioner. To the extent that agreement in conciliation council fails, the Court takes over and, after hearing, makes an award; to the extent that there is agreement reached "in council," the contract (or parts thereof) agreed upon is filed with the Court, which, "without any hearing of the dispute" may "incorporate" its terms into an award.[41] How much bargaining goes on in New Zealand before the convening of conciliation councils I do not know.

Conciliation

The conditions subject to which "assisted bargaining," or conciliation, is carried on in the Dominion are substantially paralleled in the five Australian arbitral jurisdictions. In all of them, conciliation is one of the two central processes, the other of course being arbitration. The conciliative process in all of the Australian jurisdictions appears to have precedence, in the sense at least that it is expected—in the Dominion it clearly is required—to be resorted to before arbitration.[42] Down Under, the process of bargaining *cum* conciliation is a compulsory one for all registered organizations, although registration everywhere in Australasia is optional. What amount to compulsory conciliation conferences seem to be a feature of all of the Australasian jurisdictions.[43]

How much collective bargaining (of the several sorts described above) goes on in Australia it is difficult to say.[44] One Australian writer remarks that ". . . very little voluntary collective bargaining takes place in Australia outside of the arbitration system." [45] Confirmatory of this is the conclusion of Kenneth F. Walker (University of Western Australia) that, "with the sole important exception of the metal-mining industries of Broken Hill, very little collective bargaining occurs in Australia in complete independence of an industrial tribunal of some sort." [46]

Yet Foenander contends that "through the agency of authoritative industrial arbitration . . . a powerful stimulus [has been] applied to collective bargaining through registered organizations . . ." and that a "wide scope remains for bargaining between employers and employees, whether through their organizations or otherwise." [47]

Arbitration

Arbitration, or the determination of differences between parties by "neutral" or "disinterested" outsiders, is an important process in Australia, New Zealand, and the United States. It is a procedure which has been followed for many years in all three countries. Moreover, it has been used, and continues to be used, both there and here, in commercial as well as in industrial disputes.

In the case of commercial disputes, the differences dealt with in all three countries are disputes about rights. Both Down Under and here they are handled by private arbitrators chosen by the parties, under simple, common-law sanctions, which sometimes are overlaid by statutory glosses. Moreover, the parties to disputes in commercial or business matters utilize arbitration as a simple substitute for litigation in the ordinary courts, and the disputes thus arbitrated appear always to be disputes over rights. So far as the writer knows, commercial disputes over interests are never arbitrated, anywhere. The trader or businessman doubtless would scoff at the notion that he should arbitrate on the price he was to pay for goods (or services) had and delivered. If a question should arise about what grade or quality had been agreed upon, and if the parties failed to negotiate a settlement, that would be taken in arbitral stride. Traders in goods, in other words, arbitrate the rights they have or assert in their contracts; they do not arbitrate the terms of their contracts. That they would think strange, but buyers and sellers of labor in Australia and New Zealand, in default of agreement, must go to arbitration for the determination of the prices at which labor-power of specified grades is to be paid for. In America, much of the commercial arbitration is administratively presided over by a private organization, the American Arbitration Association (AAA), which maintains panels of names of eligible arbitrators, provides hearing rooms, etc. Having begun business many years ago as a clearinghouse for the settlement of commercial disputes, it later created a Labor Arbitration Tribunal. Under the auspices of that Tribunal, many of the rights-disputes arising in the labor-management field under collective bargaining agreements are arbitrated. Indeed, the labor-dispute cases handled under AAA auspices constitute an important part of the vast operations which make up the American system of voluntary (or obligatory) arbitration. Only very rarely are labor disputes over interests arbitrated under AAA auspices.

Neither in Australia nor in New Zealand, although both countries use the foregoing techniques for settlement of commercial rights disputes, are labor disputes on rights so settled. Instead, such disputes appear to be handled Down Under (1) by strikes or other forms of direct action, (2) as a major function of the Commonwealth Industrial Court in the federal jurisdiction of Australia, and a newly created tribunal in Queensland called the Industrial Court,[48] (3) as minor functions of certain of the principal tribunals primarily concerned with (non-justiciable) disputes over interests (the Industrial Commission in New South Wales; the Industrial Court in South Australia; and the Court of Arbitration of New Zealand), (4) as major (or perhaps, exclusive) functions of subordinate, specialized subtribunals (the labor-dispute committees in New Zealand and the boards of reference in the Australian federal, Western Australian, and Victorian [49] jurisdictions), or (5) very rarely, if at all, by settlement in the way both industrial and commercial disputes over rights are settled in America, viz., by private, lay arbitrators, chosen by the parties.

Perhaps the most important of the interventionary techniques utilized in the settlement of labor disputes is this device of arbitration. Like conciliation, but unlike fact finding, it is, as has been noted, a widely used procedure in all three countries. As a technique tailored to use in labor controversies, fact finding seems to be almost nonexistent in Australasia, while here it is quite widely and frequently used. Conciliation in Australasia and conciliation and fact finding in America, moreover, seem to be put to use mostly in connection with disputes over interests. If these methods fail to bring accord, direct action or arbitration probably will supervene. If the controversy is over rights (defined in Australasia in award, or industrial-agreement, clauses and in this country in industrial-agreement clauses), redress, while attempted not infrequently through unilateral direct action, also is sought, very rarely in Australasia, but almost as a matter of routine in America, by resort to arbitration. This arbitration is *the* American "system" of private, voluntary (or obligatory) arbitration by one-man tribunals (sometimes tribunals of several men), usually operating *ad hoc*, rather than as umpires retained for the whole period of the contract. These are the disputes about rights, many of which are handled, as noted, under the administrative supervision of the Labor Arbitration Tribunal of the American Arbitration Association. This Association's Commercial Arbitration Tribunal, as noted, is concerned with disputes between businessmen about disputed clauses in their contracts. Of course, these also are "rights" disputes, and (unless they are dealt with by direct action) they are handled in all three countries in much the same way, by party-chosen private arbitrators, who operate under simple statutory rules only a step away from the English common law. One has the impression that in Australia the techniques of commercial arbitration have, much less generally than in America, dispossessed the courts of jurisdiction over these justiciable disputes.

It has been noted that resort to arbitration in cases in which labor disputes over rights are unresolved is much less common in Australia and New Zealand than it is in the United States, where, it has been suggested, the arbitration of such disputes is *the* American "system." This system may be said to have been built up on much the same common-law foundations as has commercial arbitration, both here and Down Under. Neither in Australia nor New Zealand are these (justiciable) industrial disputes over rights adjusted as are disputes in the commercial category. It is quite plain how the (non-justiciable) disputes over interests are settled in Australasia, and they will be considered presently. It is more difficult to describe the ways and means used for settlement of the justiciable labor disputes. Such disputes, commonly called in this country "grievance disputes," appear to be settled in Australasia as noted above, either by direct action or by tribunal-handling of one sort or another. But this statement of the matter is quite unsatisfactory: obviously it describes, almost equally loosely, the American as well as the Australasian methodology of dealing with justiciable disputes. The phrase "direct action" covers a variety of practices (strike, lockout, picketing, boycott, etc.), as does the less familiar expression "tribunal-handling." While the great bulk of the case load of the arbitral tribunals in Australasia is made up of (non-justiciable) disputes over interests, they do have to deal to some extent with (judiciable) disputes over rights. Moreover, as noted, there are some ancillary or subordinate tribunals which are charged primarily— perhaps exclusively—with the handling of such "rights" disputes. The tripartite boards of reference in three of the Australian jurisdictions (the Commonwealth,[50] Western Australia, and Victoria) and in New Zealand (there called "labor disputes committees") appear to be charged, in part at least, with the resolution of "rights" disputes, although their powers appear to be delineated more specifically in the awards than they are in the statutes. The Commonwealth Act, however, authorizes the Commission "to appoint, for the purposes of the award, a Board of Reference consisting of one or more persons; and . . . assign to . . . [it] the functions of allowing, approving, fixing, determining or dealing with . . . a matter or thing which, under the award, may from time to time require to be allowed, approved, fixed, determined or dealt with by the Board." [51] This language would seem to give scope to these Boards to deal with labor disputes of any variety—except such as may be prohibited to them by the terms of the governing award. However, labor disputes involving problems of interpretation would be likely to go in any case to the Commonwealth Industrial Court. But the line between what is "interpretation" for the Industrial Court and what is permissible grist for Boards of Reference is not easy for this writer to draw.

In the Australian Commonwealth jurisdiction an amendment in 1956 to the Conciliation and Arbitration Act created the Conciliation and Arbitration Commission, consisting of a president, four other judges, and nine other commissioners, and exercising the power to settle disputes over interests by hearing the parties and making awards binding upon them. Another amendment in the same year set up the Commonwealth Industrial Court, with, among other powers, the authority "to give an interpretation of an award" (Sec. 110 (1)), making it, seemingly, the dominant determiner in the federal jurisdiction of (justiciable) disputes over rights.

It has been noted that the powers of the boards of reference which the Commonwealth arbitration act authorizes to be created usually are more specifically outlined in the awards which provide for them than in the statute itself. Thus a relevant provision in The New South Wales Tramways and Omnibus (Traffic Section) Award, 1952, (No. 470 of 1951) sets up (in Clause 31) a tripartite board of reference, among whose functions are the "settlement of any dispute arising out of this award and/or any dispute between the parties within the ambits of the respective disputes concerned, *but not involving interpretation thereof.*" The Board is specifically obligated "to refer to the [Commonwealth Court of Conciliation and Arbitration, now the Conciliation and Arbitration Commission] . . . *any dispute involving interpretation of this award.*" [52] But, since creation of the Commonwealth Industrial Court in 1956, such disputes would seem to be for that tribunal.

The Anzac systems of labor dispute settlement, then, are systems, predominantly, of adjustment of labor disputes over interests by compulsory (conciliation and) arbitration. Put in somewhat different terms, they are systems of decision making structured for the handling of disputes about what the working rules are to be in the future (insofar as such disputes remain unresolved by negotiation and/or direct action) through third-party determination by specialized tribunals constituting branches or extensions of the judicial systems of the two countries. Reference to these tribunals as extensions of the judicial system, however, does not warrant characterization of them as judicial agencies in the strict sense. Except as to procedural forms and requirements (stress upon "parties," the adducing of evidence, etc.) they are more legislative than judicial. Certainly their codes of working rules for the future—called "awards"—are legislative in character, and they are fairly comparable to the private legislative codes of working rules (collective labor contracts) bargained out by unions and employers in the United States.

The apparatus in the politically unitary Dominion is relatively simple: there is one dominant tribunal, the Court of Arbitration, tripartite, presided over by a judge, flanked by two lay colleagues representing labor and industry, respectively. This is the chief tribunal in New Zealand—a court with general jurisdiction to settle disputes arising in New Zealand industries. There are a few specialized industrial tribunals in New Zealand performing functions essentially arbitral: the Public Services Tribunal, the Railways Tribunal, the Post and Telegraph Staff Tribunal, and the Waterfront Tribunal. As has been noted, disputes may not be brought to arbitration until after they have been dealt with and, if possible, settled "in conciliation council." Thus, it appears that in New Zealand there is a more emphatic (or unconditional) disallowance of arbitration until and unless disputes first have been subjected to conciliative due process than seems to be the case in the Australian jurisdiction.

While there are in the Anzac countries special tribunals for such industries as coal mining, stevedoring, railroad transportation, etc., this specialization does no more than separate particular industries for treatment by the standard techniques of compulsory conciliation and arbitration. There is no adaptation of *process* to industry. In the United States, on the other hand, there is fairly widespread adaptation of this sort. Thus disputes on interstate railroads are dealt with, under the Railway Labor Act, by means of an elaborate system of procedures, invoked when bilateral negotiations fail: (1) for disputes over interests, governmental mediation and, that failing, voluntary arbitration under the auspices of the National Mediation Board; (2) for disputes over rights, unilateral compulsory arbitration at the hands of a public, Federal tribunal (the National Railroad Adjustment Board); (3) for disputes of any type which "threaten substantially to interrupt interstate commerce to a degree such as to deprive any section of the country of essential transportation service," resort to "emergency board" fact finding, culminating in a report to the President. In several of the states, the legislatures have enacted emergency labor laws providing for the adjustment of labor disputes involving public utilities. These statutes provide for the use of a variety of settlement devices, including fact finding, plant seizure, and voluntary and compulsory arbitration. For industry at large, there is provision in the Federal jurisdiction, by way of Section 206 of the Taft-Hartley Act, for dealing with "national emergencies." That section provides that whenever "in the opinion of the President of the United States, a threatened or actual strike or lockout affecting an entire industry or a substantial part thereof . . . will, if permitted to occur or continue, imperil the national health or safety, he may appoint a board of inquiry to inquire into the issues . . . and to make a written report to him. . . . Such report shall include a statement of the facts . . . but shall not contain any recommendations." The law also authorizes the President to seek an injunction restraining the strike or lock-out for 80 days. However, although the strike may be stopped in its tracks, the underlying dispute may, nevertheless, remain unresolved. It may be wishful thinking, therefore, to describe these as "dispute-settling" arrangements.

IDEOLOGICAL DEVELOPMENTS

IDEOLOGICAL DEVELOPMENTS IN THE INTERNATIONAL LABOR MOVEMENT

CHAPTER 11

by David J. Saposs

It is proposed in these pages to sketch the ideologic developments in the international labor movement.[1] These ideologies have been adapted and modified in different parts of the world, but they were nevertheless very largely influenced and stimulated by ideologic developments in Europe. An ideology, as has been intimated, may have a variety of facets. I propose to narrow my discussion down as closely as possible to the effect that ideologies have had on industrial relations. It may be necessary to touch on some of the related aspects, but I shall reduce these to a minimum.

In general, as we all know, labor movements started first in Europe. Therefore, insofar as organized labor is concerned, the important basic ideologies of an international nature emanated from Europe.

This means that these ideologies were predicated on the basis of the social and economic conditions existing in that part of the world. I shall therefore devote a fair amount of time to the ideologies as they were developed in Europe. At present, for instance, all of the important international labor organizations still have their headquarters in Europe. The World Federation of Trade Unions, being now Communist controlled, might be regarded as an exception. It has its headquarters in Prague, Czechoslavakia, on the other side of the Iron Curtain. Thus, Europe has always been, and perhaps is even now, the originator and chief expounder of labor ideologies; it is natural, therefore, that the international labor ideologies have been largely an outgrowth of the European situation.

Industry began separating from agriculture in the handicraft stage. During feudal times and earlier, industry was a kind of appendix to agriculture. Then, gradually, the skilled workers began moving away from the plantations and from the feudal estates and manors and settling in what later became urban centers of population. So, industry and commerce, as we understand them, developed largely as urban phenomena. In this early period, the great bulk of the industrial producers, as well as the great bulk of the people engaged in commerce, were the so-called self-employed.

As long as people were self-employed, there was no need for labor organization. But gradually, as business grew and it became not only possible but necessary to employ workers, a new social group appeared on the horizon—the propertyless workers with nothing to sell but their labor power. This group, whose members were dependent on others for employment, found itself on the lowest rung of the industrial ladder. It was confronted, therefore, with very serious problems.

The social reformers and other intellectuals, who were in sympathy with this wage-earner group, began to take a serious interest in it. A few leaders came up almost immediately from the ranks of the laborers. They were some of the more assertive, more articulate, and more talented members. But, in general, it was the intellectuals who shaped the early ideologies. The workers, imitating thcir masters who were organized in guilds, had barely started to organize into what became an incipient labor movement when the sympathizing intellectuals began to realize that there were certain underlying problems that affected the workers, particularly insofar as Europe was concerned. They began to develop a philosophy, an ideology, not so much as it related to a particular country or a particular nation, but as it reflected what they considered a universal situation. So we find that, in the very early period, most of the ideologies that were developed were those largely conceived and given form by intellectuals. Hence, although workers had barely begun to organize, the idea was already formulated that there ought to be some international organization; that national organization would not be adquate to cope with the problems confronting the workers.

The first concrete evidence of international organization appeared in 1864 when the International Workingmen's Association was formed. In the parlance of the labor movement it was referred to as the First International. This organization encompassed various groups with a variety of different concepts, philosophies, and programs, but in particular there developed two important points of view. One of them was publicized by Karl Marx and Frederick Engels. Marx and Engels had already written the *Communist Manifesto* in 1848. In the *Manifesto* they had begun a diagnosis of the existing social order, evaluating it, analyzing it, and finally setting forth what they believed to be a way out.

There had been only one significant development of a concrete nature that might have suggested the need of international organization. There had been a few minor instances in Europe where strikebreakers were brought in from one country to break strikes of workers in another country. Thus, in 1864, the First International was formed with representatives from all the European countries. Actually, there were no representatives to speak of from non-European countries. The First International had barely started when a very serious ideological conflict developed. The original ideology to which this First International was committed was Marxian, based on a watered-down version of the *Communist Manifesto*.

Another articulate and assertive group was made up of anarchists led by Michael Bakunin, a Russian intellectual. The anarchist philosophy was the exact opposite of the socialist philosophy. It is pertinent here to note some of the ways in which anarchism and socialism differed. The socialist philosophy was anti-capitalist. In those days the idea was that capitalism brought nothing but evil. The anarchists were also anti-capitalist, and to that extent they were in agreement with the socialists. They had the same basic approach, but differed on how to correct the situation. Quite often we find that labor ideologists may agree on defining a social system but differ as to how to bring about its abolition and on the nature of the social order that is to replace it. Thus these two groups differed fundamentally as to the type of organization needed to promote their ideology—that is, the abolition of the capitalist system and the introduction of another social order—and as to what type of procedure, or activity would make it possible for the workers to achieve their objectives, and as to what the new social order would be like.

As regards procedure, the socialists favored political action. They felt that it was important to organize the workers politically. Through their political parties they could carry on agitation and education until ultimately they would capture the government, and then would introduce socialism. In that sense they showed remarkable foresight, because in those days there was very little of what we call universal manhood suffrage. Most of the countries, as they emerged from feudalism, had begun to develop into absolute monarchies. Insofar as there was any suffrage at all, it was limited to property rights; but, nevertheless, the socialists (largely, it seems, because Karl Marx developed his philosophy in England where the workers were already beginning to acquire rights) considered legal action the appropriate strategy. Moreover, the socialists accepted capitalistic industrialism and proposed to build their social order upon it.

The anarchists, on the other hand, were opposed to political action. They pointed to the absolute monarchies and their denial of civil rights. "What good is political action?" they asked. They favored what they called "propaganda by the deed." Now propaganda by deed simply meant illegal, terroristic, insurrectionary action—action going even to the extent of assassination. They believed that was the only way to overthrow a system, that in fighting by political action there was no chance at all because of military or police control and denial of civil rights. The anarchists also differed with the socialists in that even though they were anticapitalist they did not want to take over the capitalist system and develop it further. They wanted absolutely and completely to prevent capitalism from developing at all. In other words, they wanted to turn back the clock. They wanted to maintain the original order that had been developing under the handicraft system, in which any individual could save enough money to become self-employed and be in business for himself. Indeed, in order to safeguard the ideal of self-employment, certain elements favored stopping corporations from doing business for fear that the self-employed would be unable to compete with them.

One profession in the United States has actually succeeded in attaining this ideal. It is illegal for a corporation to practice law. Only an individual or a partnership can do legal business. In some states the certified public accountants have also succeeded in obtaining such legislation. Likewise, the anarchists aimed at a social order based on small communities entirely independent of each other—as they were in the early days of the guild system.

The socialists believed in permitting industrialism to develop but in ultimately taking it over and nationalizing or socializing it. They believed that the way to do it was through political action. The anarchists said, in effect, "We will not permit industrialism to develop. We want to preserve small-scale business and encourage small communities, with everybody in business for himself. We cannot accomplish this reform through political action because we do not have the votes and we do not have the army. The way to do it is through terroristic illegal action." Those were the two conflicting ideologies that developed in the First International. It looked very much as though the First International would be captured by the anarchists, since the whole social situation appeared to the common man to confirm the analysis of the anarchists. The only thing that saved the First International from the anarchists was that Karl Marx removed its headquarters to New York. Otherwise the anarchists would undoubtedly have won out at that particular time. When it got to New York it was definitely on foreign soil. Hence it did not last very long, and in 1874 it went out of existence.

In the meantime other local labor organizations in the various countries began to grow and develop, and to take on substance. Concurrently, the feeling grew that there should be an international organization, and by 1889 there emerged the Second International, or the International Socialist Congress as it was officially called. At the outset, no particular effort was made to categorize the participants. Anybody who was affiliated with any kind of labor organization—whether it was an educational group, a co-operative, a union, or a political organization—could join the Second International. That organization was barely started when again an ideological conflict developed. This time it was the syndicalists who challenged the socialists. The syndicalist philosophy was developed very largely by Frenchmen. "Syndicat" in French means "union"; even employers' organizations called themselves "syndicats." Syndicalism, therefore, is a philosophy based on union organization. The syndicalists, like the socialists, accepted industrialism, and in addition were anticapitalist. They accepted the anarchist concept that political action was not the best means of obtaining their objective. According to them, the proper way to abolish capitalism was to organize workers into unions, and through union activity to so weaken the system that by resort to the general strike it would finally be abolished. And in this context there is an apt illustration of how ideologies affect industrial relations. Union activity was not intended primarily to establish collective bargaining, but rather to prepare the workers for the final general strike whereby the capitalist system would be overthrown and the new social order introduced. The syndicalists differed from the anarchists also in that they wanted organizations to systematically combat capitalism. They frowned on the haphazard use of individual action to accomplish the task. They wanted to function systematically as an organization, that is, as a union. The union might incidentally interest itself in labor relations, but only incidentally. Strong unions must not be developed. As a matter of fact, unions, so it was thought, tended to develop a sort of a class divsion among workers. The key group was to be found in the militant minority, the small, sophisticated, articulate group that really knew what it wanted. There were also the masses, who were merely followers—who constituted the inert mass—and who did not actually know what they wanted. Now this inert mass would have to be humored by throwing it a sop once in a while to hold it in line. The way to throw a sop is to call a strike, thus securing a trifling increase in wages or other improvement. But strict care must be exercised not to encourage unions which would establish permanent collective bargaining because then the unions would become conservative, and the masses would lose interest in revolution. Only incidentally are unions to be permitted to conduct labor relations and industrial relations. The prime idea was that they would be the revolutionary instrument to overthrow the capitalist order through a general strike. The chief tactic was to call intermittent strikes so as to keep the workers in training for the general strike in order to achieve the ultimate objective of capturing the government.

The socialists, on the other hand, while regarding political action as the prime means of achieving their aim, nevertheless laid the foundation for what we call collective bargaining. The socialists believed it necessary to organize workers into unions, which, in addition to serving the revolutionary objective in the sense that this would educate the workers, would also take a sober interest in industrial relations—that is to say relations with employers. So, here again we see how ideology affects industrial relations. As far as the syndicalists were concerned, collective bargaining and the other systematic methods of labor relations were purely incidental. They were techniques to be suspected and certainly not permitted to develop to a point where they might interfere with the revolutionary objective. The socialists thought that unions had two functions. One was to educate the workers in the revolutionary objective; the other, to lead the workers in the development of stable collective bargaining. So the ideology of the socialists was quite different; and the general conviction on the part of students in this field is that the socialists won out and the anarchists and syndicalists lost because the latter groups would not accept this particular procedure for dealing with the problems that arose under modern industrialism.

But, within the socialist movement there developed a profound difference over strategy, which resulted in a complete ideological metamorphosis. In part, it related to the collective bargaining role of the unions. It began in about the 1880's. Each group, one led primarily by Karl Kautsky and the other by Edward Bernstein, championed a different view on how the socialist movement could best accomplish its purpose. Kautsky held that the revolutionary objectives must be given priority. Bernstein, who had lived in Britain a great deal and was considerably influenced by the Fabian concept of gradualism, contended that it was more important to emphasize improvement of the conditions of the workers at the present time. The first precept became known as stressing ultimate demands, that is, the revolutionary objective. The second concept gave primacy to immediate demands—demands that, hopefully, would bring about immediate improvements. The group that favored revolutionary objectives, the Kautskyite group, reiterated, "Do not pay chief attention to collective bargaining." The Bernsteinite group maintained that collective bargaining must be given greater consideration, since the unions must play an important part in the development of the labor movement. To further bolster his position Bernstein began to question the Marxian philosophy.

Marx had proclaimed that there was no hope of improving conditions of the workers under capitalism. Bernstein challenged this concept. In addition, Marx predicted that the conditions of the workers would progressively deteriorate. Bernstein held that it is possible to improve the conditions of workers under capitalism. Therefore, it is necessary to develop strong unions, and these unions must develop systematic and effective collective bargaining relations. Thus the whole concept of systematic, orderly industrial relations, with strong unions through collective bargaining, really was developed by what might be called the moderate element in the socialist movement.

There were two countries in which a strong trade-union movement had grown at this time that did not accept socialism. One of them was the United States, and the other was Britain. The British unions were anticapitalist in the early stages, that is, around the 1830's. First they were strongly aligned with the Chartist movement, which was a revolutionary movement that wanted land reform and reform of the political system, particularly adoption of universal manhood suffrage. Later on, the British unions became followers of Robert Owen, a textile manufacturer who conceived the idea that in order to do away with the wage system it was necessary to develop producers' co-operation. This was an anticapitalistic concept but one to be achieved through co-operation.

In the United States, up to about 1890, the dominant labor organization was the Knights of Labor, a group which consisted overwhelmingly of indigenous workers. The American Federation of Labor came into existence in 1881, but did not become really important until 1886, and did not become the dominant organization until about 1895. The Knights of Labor as an organization was against capitalism in the sense that it wanted to prevent it from developing. It stood for producers' co-operation, and the accomplishment of certain other objectives through political action, and regarded union activity as an incidental feature. The trade-union movements of Britain and the United States, as represented by the AF of L, were really the most viable trade-union movements at this particular time, that is, up into the 1890s. Likewise, the socialist movement, which was largely confined to the continent of Europe, also took on substance.

At this time, a new element came upon the scene which had considerable influence on ideology as it affected industrial relations. The continent of Europe had a very large Catholic population. Indeed, most European countries were overwhelmingly or practically entirely Catholic (e.g., France, Italy, and Belgium). The only countries on the continent of Europe that did not have a large Catholic population were the Scandinavian countries, and these must therefore be treated separately. When the trade-union movement developed in continental Europe, its recruits naturally came primarily from the Catholics, but the Catholic hierarchy showed little interest in the problems of the emerging working class. This situation gave the radicals, the socialists, the anarchists, and the syndicalists a free field in which to win over the Catholic workers to their respective movements. Notwithstanding that they were Catholics, they were won over by philosophies that were clearly materialistic and anticlerical. Marx's slogan was, "Religion is the opiate of the people." But there were certain elements among the Catholic hierarchy that began to realize that it was a mistake to be indifferent to the problems of the workers. They were mostly from the lower eschelons, and they began to press the Catholic Church to change its position and take an interest in the problems of the workers. As a result, in 1891 the historical encyclical of Pope Leo XIII, called *Rerum Novarum,* was issued.

Rerum Novarum propounded a social philosophy of the Catholic Church which took into consideration the existence of a working class laboring under undesirable conditions traceable to industrialism. The encyclical demanded that these unfavorable conditions be remedied. The encyclical further declared that the workers must organize into unions, and that the employers must recognize their right to organize. However, the workers must not join the socialist unions. These were atheistic unions. Thus, a new trade-union group gradually came into existence, particularly in continental Europe; later it spread to other parts of the world. It called itself the Christian Trade Unions, which really meant unions that were predominately Catholic.

Catholic unions began to organize in various countries with a large Catholic population, finally founding in 1906 the International Federation of Christian Trade Unions. The ideology of the Christian unions was based on the Christian ethics. They accepted capitalism, and they worked on the hypothesis that the trade-union movement must adapt itself to working under capitalism, and therefore it must develop collective bargaining procedures. The ideology also favored various types of social reform and labor legislation, such as, social insurance, workmen's compensation, reduction of hours of labor, minimum wage legislation, etc. But, unlike the socialists, they decided that they would work through Catholic parties which were in existence in these European countries, as they are even up to the present time.[2]

I should mention that the Catholics have quite a substantial following in Canada, particularly in Eastern Canada and especially in Quebec. They also have a rather small following in Latin America. As far as Britain is concerned, the situation is a bit different. In Britain, the high Episcopalian Church took the same indifferent position as the Catholic hierarchy with reference to the problems of the workers. But there was a nonconformist church in Britain. The nonconformist or the minority group worked very closely with the early British labor movement, and as a result the British labor movement never really embraced Marxism in its entirety. Besides, many of the early labor leaders also served as lay ministers among the nonconformists. Consequently, there has always been a very strong religious tinge in the British trade-union movement in contrast to that in the continental European trade-union movements.

By the beginning of the twentieth century the labor movements that advocated practical trade-union activity through collective bargaining predominated. Those that adhered to an ideology that subordinated this concept began to vanish. In the socialist movement the reformists came into the ascendency; the pure and simple trade-unions and Christian unions became firmly established. On the other hand, those organized labor groups that featured revolutionary objectives were reduced to fringe factions. The ideologies of syndicalism and anarchism were most tellingly affected. For instance, in my book on the *French Labor Movement,* which appeared in 1931, I pointed out that, following World War I, syndicalism in France was practically abandoned by the labor movement, and the same thing happened in other countries. Following World War II a complete metamorphosis in the ideology of most of these labor groups occurred. I might start with the Catholic unions, which became very aggressive, very insistent in the labor-management relations field as well as in political activity. On the industrial field they were quite aggressive and quite active and carried on the same kind of collective bargaining practices that the other unions did. On the political field, they became the left-wing among the Catholic parties. I talked to many of their leaders in various parts of Europe. They always were interested in a coalition government of the Catholics and the socialists because, they said, if there were a coalition government of the Catholics and the socialists as the left wing of the Catholic party, they could vote with the socialists without violating any particular loyalty to the Catholic party. And they said they actually had more in common with the socialists by way of an interest in social reform than with their own party, because the Catholic parties in Europe are really more of a cross section of society, somewhat similar to the parties in the United States. They were a cross section of social life in general, and quite largely dominated by conservative elements; therefore these Catholic trade-union groups felt closer to the moderate socialists, who now stress welfare statism. A concrete example of Christian trade-union ideological transformation is presented in Germany in connection with the issue of co-determination. This concept calls for worker participation in the management of industry by the electing of workers to become members of boards of directors. The Catholic unionists serving in the Bundestag, the parliament of Germany, voted with the socialist unionists for co-determination legislation.

What, then, has happened ideologically to the pure and simple trade-unions as represented by the American Federation of Labor in the United States? The AF of L, when it came into existence and superseded the Knights of Labor, was composed of two immigrant groups, one from the United Kingdom, and the other from Germany. The Germans were socialists. Indeed, they introduced socialism into the United States. There happened to be certain industries in the United States that were exclusively German—the owners, the supervisors, and the workers. Hence, the unions in these industries subscribed to the socialist ideology. At a later period the same situation prevailed in the needle trades, dominated by the Jews. They, too, organized their own unions that adhered to socialism, which they also had brought with them from abroad.

On the other hand, the other industries, mostly the heavy industries—metal, steel, machine manufacturing, and so forth—were dominated by the Anglo-Saxons. The British unionists at that time were not socialists. They did not embrace socialism until after World War I. Hence, in the early 1890's conflict arose within the AF of L, between the socialists and the nonsocialists. The nonsocialists won out. Their leader was Samuel Gompers, a man of great intellectual prowess, although of a limited formal education. In his early trade-union career he was friendly to the socialists, but as the differences became clarified, he threw in his lot with the nonsocialists, becoming their leader. In this conflict the nonsocialists won out, gaining control of the AF of L. In addition to union activity, the socialists advocated political action as a means of securing labor and social reform legislation and agitating for socialism. On the other hand, the AF of L leaders, realizing that our government and our whole social life was dominated by the business elements, thought it best to adapt itself to the social order as it existed. Hence, the AF of L accepted capitalism by working within the existing order, concentrating on union organization that would work in the practical areas of securing immediate improvements through collective bargaining. Because they were pressed by the socialists to embark on independent political action and to advocate social legislation, they resisted this form of activity. Gradually they hammered out a new ideology, which they called "voluntarism."

Unions are voluntary organizations for the protection and

promotion of the interests of the workers. The workers must rely entirely on their unions. If the government does anything for them, if the employer does anything for them, then they will show less interest in the union. Therefore, the AF of L, in this early period, was opposed to political action. It was also opposed to most forms of labor and social legislation. It opposed, for instance, workmen's compensation and accident insurance legislation. The AF of L originally, around the turn of the century, opposed regulating the hours of labor of men. It opposed any kind of social legislation, such as social insurance and unemployment compensation, up to the time of the New Deal, largely because these things were advocated by the socialists who were very strong up to the time of the World War I in the United States, and because it wanted to ingratiate itself with the business elements who dominated both industry and the government. As a matter of fact, the AF of L played up the idea that it was going to save the business elements from socialism, in the hope that on that basis the business elements would recognize its unions. The business elements wined and dined the labor leaders but did not recognize their unions. Thus, we had in the United States an antisocialist voluntarism which even opposed almost any kind of labor and social legislation.

By the time of World War II, and mainly because of experiences during the unprecedented depression in the United States, certain trade-union elements led by John L. Lewis concluded that the voluntaristic philosophy was a mistake. They felt that the government had a definite responsibility to ameliorate the hardships from which the workers were suffering, particularly because of immense unemployment. They insisted that the AF of L demand such legislation and government administrative action. In due course they committed the AF of L to social legislation, which ultimately developed into a full-fledged welfare state ideology. In this connection, the dissident elements also introduced the idea that only through industrial unions could the workers in the mass-production industries be organized. And since the influential AF of L leaders addicted to craft unionism opposed the innovation of industrial unions, a schism occurred which resulted in the founding of the Congress of Industrial Organizations, the CIO.

Slowly the AF of L began to realize that the government also had a very important role to play in promoting the welfare of the workers, that by themselves the unions could not cope with these problems. Hence, the AF of L also became welfare state in ideology. It favored social security, housing, and other types of labor and social reform legislation, and sympathetic government administration. Thus, when the merger with the CIO occurred in 1955 the question of ideology did not arise, since both now had the same outlook. For instance, at the present time the AFL–CIO recognizes that the bothersome problems of automation, race discrimination, racketeering, and unemployment cannot be solved by the unions alone, but that the government, and indeed management, must do their part in coping with these problems.

On the problem of racketeering, first the AF of L announced that it alone would handle and correct this evil. However, the leaders have now acknowledged that racketeering in the labor unions is too big a problem for the unions themselves to handle, and that the government, especially, must take a hand in it. More recently, when the question of race discrimination in the unions became acute, particularly in the building trades which the highly skilled workers dominate, George Meany, the president of the AFL–CIO, declared that, while racial discrimination must be met and attacked by the unions, the unions alone cannot handle it. Later, the AFL–CIO officially declared that the government must assist. A similar attitude is now expressed with reference to other profound social problems. Thus, although the AFL–CIO has definitely embraced the welfare state ideology, it has not abandoned collective bargaining. Indeed, it has actually enlarged collective bargaining procedures. The Australian, New Zealand, and Israeli labor parties are also welfare state in outlook, and so are their trade-union movements.

This organized labor ideological metamorphosis presents a global situation. In the Western-oriented countries, i.e., Western Europe, North America, Australasia, and Israel, the labor movements have definitely become welfare state in ideology. These countries are recognized as supremely socially stable, which seems to be the concomitant ingredient for viable labor movements.

Moreover, it should be noted that the welfare state concept in the Western-oriented countries has now been accepted by practically all political parties. In Britain, when the Tories defeated the Labor Party and came into power, they did not undo the nationalization that the Labor Party had introduced. They tried to denationalize the steel industry, and even there they have not entirely succeeded because the Labor Party had announced that when it regained power it would nationalize it again. Hence, private enterprise is hesitant and the steel industry is really not denationalized. The only business completely denationalized was long-haul trucking. In regard to social reform legislation, the major competition now is between the Tories and the Labor Party over the introduction of social reform legislation. The former claims that it is doing more than the Labor Party. A similar situation exists in the United States. Former President Eisenhower talked about "creeping socialism," but he did nothing to undo any of the basic social reform policies adopted under the New Deal. As a matter of fact, during his administration some of the measures were improved and even extended. Thus, so far as Western-oriented countries are concerned, all political parties are welfare statist in some degree.

Now with reference to the underdeveloped countries: as pointed out by Mr. Mehta, all of the parties in India are socialist. At least, they claim that they are. Take, for instance, most of the other Asian parties—Sukarno of Indonesia proclaims his own brand of socialism; Nasser of Egypt actually has set the pattern by declaring for Egyptian socialism. What kind of socialism do they profess? I think it is an entirely different kind of socialism from that advocated originally by the Western socialists. Likewise, the labor movements that are being organized in the underdeveloped countries generally proclaim themselves as socialist adherents. In Latin America the labor movements are also anticapitalist, socialist, or communist. In Africa, the same attitude prevails. A close analysis reveals that the socialism advocated in these newly developing regions is rather vague. Indeed, it more nearly resembles welfare statism.

So far as the labor movements of the Western countries are concerned, this ideological transformation simply means emphasis on empirical activity and practical achievements through trade-union and political action. Insofar as the underdeveloped countries are concerned, the interest for the time being is chiefly with political rather than industrial aspects, because they are just passing out of colonialism and feudalism.

INDUSTRIAL RELATIONS AND THE NEW ZEALAND ECONOMY

CHAPTER 12

by Arthur Tyndall

I propose first to give a short economic background on New Zealand; then a history of the labor movement, political and industrial; some comments on the investigation of union elections and other legislation dealing with the control of unions; contributions and levies for political purposes; relations between the industrial and political labor movements; the status of the New Zealand Federation of Labor (the dominant labor organization in the country) ; and, finally, a few remarks on the part that communism has played in the political and industrial arenas.

It must first be realized that New Zealand is primarily an agricultural and pastoral country. Ninety-four per cent of her exports are pastoral products. The main items are wool, meat, and dairy products, and such by-products of those industries as skins, hides, tallow, and so forth. The farmers claim that they are the backbone of the country. For a long period the influence of the farming interests has been very strong in the political field. The attitude of the farmers to the workers' unions for many years was one of hostility, and also I think it would be fair to say that their attitude to the Court of Arbitration prior to 1935 was similar. Attempts to bring agricultural workers under the Industrial Conciliation and Arbitration Act or some system of wage regulation were unsuccessful until the labor government was elected to power in 1935. Indeed, many years ago, when an attempt was made to bring farm workers within the jurisdiction of the Court, the Court itself refused to accept jurisdiction. Agricultural workers for the most part do not even now come within the scope of the ordinary activities of my Court (the New Zealand Court of Arbitration), although in certain circumstances we may be called upon to make recommendations to the Minister of Labour as to the minimum rates of wages and the working conditions which should prevail.

The history of the trade-union movement in New Zealand prior to 1894 was similar to that in Australia and Great Britain. In 1890, however, there was a major maritime strike which seriously affected both Australia and New Zealand. The conditions prior to the introduction of the Industrial Conciliation and Arbitration Act were described in depressing terms by Professor J. B. Condliffe in his book, *New Zealand in the Making*.[1] Unemployment was aggravated by the exploitation of the labor of women and minors. This was most serious in the clothing trades, where a vicious system of subcontracting and homework had grown up. Wages were desperately low, hours were long and were lengthening, and working conditions were very bad. Adult male labor had escaped the worst of such conditions by standards of hours set early in the colony's history. But the sweating of female and child labor tended to lower wages and accentuate male unemployment even if it did not materially worsen the conditions of labor. The trade-unionists therefore felt a vital interest in the welfare of the unorganized workers in home industries. It was partly a problem of depression, low wages, and falling prices, but also it was largely a lack of government regulation. Inadequate organization of labor contributed by making possible the abuse of the apprenticeship system and the growth of subcontracting. As always in such cases, it was the home workers whose conditions were the worst and whose competition brought down general standards. The chief need, therefore, was such government regulation as would enable the more efficient employers to withstand the competition of their weaker and less scrupulous rivals. There were very few laws at that time (the period preceding 1890) to protect the workers.

I have mentioned that in that year a devastating maritime strike took place in Australia and New Zealand. At about this time a new government came into power in New Zealand. The party was called the "Liberal and Labor Party" and was headed by a notable figure by the name of Richard John Seddon, who was to be premier for 13 years. The government started off with a kind of "new deal," and more rigid regulations were applied to factories, shops, and offices. Old-age pensions were introduced and much liberal legislation was passed. One of the new statutes introduced by that government was the Industrial Conciliation and Arbitration Act, which was enacted in 1894, and which has come to be referred to generally as the "I. C. & A. Act."

The first attempts of the liberal government to put through an industrial conciliation and arbitration bill were frustrated by the legislative council (the upper chamber) [2] which was dominated by supporters of the defeated government. In their first year in office the liberals made their first attempt to enact a conciliation and arbitration act, which was followed by another in 1893, and then by the successful passage of the statute in 1894. Other laws were passed which made great improvements in working conditions. These were the first effective labor laws in the country. Incidentally, there was such a division of opinion over the I. C. & A. Act between the house of representatives and the legislative council, that a committee from both houses had to be set up to try to arbitrate the differences. One of the matters that figured prominently in the debates was the picture, drawn by some of those opposed to the proposal, of the very unfortunate possibilities that might arise in connection with the dignity of judges. The original provision was that a supreme court judge should do the work of the Court of Arbitration, which was estimated to be only a very small part-time job. But the people who opposed this scheme were very concerned about how the dignity of a supreme court judge might be affected by the vigorous advocacy arguments and attitudes of both sides in labor disputes.

Things went on relatively quietly until about 1912 when the liberal government then in office was replaced by a conservative government with strong support from the farming community. Just prior to World War I, there was a miner's dispute at the Waihi mine, which culminated in a serious strike. The mine was New Zealand's largest gold mine, and the conflict between the employer and the workers and between rival groups of workers was very bitter. There were riots and violence and a man was killed. The incident left a black mark on New Zealand's industrial history.

In 1913 there were similar troubles on the waterfront, in which farmers and business men were sworn in as special constables. Feelings were running very high at the time and there were many cases of violence. Civil servants were called out and equipped with batons to help in dealing with the strikers. It was an unfortunate time industrially, and one of the results was the passing, in 1913, of a subsidiary act called the Labor Disputes Investigation Act. The whole situation, of course, changed with the outbreak of World War I.

During the war, the arbitration court functioned and awarded what were called cost-of-living bonuses, based on the war-induced increases in the cost of living. After the war, certain general adjustments were made to minimum rates of wages throughout the country in 1919, 1920, and 1923. Several adjustments provided for increases and one or two for reductions. Here it should be mentioned that during World War I a coalition government functioned. It was constituted of the leaders of the conservative party and the liberal party which had been ousted from office in 1912. After the war ended, the coalition was terminated and an election was held. The conservative party was returned to office and remained in power until 1928. As already noted, the farming community strongly supported that government and the prime minister, Mr. J. G. Coates, who was a farmer. Between the war and the depression of the 1930s, a third political party, the Labour Party, grew stronger and stronger.

In 1928, an industrial conference was held under the aegis of the government. It was comprised of representatives of many interests, including farmers, well-known professors of economics, employers, and trade-unionists. The whole arbitration system came under critical review. The arbitration court was held up to ridicule, particularly by the economists. One matter that was played up was the fact that the arbitration court on one occasion had been called upon to decide whether the putting of jam and cream on cakes was or was not unskilled work. Interestingly enough, that very same incident was referred to my court only a few weeks ago in the course of the general order case now being heard, showing how these matters echo and re-echo over the years.

In 1928 there was a change of government. A new party called the United Party emerged and won a certain number of seats. The Labor Party obtained more seats and the United Party and the Labor Party joined to defeat the conservative government. The United Party became a minority government, being kept in office with the assistance of the members of the Labor Party. Incidentally, during the war several important labor leaders, including a labor member of Parliament, were imprisoned for making subversive speeches. The principle mainly espoused in those speeches was that the policy of the country in wartime should be to conscript wealth before human beings.

Then came the economic depression. Again the emergency produced a coalition government. The United Party and the conservative party formed a coalition for the purpose of coping with the serious economic problems arising out of the depression. Our money was devalued to the extent of 25 per cent, compared with English sterling, mainly to assist the farming industry. Agricultural and pastoral activities are such vital features of our economy that, naturally, a government that had any interest in the welfare of the farmers had to do something of the kind. This step helped the farming community and the exporters, but of course it also affected the cost of all imports and this was resented by organized labor. During the depression we had a large number of unemployed and the government organized relief works on which the workers were paid about three pence an hour plus their keep. They worked largely on road improvements. Local authorities were also assisted by the government to find work for the unemployed, and many civic improvements were carried out at low cost to those authorities. There were a few riots of the unemployed in our main centers, during which shop windows were broken and some pilfering occurred.

In 1935 there was a general election. The policy of the coalition government, combined with the effect of the depression, resulted in a political landslide, and for the first time in the history of New Zealand the Labor Party was returned with a solid majority. I should mention that the Court of Arbitration continued to function in its normal way until 1932. In 1931 the first Finance Act of that year empowered the Court to vary all minimum prescribed rates of wages by general order. Interestingly enough, it was no doubt the farming community and the employers who pressed for the introduction at that time of this very important power. As a result of that legislation, the Court of Arbitration, in 1931, made a general order under which all minimum rates determined by awards and industrial agreements were reduced by 10 per cent. In the following year, however, Parliament decided to reduce the powers of the Court. The effect of the legislation was to continue conciliation but to abolish compulsory arbitration. The parties were required to confer, but, if they did not succeed in reaching an agreement, there was no right of either side to bring the issues before the Court. If they wanted to do so, the parties could have gone to the Court voluntarily. So, from 1932 until 1936 compulsory arbitration as we know it was abolished. The result was that numerous awards expired and were not replaced, so that many workers were at the mercy of their employers who, in fact, because of the surplus of labor were able to reduce wages considerably. This development no doubt contributed to the success of the Labor Party in the 1935 elections. The platform of the Labor Party was, broadly, to improve the economic status and conditions of employment of the lower-paid workers.

In 1935 the general election in New Zealand was held near the end of the year, and in 1936 the labor government introduced a new era into many fields of human activity, and particularly into industrial relations. A flood of fresh legislation included provisions for complete restoration, and indeed substantial extension, of the powers of the Arbitration Court. It is interesting that the personnel of the first labor cabinet reflected the fact that the trade-union movement had been cradled in the mining industry. A majority of the members of that cabinet had been either coal or gold miners at some stage of their lives.

The legislation that was passed in 1936 included a general provision for a maximum working week of 40 hours at ordinary rates of pay. It was the idea of the labor government that there was not enough work to go around during the depression, and therefore the ordinary hours of work should be reduced. At the same time, discretionary powers were given to the Court of Arbitration to determine whether longer hours up to 44 per week at ordinary rates of pay should be permissively worked in any particular industry, which, after hearing the parties, the Court considered could not be carried on efficiently within the 40-hour week. These discretionary powers have remained with the Court up to the present, but in 1945 the 40-hour week was compulsorily applied by the legislature to all factories, whereas between 1936 and 1945 there were many exceptions. The 40-hour week was also applied by statute to shops and offices in 1945. For all practical purposes the 40-hour week is now almost universal. The 40-hour week, of course, does not mean that the workers work only 40 hours. Under conditions of over-full employment there are many workers who do not adhere to the

40-hour week. The employers in some industries regularly offer overtime work, and many workers regard the offer of overtime work as an inducement to start with an employer instead of the reverse. So the 40-hour week, so far as actual working hours are concerned, is largely a mythical concept. I was reminded of one situation the other day when I read about the electrical workers in New York City reaching agreement with the employers for a 25-hour week, but I understand they have five hours guaranteed overtime, paid for at time-and-a-half rates. The legislation in New Zealand prescribes that coal miners shall work a maximum of 35 hours a week at ordinary rates of pay.

Another very important matter introduced in 1936 was compulsory union membership. An amendment to the I.C. & A. Act was passed, providing that the Court of Arbitration in making any award should insert a provision requiring all workers covered by the award to become members of a union of workers bound by that award. There may be more than one union, of course, bound by any particular award, but provided the workers were the members of any such union, they complied with the law. There were penal provisions against workers who did not comply, and also penal provisions against employers who employed workers who were not members of an appropriate union. The statute provided further that all industrial agreements should be deemed to include similar provisions. The foregoing compulsory requirements have been in effect for the last 26 years and have operated successfully. Now the matter is in a state of legislative flux, of which I shall speak presently.

The amendments of 1936 imposed upon the Court of Arbitration the obligation to fix a basic wage, somewhat similar in concept to the basic wage in Australia. The Court fixed such a wage in 1936, but never again exercised the power. This part of the legislation was abandoned some years afterwards, and in 1945 it was in effect replaced by the Minimum Wage Act in which Parliament fixed the minimum rates, which were appreciably lower than the minimum rates prescribed in awards of the Court. The Act protects domestic workers and any other

workers who are not covered by awards or industrial agreements or orders of tribunals, but is limited in its application to
adult male and female workers.

As a matter which affects the income of a worker's family,
mention should be made of the payment, under our social security scheme, of 15s. per week in respect of every child under 16
years of age and, under certain conditions, up to 18 years of
age. The Maoris, our native race, of which there are 150,000
out of a total population of about 2½ million, are very prolific.
Their present rate of natural increase is 4 per cent per annum
compared with 2 per cent for Europeans; consequently they
derive considerable benefit from the children's allowance.
There are four Maori members of Parliament, out of 80 members for the whole country, and they are directly elected by the
Maori people. Since the end of World War II, every Maori representative has been a supporter of the labor government, and
no doubt the social security benefits introduced by a labor
government have been a contributing factor.

In the postwar years other statutes have had a beneficial
effect on the welfare of workers. One is the Annual Holidays
Act, making a minimum of two weeks annual leave compulsory
for all workers. As the result of recent decisions in Australia
granting three weeks annual leave to many workers, there is
agitation developing in New Zealand for similar treatment.
The Court of Arbitration has power to grant annual leave to
any extent it deems fit, provided it does not award less than the
Annual Holidays Act prescribes. For example, it has in a
number of cases awarded regular-shift workers three weeks'
annual leave because of the disabilities associated with shift
work. Likewise, partly due to the generosity of employers and
partly due to decisions of the Court, we have a number of
awards and industrial agreements in which three weeks' annual leave is prescribed after 10 years of continuous service
with the same employer.

I mentioned that the farmers as a group have for many years
been opposed to any regulation by the government or by the
Arbitration Court of the conditions of work of their employees,
but the labor government in 1936 introduced a statute called

the Agricultural Workers Act. Under that statute provision is made for negotiations or collective bargaining between authorized representatives of the farming community or any section of it and a certain union that includes agricultural workers within its authorized coverage, called the New Zealand Workers Union. The parties have usually settled the minimum rates of wages and conditions, following which event an order in council has been issued in terms of the settlement which binds all farmer employers for a prescribed period. Similar orders have also been negotiated and issued for specialized branches of the farming industry such as orchards, tobacco farms, and so forth. I should mention as an exception that for many years there have been awards of the Court of Arbitration covering the employment of workers engaged in the shearing of sheep. One interesting feature of the shearers' award in our country is that minimum wage rates, including piece-work rates, are computed by a formula which varies from time to time depending upon the negotiating capacity of the parties. In general, the formula is based on the price received by the farmers for their wool. I think that is the only award we have in the country of such a nature. Farmers, however, have to compete for labor against growing secondary industries in the cities and towns and have been forced to pay rates in excess of the minimum award rates. Indeed, throughout all industries in New Zealand the average gap between the minimum rates of wages prescribed in awards, agreements, and orders in council and the actual wages paid has been increasing steadily ever since the end of World War II.

In 1943, an amendment to the I.C. & A. Act was passed, strengthening the protection of workers against victimization for engaging in union activities or for appearing as witnesses or taking any action in the interest of their fellow workers. The enforcement of that legislation is in the hands of the Court.

After World War II broke out in 1939, many emergency regulations were promulgated. One such was called the "Rates of Wages Emergency Regulations 1940." The object of these regulations was to vest the Court of Arbitration with power by general order to increase or reduce all rates of remuneration prescribed in awards and industrial agreements after taking into account the economic and financial conditions in the country and any changes in the cost of living. The idea was to enable the Court to make rapid adjustments in the wage structure which might be desirable as the result of changes brought about by the war. The regulations have been varied many times in the intervening years, but the basic authority still remains with the Court.

The first general order under the regulations was made in August, 1940. Since then the Court has dealt with 12 further applications for such orders or orders of a similar nature and is now engaged in hearing the fourteenth application. After the War, when the cancellation of emergency regulations was under consideration, the provisions for making general orders were not repealed, and these special powers with certain modifications have remained with the Court down to the present time. The employers have made many requests to several successive governments that the powers should be withdrawn, but without success. The workers' organizations desire the retention of these powers.

In December, 1942, economic stabilization was introduced into New Zealand. An interesting result was that the Court of Arbitration was made one of the instruments for the effective administration of stabilization in relation to all salaries and wages whether or not covered by awards or industrial agreements. Salaries and wages were frozen, subject to certain conditions. Conciliation commissioners were given authority to approve in special circumstances departures from the general scheme of stabilization, with the right to appeal to the Court of Arbitration. That system theoretically prevailed until 1950, when it was abandoned.

After the war, from 1945 onwards, there were signs of unrest among labor organizations, and various steps were taken to obtain general increases in wages. The labor government, which had been in power since 1935, was defeated in the 1949 general election, and the National Party under the leadership of Mr. S. G. Holland (later Sir Sidney Holland) became the government. The defeat of the Labor Government in 1949 was probably due partly to the swing of the pendulum, which is characteristic of democracies, and to a growing feeling of irritation among some people over the attitude and actions of a few militant labor unions, notably the waterside workers.

Among the policies announced by the National Party in its election campaign was the abolition of compulsory unionism, but when the legislation was framed to implement the policy and evidence was heard before the Labor Bills Committee of the House of Representatives, it was not supported by either employers' or workers' organizations, with the result that the government dropped its proposal for abolition.

In 1950, the new government reduced some of the subsidies on certain necessities which had been introduced during the war to assist the lower-income groups; this step was resented by the labor organizations. However, my Court, of its own motion, made a general order increasing minimum rates of wages by 5 per cent, to balance the effect of the reduction in subsidies on the living costs of the working man. In 1951 the country was benefiting from high prices for its exports as a result of the Korean War. The price of wool advanced tremendously, and the national income rose appreciably. After hearing submissions and evidence from workers' and employers' organizations, the Court made another general order in 1951 increasing all minimum rates of wages by a further 10 per cent, making 15 per cent in all. The manner in which this increase was applied to the waterside workers produced discord; the new government was faced with a general waterside strike, which spread to some other industries in which the workers were in sympathy. The waterside workers were not directly within the jurisdiction of the Arbitration Court, having been placed under the control of a separate authority early in 1940. This 1951 strike, which continued for several months, was the most serious industrial disturbance we have had in many years. The government utilized military forces on the wharves to help unload and load the ships. The attitude of the New Zealand Federation of Labor, which is the dominant labor organization in the country, was expressed in the following resolution: "That in negotiations there shall be no departure from the policy of the Federation of Labor, namely, conciliation and arbitration, and that representatives of the watersiders, miners, and freezing workers or any other unions not affiliated with the Federation of Labor taking part shall first state in writing that they accept this condition. Failing such assurance by the watersiders, this conference has no option but to inform our affiliated unions that we cannot and will not lend any further support to this dispute." That was a forthright statement, and no doubt proved of considerable help to the national government.

The strike ultimately collapsed. This was due to several causes, an important one being the attitude of the then President of the Federation of Labor, Mr. Fintan P. Walsh. Other drastic actions were taken by the government, such as freezing the funds of several of the striking unions. These actions were very strongly criticized and challenged as being contrary to the principles of freedom of association and independence of organized unions of workers. Nevertheless, the collapse of the strike resulted in the fragmentation of the waterside workers' unions and the freezing of workers' unions, two of the most militant and powerful groups in the country. By fragmentation I mean that the national union of waterside workers was broken up into several unions, and while some integration has since been achieved, the original position has not yet been fully restored.

The New Zealand economy and the public interest suffered very greatly from the 1951 strike. It is estimated that New Zealand lost in export trade a sum of from 30 to 40 million pounds. Because of the strike we lost the advantage of the sale of a large quantity of wool at peak prices.

The strike and the attitude of the Federation of Labor resulted in the expulsion from the Federation of Labor of the waterside workers and certain other unions, such as the coal miners, and the freezing of workers who had struck in sympathy with the watersiders. A rival organization called the Trade Union Congress was organized but very soon faded out of existence. There was a great deal of public debate on the way in which the government had handled the strike and on the attitude toward it of the Federation of Labor. The Prime Minister of the day (Mr. S. G. Holland) decided to test public opinion, and on very short notice called for a general election. His government was returned with a substantially increased majority, showing that the electors supported the government's policy and its drastic actions against the strikers. Following the restoration of industrial peace, Parliament passed the Waterfront Industry Act 1953, and this statute still governs activities on the waterfront.

In 1957 the labor government was again returned to office. Deterioration took place at this time in our terms of trade because of the drastic falling off in prices paid overseas for our dairy produce. Our overseas balances started to fall rather seriously and the labor government brought out a bold budget in 1958 which increased indirect taxation to such an extent that it came in some quarters to be called the "black" budget. Naturally, the cost of living was affected, with the result that in 1959 an application was made to the Court of Arbitration for a general order increasing all minimum rates of wages. An issue debated at length before my Court was whether, in reaching a decision, the Court should take fully into account the effects of the emergency budget on the consumers' price index.

In 1960 there was another swing of the political pendulum, the National Party being again returned to office, and, for the second time, it included in its platform a proposal to abolish compulsory unionism. In 1961 a bill was introduced accordingly. It underwent much modification during the debate in Parliament but was ultimately passed. The attitude of the Federation of Labor was expressed in this resolution: "That having regard to the present government's decision to abolish compulsory unionism and its refusal to enforce the law thereon that has been in operation and enforced by all previous governments for the past 25 years, it be recommended that conference not reaffirm its previously adopted principle of compulsory conciliation and arbitration, which includes its present attitude to the Court of Arbitration, and that this whole subject be referred to the incoming national executive to deal with, having regard to the legislation the government proposes to intro-

duce on the abolition of compulsory unionism and industrial
matters generally."

This resolution indicates the impact of the legislation on the
attitude of organized labor. The new law provided that, where
awards included a provision for compulsory unionism, it continued in effect until they were replaced by other awards or
amended during their currency. After fifteen months following
March 1, 1962, the old compulsory unionism provisions will
automatically expire and be replaced by qualified preference
clauses unless previous action has been taken to substitute
unqualified preference clauses. The amending act provides for
unqualified preference under certain conditions, and, in practice, there is not a great deal of difference between unqualified
preference and compulsory unionism. One technical difference
is that the statute provides that under an unqualified preference clause a worker must join the appropriate union within 14
days or such shorter period as may be prescribed in the award
or industrial agreement. Previously the worker was required to
be a member of the union before he was employed. Another
change introduced by the amending act is that in the future
enforcement of clauses dealing with membership of workers'
unions will be in the hands of unions and not of the Labor
Department. The employers in almost every instance have
agreed in conciliation council to unqualified preference clauses
in new awards and industrial agreements; consequently there
is not likely to be much practical change, so little indeed that
the opposition to the new law is fast waning.

Another jurisdiction vested in my Court is to conduct inquiries into any alleged irregularities in union elections. An application for such an inquiry must be made to the registrar of
industrial unions, who makes a preliminary investigation to
ensure that the Court is not troubled with trifling matters, and,
if the registrar thinks there is some reasonable basis for com-
plaint, he refers the application to my Court, and a formal
public inquiry is held. This particular jurisdiction is vested in
the judge alone. I have conducted several such inquiries and
have declared some elections void and ordered new elections.

The auditing of union accounts is now required by law in

New Zealand. There is no provision for making detailed accounts available to the public, but any member of a union is entitled to have a copy of his union's audited accounts. The only obligation of the Department of Labor is to see that the accounts are audited by members of the New Zealand Society of Accountants.

Under certain conditions unions may make contributions to the funds of political parties in New Zealand.

I now offer a few comments about the relations between industrial unions and the political labor party. The New Zealand Federation of Labor is the dominant industrial labor organization, yet all industrial unions of workers are not affiliated with it. It has its own domestic troubles, and sometimes it expels unions and at other times unions take action to secede from it, but at present it probably has two-thirds of the organized labor unions in the country affiliated to it. It has an important place in the community and, if invited by one of its affiliates, takes an active part in trying to settle any strikes or major disturbances that may occur. The particular unions involved often hand over the negotiations with the employers to the Federation of Labor. The Federation, representing the industrial labor movement, to some extent keeps aloof from the political labor movement, represented by the political labor party in the House of Representatives. There are occasional clashes of opinion between industrial labor and political labor, but sometimes these clashes involve personalities rather than principles. The former Prime Minister, Mr. Walter Nash,[3] who is now leader of the labor opposition in Parliament, has long been a highly respected figure in New Zealand. Mr. F. P. Walsh,[4] for many years President of the Federation of Labor, was an outstanding character, a rugged personality, and a forceful leader. His tactics and utterances were often strongly criticized. On many occasions he appeared before my Court and I have no criticisms to make as to his conduct of cases.

We have no political party in New Zealand comparable to the Democratic Labor Party in Australia. One was launched about 20 years ago, but it faded from the scene. The main parties are the National Party, which is presently in power, and the Labor

Party, which lost power in 1960. A third party is the Social Credit Party, which in the general elections obtains roughly about one hundred thousand votes out of 11 or 12 hundred thousand, but has never yet won a seat in Parliament. A fourth party is the Communist party, and it also has never yet won a seat in Parliament. In the 1960 election it obtained only 2,400 votes in the whole country. Its candidates almost always forfeit their deposits, and its adherents appear to have declined in number in the last few years, the Hungarian incident being mainly responsible.

There is still talk about nationalization in New Zealand. The political labor party holds an annual conference and so does the Federation of Labor, and hundreds of remits are considered by the conferences. I noticed recently a proposal that all the banks should be nationalized. The principal bank in our country is the Bank of New Zealand, whose private shareholders were bought out by the government some years ago during a labor regime. It is operated as a government-owned corporation. We have also a government-owned Reserve Bank which exercises a measure of control over the trading banks, all of which, except the Bank of New Zealand, are privately owned.

Our present economic situation is rather precarious; our overseas balances, due to a drop in prices of our exports, are not in a very good state. At present we have only about 50 million pounds in overseas reserves, whereas the Royal Commission, of which I was chairman some years ago, recommended we should endeavor to maintain a reserve of about 150 million pounds. At present we are borrowing in New York and London to maintain existing standards of living. During the last year or two we have really been living beyond our means. The policy of the present government is not to adopt crash tactics to cure the situation but to take steps in a steady manner to restore our former economic equilibrium.

There are clouds on the horizon because of the discussions that are taking place over the entry of Great Britain into the European common market. Some people, particularly in the farming community, regard the proposal as a menace. Great

Britain has promised to look after the interests of New Zealand if it does join the common market.

Our situation as far as employment is concerned is that there are still many more jobs than workers available to fill them. As a result, the farmers have to compete with secondary industries for labor, and this situation, in their view, has tended to raise unduly the ruling rates of wages.

The labor government, which went out of office in 1960, entered into a number of agreements for starting new secondary industries, and their policy is based on the fact that the numbers of workers employed in primary industry over the last six years had been relatively static. Production has advanced because of considerable mechanization. We have a moderate immigration policy and a good birth rate, and the feeling of the labor party is that secondary industries must be expanded to ensure employment for our people in the future. The farmers are apprehensive of new industries being started in the country because they think some will be uneconomic and will cause their costs to rise at a time when the return for our primary products is on the decline. This is the atmosphere at present in which a case is being heard by the New Zealand Court of Arbitration, involving a claim by the Federation of Labor for an increase of 10.4 per cent in all minimum rates of remuneration while the farming community, through one of its agencies, is applying for a 10 per cent reduction.[5]

APPENDIX I Code of Discipline in Industry [1]

I. *To Maintain Discipline in Industry* (both in public and private sectors) there has to be (i) a just recognition by employers and workers of the rights and responsibilities of either party, as defined by the laws and agreements (including bipartite and tripartite agreements arrived at all levels from time to time), and (ii) a proper and willing discharge by either party of its obligations consequent on such recognition.

The Central and State Governments, on their part, will arrange to examine and set right any shortcomings in the machinery they constitute for the administration of labour laws.

To ensure better discipline in industry

II. *Management and Union(s) Agree*

(i) that no unilateral action should be taken in connection with any industrial matter and that disputes should be settled at the appropriate level;

(ii) that the existing machinery for settlement of disputes should be utilised with the utmost expedition;

(iii) that there should be no strike or lockout without notice;

(iv) that, affirming their faith in democratic principles, they bind themselves to settle all future differences, disputes and grievances by mutual negotiation, conciliation and voluntary arbitration;

(v) that neither party will have recourse to (a) coercion, (b) intimidation, (c) victimisation or (d) go-slow;

(vi) that they will avoid, (a) litigation, (b) sit-down and stay-in strikes and (c) lockouts;

(vii) that they will promote constructive co-operation between their representatives at all levels and as between workers themselves and abide by the spirit of agreements mutually entered into;

(viii) that they will establish upon a mutually agreed basis, a grievance procedure which will ensure a speedy and full investigation leading to settlement;

(ix) that they will abide by various stages in the grievance procedure and take no arbitrary action which would by-pass this procedure; and

(x) that they will educate the management personnel and workers regarding their obligations to each other.

[1] Ministry of Labour and Employment, Government of India, New Delhi, 1961.

III. *Management Agrees*

(i) not to increase work loads unless agreed upon or settled otherwise;

(ii) not to support or encourage any unfair labour practice, such as (a) interference with the right of employees to enrol or continue as union members, (b) discrimination, restraint or coercion against any employee because of recognised activity of trade unions and (c) victimisation of any employee and abuse of authority in any form;

(iii) to take prompt action for (a) settlement of grievances and (b) implementation of settlements, awards, decisions and orders;

(iv) to display in conspicuous places in the undertaking the provisions of this Code in local language (s) ;

(v) to distinguish between actions justifying immediate discharge and those where discharge must be preceded by a warning, reprimand, suspension or some other form of disciplinary action and to arrange that all such disciplinary action should be subject to an appeal through normal grievance procedure;

(vi) to take appropriate disciplinary action against its officers and members in cases where enquiries reveal that they were responsible for precipitate action by workers leading to indiscipline; and

(vii) to recognise the union in accordance with the criteria (Annexure I) evolved at the 16th session of the Indian Labour Conference held in May, 1958.

IV. *Union (s) Agree*

(i) not to engage in any form of physical duress;

(ii) not to permit demonstrations which are not peaceful and not to permit rowdyism in demonstration;

(iii) that their members will not engage or cause other employees to engage in any union activity during working hours, unless as provided for by law, agreement or practice;

(iv) to discourage unfair labour practices such as (a) negligence of duty, (b) careless operation, (c) damage to property, (d) interference with or disturbance to normal work and (e) insubordination;

(v) to take prompt action to implement awards, agreements, settlements and decisions;

(vi) to display in conspicuous places in the union offices, the provisions of this Code in the local language (s) ; and

(vii) to express disapproval and to take appropriate action against office-bearers and members for indulging in action against the spirit of this Code.

Annexure I: Criteria for Recognition of Unions

1. Where there is more than one union, a union claiming recognition should have been functioning for at least one year after registration. Where there is only one union, this condition would not apply.

2. The membership of the union should cover at least 15% of the workers in the establishment concerned. Membership would be counted only of those who had paid their subscriptions for at least three months during the period of six months immediately preceding the reckoning.

3. A union may claim to be recognised as a representative union for an industry in a local area if it has a membership of at least 25% of the workers of that industry in that area.

4. When a union has been recognised, there should be no change in its position for a period of two years.

5. Where there are several unions in an industry or establishment, the one with the largest membership should be recognised.

6. A representative union for an industry in an area should have the right to represent the workers in all the establishments in the industry, but if a union of workers in a particular establishment has a membership of 50 per cent or more of the workers of that establishment it should have the right to deal with matters of purely local interest, such as, for instance, the handling of grievances pertaining to its own members. All other workers who are not members of that union might either operate through the representative Union for the industry of seek redress directly.

7. In the case of trade union federations which are not affiliated to any of the four central organisations of labour, the question of recognition would have to be dealt with separately.

8. Only unions which observed the Code of Discipline would be entitled to recognition.

APPENDIX II: Conference Participants

IWAO F. AYUSAWA

Professor of Labor Problems and International Relations; Chairman of the Social Science Division at the International Christian University, Tokyo. First Friend Peace Scholar at Mid-Pacific Institute, Honolulu, 1911–1913. Senior staff member at the International Labor Organization, Geneva, 1922–1934. Director of ILO Tokyo Office, 1934–1938.

Was one of the draftsmen of the Trade Union Law of 1945 and the law on conciliation, mediation, and arbitration, the Law for Adjustment of Labor Relations of 1946. Was the first director of the Central Labor Relations Commission. Author of many studies on Japanese and International labor questions.

Senior Visiting Scholar at the East-West Center, Honolulu, 1961/62.

PAUL F. BRISSENDEN

Visiting Colleague in Industrial Relations, University of Hawaii. Professor of Economics, Columbia University, 1921–1955. Professor Emeritus of Economics, Columbia University, 1955—.

A.B., University of Denver, 1908; A.M., University of California, 1912; Ph.D., Columbia University, 1917.

Special agent of the U. S. Commission on Industrial Relations; vice chairman and public member of the Second Regional Board of the National War Labor Board; member of the Clothing Advisory Committee of the War Production Board. Served as arbitrator under various labor agreements and has been a member of many commissions, including those setting minimum wages for workers in industry.

Has written widely on labor and management, the Hawaiian dock strike, the injunction, and, more recently, a comparative study of the arbitration systems of Australia, New Zealand, and the United States. Among his major studies are those on the Industrial Workers of the World, labor turnover, and the wages of factory workers.

Senior Visiting Scholar at the East-West Center, Honolulu, 1962/63.

A. W. R. CARROTHERS

Director of the Institute of Industrial Relations and a member of the Faculty of Law, University of British Columbia. Bachelor degree in Economics and degree in law at University of British Columbia. Master of Law degree, Harvard.

Has served on the Board of Reference under the Civil Service Act of British Columbia and on the Conciliation and Arbitration Board. Is a Scholar of the Canadian Bar Association and President of the Canadian Association of University Teachers. Has written on the Trade Union Act of British Columbia, the Law of Picketing, the use of labor injunctions, and compulsory arbitration.

KINGSLEY M. LAFFER

Senior Lecturer in Economics; in charge of the teaching of Industrial Relations at the University of Sydney. Editor of the *Journal of Industrial Relations* (Sydney).

Formerly professor at the universities of Western Australia and Melbourne.

Founder and honorary secretary of the Industrial Relations Society. Authority in the field of arbitration.

Has written numerous articles on the subject of the machinery of arbitration, as well as on the problems of Australian compulsory arbitration. Is currently working on arbitration in seamen's disputes in Australia.

A. S. MATHUR

Professor in the Institute of Social Sciences at Agra University, India. Is in charge of the Industrial Relations Specialists course at the Institute of Social Sciences, Agra.

Is an authority on problems of trade-union leadership and trade-union rivalry, and is at present engaged in studying recent trends in industrial relations in India.

ASOKA MEHTA

Member of the Indian Parliament for many years. At present, deputy chairman of the Indian Planning Commission.

Has served as chairman of the Food-Grain Inquiry Committee and on many government committees connected with labor and industry, including the Central Wage Boards. Has been intimately connected with the work of the Planning Commission and serves on many of its panels.

As pioneer and leader of social and economic reform in India has been intimately concerned with labor and peasant movements. Took a prominent part in National Liberation Movement.

Has written several books on political, social, and economic problems in India.

HAROLD S. ROBERTS

Director of the Industrial Relations Center and Chairman of the Department of Personnel and Industrial Relations of the College of Business Administration, University of Hawaii. B.A. and Ph.D., Columbia University.

Has served on the Interstate Commerce Committee of the U. S. Senate; with the National Labor Relations Board, the U. S. Department of Labor, and the National War Labor Board; as chief of the Collective Bargaining Division of the Bureau of Labor Statistics, U. S. Department of Labor; on state public utility mediation and emergency boards, and as arbitrator under contracts.

Has written widely in the field of labor legislation, collective bargaining, and arbitration.

Member of the American Arbitration Association Panel of Arbitrators and of the Federal Mediation and Conciliation Service panel.

DAVID J. SAPOSS

Lecturer in International Labor Relations at American University. Undergraduate work at the University of Wisconsin; graduate work at Columbia.

Has served as staff member of the United States Commission on Industrial Relations; research associate of the Twentieth Century Fund Study on Labor and the Government; chief economist of the U. S. National Labor Relations Board; Labor Consultant to the Co-ordinator of Inter-American Affairs; chief economic advisor of the Labor Production Division of the War Production Board; chief of the Reports and Statistics Branch of the Man Power Division, Office of the U. S. military government of Germany; and labor advisor to the ECA in Paris.

Was one of the authors of the two-volume *History of Labor in the United States*. Has written widely in the field of labor history, including a volume on the labor movement of postwar France, a study of left-wing unions, and readings in American trade-unionism. Has recently published authoritative studies on communism in American unions and communism in American politics.

TAISHIRO SHIRAI

Senior Researcher with the Japan Institute of Labor. Graduate work in the field of labor problems at Tokyo University.

Lecturer at the Yamanashi Gakuen College and at the Chubu Social Welfare College. Member of the Commission for Compiling the Documentary History of the Japanese Trade Union Movement, an interuniversity project with financial grant from the Ford Foundation.

Has written on the historic development of the Japanese labor movement and the reappraisal of trade-unionism in Japan.

EDWARD I. SYKES

Professor of Public Law, University of Queensland. An authority on private and public law in their relation to industrial relations.

Author of two books dealing with labor law and labor relations in Australia: *The Employer, the Employee, and the Law*, and *Strike Law in Australia*. Two other books and numerous articles dealing with private law and labor law.

Under the auspices of Carnegie Corporation and Fulbright Foundation, 1955/56, visited the United Kingdom and the United States to study labor law and labor relations in those countries.

SIR ARTHUR TYNDALL

Chief Justice of the New Zealand Court of Arbitration. Has held the post of Justice of the Court for the past 22 years.

Visiting Lecturer at the Massachusetts Institute of Technology, Princeton, McGill, and Harvard Law School. Honorary secretary for Massachusetts Institute of Technology in New Zealand and president of the New Zealand–American Association.

Has served as Undersecretary of Mines and Director of Housing Construction in New Zealand. Was a member of the International Labour Organization delegation to Pakistan in 1953 and to Bolivia in 1957. Chairman of the Royal Commission on Monetary, Banking, and Credit Systems of New Zealand, 1955/56.

Has written on the New Zealand system of Industrial conciliation and arbitration and on the general subject of the settlement of labor disputes in New Zealand; has published many outstanding decisions to be found in the *New Zealand Book of Awards*.

NOTES

CHAPTER 1

1. The proceedings of the conference have not been published, but, since they are of some historic interest, they probably will be made available in some form by the Industrial Relations Center of the University of Hawaii within the next few years. The Industrial Relations Center was co-sponsor and its Director was chairman of the conference as well as a participant in the discussions.
2. Iwao Ayusawa, Paul Brissenden, and Harold S. Roberts.
3. The original proposal contemplated twelve countries, but financial and other considerations reduced the number to six. Invitations were extended to persons in seven countries: Australia, Canada, New Zealand, India, Japan, the Philippines, and the United States. Unfortunately, the delegate chosen to represent the Philippines was unable to attend.
4. The verbatim record should indicate to those interested the more detailed explanations of the practices within the countries.
5. Arbitration which results from the voluntary agreement of parties under a collective bargaining contract to submit future disputes under the terms of the contract to a third party for settlement. The parties have obligated themselves to arbitrate. Some collective contracts may also contain provisions obligating the parties to settle new contract terms by arbitration. In current usage, the phrase "obligatory arbitration" is encompassed in the phrase "voluntary arbitration."
6. The International Labour Organization convened a conference at the end of 1962, in Melbourne, Australia, which was a follow-up of the seminar in Kuala Lumpur, 1961. For further details see *Prevention and Settlement of Industrial Disputes in Asia* (Labour-Management Relations Series No. 15) (Geneva: ILO, 1962), and *Government Services for the Improvement of Labour-Management Relations and Settlement of Disputes in Asia* (Labour-Management Relations Series No. 16) (Geneva: ILO, 1963).

CHAPTER 2

1. Tokyo: Ministry of Agriculture and Commerce, 1903; 5 vols.
2. Tokyo: Kyobunkan, 1899.
3. *Nippon No Rodo Undo* (Tokyo: Rodo Shimbunsha, 1901).
4. The Ministry of Labor includes bureaus of Employment Stabilization, Women and Juvenile Workers, Labor Standards, Labor Policy, etc., with their respective branches at the local or prefectural level. These agencies conduct researches in their specialized fields, and, as such, provide basic materials and data for the study of industrial relations.

5. Kazuo Okochi, ed., *Sengo Rodo-kumiai no Jittai* (Tokyo: Nippon Hyoronsha, 1950).
6. *Rodo Kumiai no Kozo to Kino* (Tokyo: Tokyo Daigaku Shuppankai, 1959).

CHAPTER 3

1. Clark Kerr and Abraham Siegel, "Inter-Industry Propensity to Strike—An International Comparison," in Arthur Kornhauser, Robert Dubin, and Arthur M. Ross, eds., *Industrial Conflict* (New York: McGraw-Hill, 1954), pp. 189–212.
2. Alfred W. Carrothers, *Labour Arbitration in Canada: A Study of the Law and Practice Relating to the Arbitration of Grievance Disputes in Industrial Relations in Common Law Canada* (Toronto: Butterworth, 1961).

CHAPTER 4

1. His most recent publication is a book on Australian trade-union law, *Trade Unionism in Australia; Some Aspects* (Sydney: Law Book Co. of Australasia Pty., Ltd., 1962).
2. *The Development of Australian Trade Union Law* (Carlton: Melbourne University Press, 1958).
3. *Strike Law in Australia* (Sydney: Law Book Co. of Australasia Pty., Ltd., 1960).
4. Melbourne, 1929.
5. *Judges in Industry: A Study of Labor Arbitration in Australia* (Carlton: Melbourne University Press, 1954).
6. *Industrial Relations in Australia* (Cambridge: Harvard University Press, 1956).
7. Industrial Relations Research Association, *News Letter* (1961).

CHAPTER 5

1. In Australia, I have been known to some extent as a critic of compulsory arbitration, recently having been described at home as a "well-known advocate of collective bargaining." But, when in England a few years ago, I was considered an advocate of compulsory arbitration. For the record I wish to say that I would like to see the cautious development of more collective bargaining in Australia. See Kingsley Laffer, "Problems of Australian Compulsory Arbitration," *International Labour Review*, May, 1958; "Compulsory Arbitration *and* Collective Bargaining," *Journal of Industrial Relations* (Sydney), October, 1962.
2. See K. F. Walker, *Industrial Relations in Australia* (Cambridge: Harvard University Press, 1956), Chap. 2, for a discussion of the various systems; also D. C. Thomson, "A Survey of Australian Arbitration Tribunals," *Industrial Law Review*, July, 1955.

3. See Paul F. Brissenden, "Arbitration in Australia and the United States," *Labor Law Journal* (Chicago), June, 1960; "Industrial Arbitration and the Arbitral Process in Australia and in America," *Journal of Industrial Relations* (Sydney), April, 1962.

4. See Commonwealth Bureau of Census and Statistics, *Incidence of Industrial Awards*, February, 1956, reprinted in Department of Labour and National Service, *Industrial Information Bulletin*, March, 1956, pp. 292–294.

5. Marjorie Barnard, *A History of Australia* (Sydney: Angus & Robertson, Ltd., 1962), p. 68.

6. For an example, see N. G. Butlin, "Collective Bargaining in the Printing Industry 1880–1900," *Economic Record*, December, 1947, p. 23. See also E. O. G. Shann, *Economic History of Australia* (Cambridge [England]: The University Press, 1948), pp. 397–400.

7. Ernest Aves, *Report . . . on the Wages Boards and Industrial Conciliation and Arbitration Acts of Australia and New Zealand*, Cmd. 4167 (London: Darling & Son, 1908).

8. For a fuller discussion of the points made in this section, see D. W. Oxnam, "Industrial Arbitration in Australia: Its Effects on Wages and Unions," *Industrial and Labor Relations Review*, July, 1956.

9. There are some "conciliators" who lack the power to arbitrate, but these are fairly new and have so far been of minor importance in the operation of our system.

10. See articles by J. H. Wootten and J. B. Sweeney in *Lectures in Industrial Law* (mimeographed; University of Sydney, Department of Law, 1961). See also J. H. Portus, *The Development of Australian Trade Union Law* (Carlton: Melbourne University Press, 1958), pp. 179–180.

11. See Department of Labour and National Service, *Industrial Information Bulletin*, May, 1959, pp. 407–409, for a statement by Judge A. W. Foster, in a basic wage judgment, concerning the legislative nature of the Commonwealth Arbitration Commission's work.

12. For a statement of the principles followed, see Frank T. deVyver, "Concept of Wages in Australia," *South Atlantic Quarterly*, Summer, 1962, p. 399.

13. See Raymond O'Dea, "Some Features of the Professional Engineers' Case," *Journal of Industrial Relations*, October, 1962, for a fuller story, which, incidentally, illustrates very well a number of aspects of the working of the Australian system. The case itself is reported at 97 *Commonwealth Arbitration Reports* 233 (Print No. A-7855). The award, *ibid.*, 344 (Print No. A-7856).

14. See J. R. Kerr, "Procedures in General Wages Cases in the Commonwealth Arbitration Commission," *Journal of Industrial Relations*, October, 1961.

15. See E. I. Sykes, *Strike Law in Australia* (Sydney: Law Book Co. of Australasia Pty., Ltd., 1960) for details.

16. See C. P. Mills, "The Enforcement of Penalties Against Strikes," *Journal of Industrial Relations*, April, 1960; J. E. Isaac, "Penal

Provisions under Commonwealth Arbitration," *Journal of Industrial Relations*, October, 1963.

17. For some examples of Judge Foster's approach, see Department of Labour and National Services, *Industrial Information Bulletin*, Vol. 8, no. 6, pp. 374–376; Vol. 9, no. 6, p. 382; Vol. 10, no. 3, pp. 157–158; Vol. 10, no. 4. pp. 288–291; Vol. 10, no. 5, p. 446.

18. See R. M. Martin, "Australian Trade Unionism, 1962," *Journal of Industrial Relations*, April, 1963, pp. 53–54.

19. See Orwell de R. Foenander, *Trade Unionism in Australia: Some Aspects* (Sydney: Law Book Co. of Australasia, Pty., Ltd., 1962), Part II, for a discussion of trade-union regulation under the Commonwealth Arbitration system.

20. See DeVyver, *op. cit.*, for a simple account of the different levels in the Australian wage structure.

21. See K. J. Hancock, "Wage Policy and Price Stability in Australia," *Economic Journal*, September, 1960, and R. I. Downing and J. E. Isaac, "The 1961 Basic Wage Judgment and Wage Policy," *Economic Record*, December, 1961. For a partial defense of the Commission, see H. R. Edwards and K. M. Laffer, "Some Issues in Australian Wage Determination," *Economic Record*, June, 1963; *Economic Record*, September, 1963, p. 377.

22. See R. I. Downing and J. E. Isaac, *op. cit.*

23. See D. C. Thomson, "The Federal Long Service Leave Code," *The Journal of Industrial Relations*, April, 1959.

24. See Kingsley Laffer, "Problems of Compulsory Arbitration in Australia," *International Labour Review*, May, 1958, and *Journal of Industrial Relations*, October, 1962; J. E. Isaac, "The Prospects for Collective Bargaining in Australia," *Economic Record*, December, 1958; Keith Hancock, *Journal of Industrial Relations*, April, 1962, for the reverberations of an Australian controversy concerning this and related questions.

25. See M. Bucklow, "A Note on Personnel Management in Australia," *Journal of Industrial Relations*, October, 1961; F. G. Lesieur, *The Scanlon Plan* (New York: Technology Press of M. I. T., 1958); Kingsley Laffer, "The Development of an Industrial Relations System," *The Australian Journal of Social Issues*, Spring, 1963.

CHAPTER 6

1. "Union" and "central" government have the same meaning as "federal" in the United States.

2. The author, in a letter to the editor, dated February 14, 1964, writes: "Word 'adjudication' is used for compulsory judicial determination of industrial dispute through courts and tribunals." Where it has seemed desirable for clarity the word "arbitration" or the phrase "compulsory arbitration" has been substituted for "adjudication."—Ed.

3. Apparently the expression "standing orders," as used in this context, means working rules in an industrial establishment.—Ed.

CHAPTER 7

1. The Code is to be found in Appendix I to this volume, pp. 203–205.

CHAPTER 10

1. The Kansas statute provided arrangements for the compulsory arbitration of labor disputes in public utilities, transportation, production of fuel and food, and the manufacture of clothing (c. 29, Laws, 1920). In a series of cases culminating in *Dorchy v. Kansas* (47 Sup. Ct. Rep. 86; Oct. 25, 1926), the United States Supreme Court held that compulsory arbitration of labor disputes in such industries as the production of fuel and food (*Dorchy* case, *supra*, and *Charles Wolff Packing Company v. Court of Industrial Relations*, 262 U. S. 522, decided June 11, 1923) was unconstitutional as in contravention of the Fourteenth Amendment, Section 1, which declares: "No state shall make or enforce any law which shall abridge the privileges or immunities of citizens of the United States; nor shall any State deprive any person of life, liberty or property without due process of law. . . ." As one writer has summed it up (in the Wolff case) : "The ultimate question was, 'Are strikes in the packing industry fraught with more social harm than would come from the restrictions upon individual rights involved in compulsory arbitration?' The state court answered this question in the affirmative and upheld the law. . . . The United States Supreme Court answered it in the negative and declared the law unconstitutional to the extent that it permitted compulsory arbitration in packing plants and coal mines." (Edward Berman, "The Supreme Court and Compulsory Arbitration," *American Economic Review*, July, 1928, pp. 19–44. The Court's implication in the Kansas cases is that compulsory arbitration in transportation and public utilities might be held Constitutional. That question, however, was not before it.

2. And there is some collective bargaining today, both in the Dominion and in the Commonwealth. There is, in fact, provision in most of the Australasian arbitration statutes for the negotiation of "industrial agreements" which in most respects have the effect of awards and, at least in New Zealand, may be made into awards on application to the Court. Also, some bargaining goes on in certain industries, e.g., coal mining in both the Dominion and the Commonwealth, metal mining and other employments in Broken Hill, New South Wales.

3. A perceptive study of management prerogatives in Australia and the United States has been made by Professor Frank T. deVyver of Duke University, Durham, North Carolina: "The Weakening of Managerial Rights," *Business Horizons* (Indiana University), Spring, 1959. Mr. deVyver points out that, while American employers in increasing numbers may discharge or discipline only for "just cause," must observe seniority rules, etc., Australian employ-

ers are, relatively, only very slightly inhibited in these and cognate matters. The American employer is frequently heard to complain that he is "married" to his employees and cannot get a divorce. Evidently such complaints are rarely heard among Australian employers.

4. There has been much disputation in America, and elsewhere as to the nature of collective labor agreements. They probably are more in the nature of treaties than authentic contracts, but in this country more and more they have come to be recognized, and treated, as being in a significant sense contracts.

5. *U. S. Code*, Title 29, c. 6, Sec. 113 (c).

6. *Industrial Conciliation and Arbitration Act 1961*, Sec. 5.

7. *Industrial Arbitration Act*, 1912–1963, Sec. 6.

8. One of the six "arbitration-court" jurisdictions—the Commonwealth of Australia—is precluded for constitutional reasons from dealing with "industrial matters" at large, and may concern itself only with the settlement by conciliation and arbitration of industrial disputes which extend "beyond the limits of any one state." New Zealand's parliament has plenary power under an unwritten constitution of the British type, and by virtue of that power has been free to legislate for the control of industrial "matters" as well as disputes.

9. Orwell de R. Foenander, *Industrial Conciliation and Arbitration in Australia* (Sydney: Law Book Co. of Australasia Pty., Ltd., 1959), p. 169. Foenander says that roughly half of the 90 per cent are covered by Commonwealth (or federal) awards or agreements, the remainder by awards from the respective arbitral authorities of the four state jurisdictions of New South Wales, Western Australia, South Australia, and Queensland (*id.*).

10. *The Settlement of Labor Disputes in New Zealand* (Cambridge: Industrial Relations Section, Massachusetts Institute of Technology, 1953), p. 53. According to Judge Arthur Tyndall, about 250,000 workers come under the Industrial Conciliation and Arbitration Act, the "percentage of total wage earners on the rolls of registered unions" being "probably about 50 per cent today" (1953), *ibid.*, pp. 11, 53.

11. Tyndall, *The Settlement of Labor Disputes in New Zealand*, pp. 53–54. Sir Arthur (p. 54) reports that for the first nine months of 1952, 4,884 coal miners and 4,244 waterside workers were involved in strikes, while the total number of workers involved in strikes in all other industries was only 3,236. His figures suggest that there are about 14,000 workers in the waterfront industry. In Australia, also, the same two industries (coal mining and stevedoring, both of which in the Commonwealth are within the coverage of the arbitration systems) are the centers of abnormally large proportions of all strike activities. The Australian Minister for Labour and National Service has stated that 60 per cent of the working time lost through strikes in Australia occurred among the 1 per cent of the workers employed in these two industries. "Australia Tackles the Strike Problem," reprinted from *Optima* (n.d., 1957?), p. 4.

12. *The Development of Australian Trade-Union Law* (Carlton: Melbourne University Press, 1958), p. 203. "Generally . . . no distinction is made between strikes by members of unions registered under the arbitration system concerned and strikes by members of unions not so registered. Also, a strike is illegal whether the matter in issue has been determined by an arbitral authority or not. . . . It cannot be said that the unions have the alternative of retaining the right to strike or using the arbitration machinery. The right to strike is taken away whether or not the employees concerned use the arbitration machinery" (*id.*).

13. *New Zealand Industrial Conciliation and Arbitration Act* 1954, Sec. 195 (2).

14. *The Settlement of Labor Disputes in New Zealand*, p. 49. The text of the 1913 law appears in "An Extract from the Public Acts of New Zealand, 1908–1931 (reprint), *Industrial Disputes* (pamphlet; Wellington, 1950), p. 1017.

15. E.g., *The Seamen's Award*, 1955; *see* n. 19, *infra*.

16. *Industrial Conciliation and Arbitration Act 1961*, Sec. 98 (1). The penalty: "Any person who contravenes any provision of this section shall be . . . liable to a penalty, in the case of an employer or industrial union, not exceeding two hundred and fifty pounds, and in any other case not exceeding twenty pounds" (*id.*).

17. *Industrial Arbitration Act 1940–1959*, Sec. 98.

18. *Id.*, Sec. 99. Sec. 99A makes an exception (to sub-sec. (b) of Sec. 99) with respect to notice of intent to strike—an exception not understood by this writer.

19. For example, see the order made on December 23, 1959, by the Commonwealth Conciliation and Arbitration Commission (J. Foster, Deputy President) varying the *Seamen's Award 1955* (81 *Commonwealth Arbitration Reports*, hereafter "*CAR*") at 205. The varying order appears in 93 *CAR* at 324, with judgment at 819.

20. Portus, *The Development of Australian Trade Union Law*, p. 224. *The Commonwealth Conciliation and Arbitration Act* provides, in Sec. 119, for the imposition of money penalties by the Industrial Court for "breach or non-observance" of award provisions.

21. Portus, *The Development of Australian Trade-Union Law*, pp. 224, 226.

22. Mr. Justice Alfred W. Foster, in a letter to this writer, dated October 5, 1959. In another letter, dated February 26, 1960, Mr. Justice Foster remarks that imposition of heavy penalties "makes working men genuinely striving for better conditions, criminals, and very resentful, and prevents effectively any attempts [to bring about] better industrial relations. I agree that sanctions are necessary . . . [but I would invoke them] by either automatically or as a matter of discretionary determination withdrawing or modifying beneficial award grants for any breaches of . . . award; this method has proved successful . . . and is commencing to have deterrent effects and produces little resentment, the men realizing that they can't have the benefits of arbitration while defying . . . the award."

23. Portus, *The Development of Australian Trade Union Law*, n. 9, p. 167.

24. *State Experiments in Australia and New Zealand* (London, 1902), Vol. II, p. 167.

25. 11 *CAR* at 516. Quoted by Portus, *The Development of Australian Trade Union Law*, p. 230.

26. *Building Workers etc. Deregistration Case* (1948), 61 *CAR* 128 at 136. (Quoted by Portus, *op. cit.*, p. 230.)

27. Kenneth F. Walker, "Australia" (Chap. 3), in Walter Galenson, ed., *Comparative Labor Movements* (New York: Prentice-Hall, 1952), p. 216.

28. Orwell de R. Foenander, *Industrial Conciliation and Arbitration in Australia.* (Sydney: Law Book Co. of Australasia Pty., Ltd., 1959), p. 54.

29. W. A. Baker, *The Commonwealth Basic Wage, 1907–1953* (pamphlet; Sydney: Metal Trades Federation, [1953]), p. 26.

30. 68 *CAR* 698. An increase of one pound in the basic wage was decreed (C. J. Kelly, dissenting). There were 54 separate disputes involved. Foenander's discussion appears in Chapters VI and VII of his *Studies in Australian Labor Law and Relations* (Carlton: Melbourne University Press, 1952).

31. Here Foenander quotes J. A. Hobson as saying, "Though principles of equity are sometimes cited, every arbitrator recognizes that his real task is one of sheer compromise, winning the acceptance of both sides to some more or less ingenious splitting of the difference" (*Wealth and Life*, New York: Macmillan, 1929, p. 178).

32. Foenander, *Industrial Conciliation and Arbitration in Australia*, pp. 161, 163–164.

33. United States Supreme Court in *Textile Workers' Union v. Lincoln Mills* (June 3, 1957; October Term, 1956), 353 *U. S. Reports*, at 448.

34. As noted, in Australia (in the Commonwealth and perhaps in some state jurisdictions), rights disputes involving the interpretation of award clauses *seem* to be put beyond the authority of the boards of reference. In the Commonwealth jurisdiction, such disputes are for the industrial court, although there are intimations that now and again a flexible handling of the word "interpretation" brings them within the reach of boards of reference.

35. *New Zealand Industrial Conciliation and Arbitration Act 1954,* Secs. 176–180.

36. Legally, of course, even so large an employer as the General Motors Corporation is only one legal person. But no one questions that its negotiations with the United Auto Workers Union are collective bargaining proceedings.

37. In Australia and New Zealand, where collective bargaining is far less pervasive than in America, such bargaining is not even conditionally compulsory, though it is mandatory for the parties to assemble for the purpose of being helped to bargain. The italicized words in the definition are emphasized by this writer in connection with disputes over rights in view of the discussion (to follow in the

text) of collective bargaining conceived of as a process which may continue during the period of the contract.

38.   In contrast to the "contract" disputes, in which the parties, upon failure of agreement by negotiation, often call in mediators or conciliators from an appropriate governmental agency, similar failure of agreement in grievance disputes almost never is followed by resort to mediation. Deadlocked grievance negotiations thus are followed by resort to direct action, or by resort to "voluntary" (grievance) arbitration, sometimes called "obligatory" arbitration.

39.   See, for example, *West Coast Engine Drivers' Agreement 1956–1958*, between Charming Creek–Westport Coal Co., Ltd. [and 8 other mines], the Minister of Mines for the Dominion of New Zealand [and] the Inangahua Coal Mine Owners' Association and the Brunner Mine Workers' Union, Charming Creek Miners' Union; and [printed with it in the same pamphlet] the *West Coast Coal Mines Agreement 1956–1958*, between some of the same parties. See Tyndall *The Settlement of Labor Disputes in New Zealand*, p. 53. The Dominion Government owns and operates some of the coal mines and appears therefore as an employer-party to many of the agreements. "The number of coal miners ordinarily employed is less than 6000" (p. 53). But as noted in the text some organizations, even in the coal-mining industry, have elected to come under the arbitration system. See, e.g., *Otago Coal Mines' Employees—Award* (pamphlet; dated February 27, 1957, published by the New Zealand Government Department of Labour). This award, however, is a consent decree and "embodies the terms of settlement arrived at by the assessors in Conciliation Council" (57 *Book of Awards* at 129).

40.   Tyndall, *op. cit.*, p. 50.

41.   *Industrial Conciliation and Arbitration Act 1954*, Sec. 130 (1).

42.   E.g.: Australia, *The Commonwealth Conciliation and Arbitration Act 1904–1961*: ". . . if it appears to a Commissioner that an industrial dispute has occurred or is likely to occur, he shall . . . take such steps as he thinks fit for the prompt prevention or settlement of that dispute by conciliation, or, if, in his opinion, conciliation is unlikely to succeed or has failed, by arbitration," Sec. 28–(1). The Dominion: *Industrial Conciliation and Arbitration Act 1954*: "No industrial dispute shall be referred to the Court [of Arbitration] until it has been first referred to a Council of Conciliation . . ." Sec. 111 (1).

43.   Even Tasmania (whose system of industrial regulation, like Victoria's, is the wages board type) has a provision for compulsory conferences. *Wages Board Act*, Sec. 77 (1). Some Australian authorities bracket the Tasmanian and Victorian systems with the four arbitral-court states and the Commonwealth jurisdiction as parts of the Australian system or systems of industrial arbitration.

44.   The most important Australian segment of the coal-mining industry —that in New South Wales—is, unlike that industry in New Zealand, arbitrally regulated, and concurrently by two governments: federal (*Coal Industry Act, 1946–1958*) and state (*Coal Industry*

Act, 1946–1957). But in the great metal-mining center at Broken Hill, New South Wales, the Australian arbitral writs, whether federal or state, do not seem to run; there a system closely resembling our collective bargaining regime seems to prevail.

45. D. W. Oxnam, "Industrial Arbitration in Australia," *Industrial and Labor Relations Review*, July, 1956, pp. 610, 611.

46. Walker, "Australia," in Walter Galenson, ed., *Comparative Labor Movements*, p. 173, at 218.

47. *Industrial Conciliation and Arbitration in Australia.* (Sydney: The Law Book Co. of Australasia Pty., Ltd., 1959), p. 50, n. 34, and p. 4.

48. In 1961, a sweeping series of amendments to the Queensland Act reshaped its apparatus much along the lines of the federal system, with an Industrial Conciliation and Arbitration Commission and an Industrial Court. The Court evidently handles justiciable disputes, the Act authorizing it to interpret awards and industrial agreements (Act, Sec. 8(9)) and leaving the non-justiciable disputes on interests to the Commission. There are no boards of reference in Queensland.

49. In Victoria, the dominant (or "curial") Australian form of industrial arbitration does not exist except insofar as the federal system penetrates the state. The Victorian boards of reference appear therefore to be ancillary to wages boards rather than to ordinary arbitration tribunals.

50. In the Commonwealth jursidiction a board of reference "may consist of or include a Commissioner or a Conciliator," *Act*, Sec. 50. However, some awards promulgated under the Act evidently often provide that they shall be tripartite. E.g., *Metal Trades Award*, clause 23, 95 *CAR* 905 at 946; reprinted as varied to August 15, 1963: Print A 9020.

51. *Commonwealth Conciliation and Arbitration Act, 1904–1961*, S. 50 (1).

52. The language quoted is that of Clause 31 (b) (i) and (b) (ii). Clause 31 (c) provides that "[a]ny dispute arising out of this award shall be referred to the Board of Reference." This seems to mean that *any* dispute is to be so referred, but that, if it is one "involving interpretation," it is to be referred by the Board to the Commonwealth Industrial Court. The text of the *Tramways Award* appears in 73 *CAR* 703 at 728; the award having been made in settlement of a dispute brought before the Court of Conciliation and Arbitration (now the Commission) under the title *Australian Tramway and Motor Omnibus Employees' Association and Brisbane City Council; re Commissioner for Road Transport and Tramways, New South Wales.*

CHAPTER 11

1. For a more comprehensive treatment of this subject, see my "Ideological Conflicts in the International Labor Movement," in Everett Malcolm Kassalow, ed., *National Labor Movements in the Post-War World* (Chicago: Northwestern University Press, 1963); and "The

Split Between the Asian and Western Socialists," in Wladyslaw Josef Stankiewicz, ed., *Political Thought Since World War II* (Glencoe, Ill.: Free Press, 1964).

2. In some countries Protestant unions also emerged. For instance, in Holland and Switzerland there are small groups of Protestant unions, usually aligned with the Christian International.

CHAPTER 12

1. Second edition, revised. New York: Macmillan, 1959.
2. New Zealand at that time had a bicameral legislature consisting of the legislative council and the house of representatives. The former was abolished in 1950.
3. The Right Honorable Walter Nash resigned leadership of the Labour Party in 1963.
4. Mr. F. P. Walsh died in 1963.
5. A general order was made on July 4, 1962, granting an increase of 2½ per cent.

SELECTED BIBLIOGRAPHIES

AUSTRALIA

"Action Against Communism in Unions," *Notes on Labor Abroad*, No. 15, August 1950.

"Arbitration or Collective Bargaining," *Employers' Review*, August 1956.

"Arbitration Reform," *Institute of Public Affairs Review*, June 1947; May 1950.

"Arbitration System," *Current Affairs Bulletin*, April 13, 1959.

Australia. Commonwealth Conciliation and Arbitration Commission. *Annual Reports, 1956—*. Canberra: Government Printer.

—— —— *Basic Wage Judgment, 1958*. Melbourne: Government Printer, 1958.

—— —— *Basic Wage Judgment, 1959*. Melbourne: Government Printer, 1959.

—— Commonwealth Court of Conciliation and Arbitration. *Annual Reports by the Chief Conciliation Commissioner, 1948–1955*. Canberra: Government Printer.

—— —— *Annual Reports by the Senior Judge, 1948–1955*. Melbourne: Government Printer.

—— —— *A Report of Cases, 1905–1961*. Sydney: Law Book Co.

—— Department of Labour and National Service. *A Note on Some Aspects of Conciliation and Arbitration in the Commonwealth*. Melbourne: Government Printer, 1956.

—— —— *Industrial Disputes in Australia*. Melbourne: Government Printer, 1958.

—— Laws, Statutes, etc. *Arbitration Act, 1902–1957*. Sydney: Government Printer, 1960.

—— —— *Conciliation & Arbitration Act, 1904–1959*. Canberra: Government Printer, 1959.

—— —— *Conciliation & Arbitration Act, 1959* (Act No. 40). Canberra: Government Printer, 1959.

—— —— *A Bill for the Conciliation & Arbitration Act (No. 2), 1960*. Canberra: Government Printer, 1960.

—— —— *Stevedoring Industry (Act) No. 66 of 1962; An Act to Amend the Stevedoring Industry Act 1956–1961* (Bound with *Stevedoring Industry Act No. 53 or 1956*). Canberra: 1962.

—— Stevedoring Industry Authority. *Reports, 1920/1–1961/2*. Sydney: 1921–1962.

"Australian Trade Union Movement," *International Labour Review*, November–December 1947.

Australian Workers' Union. *The "Workers" First 70 Years: Souvenir*. Brisbane: 1960.

Blackburn, M. *Trade Unionism: Its Operation Under Australian Law*. Melbourne: Victorian Labour College, 1940.

Blair, Leo. "Arbitration in the Federal Public Service in Australia," *Public Administration Review*, Spring 1956.

Brissenden, Paul F. "Arbitration in Australia and the United States," *Labor Law Journal*, June 1960.

―――― *Industrial Arbitration and the Arbitral Process in Australia and in America*. Honolulu: University of Hawaii, Industrial Relations Center, 1962.

Cameron, R. J. "Role of the Arbitration Court," *Historical Studies, Australia and New Zealand*, May 1954.

Campbell, Ernest William. *History of the Australian Labor Movement, A Marxist Interpretation*. Sydney: Current Book Distributors, 1945.

Churchward, L. G. "Trade Unionism in the U. S. and Australia: A Study in Contrasts," *Science and Society*, Spring 1953.

"Compulsory Arbitration in Australia," *Current Affairs Bulletin*, September 24, 1951.

"Conciliation and Arbitration in Australia: Commonwealth Act of 1947," *International Labour Review*, September 1947.

"The Conciliation and Arbitration System," *Round Table*, March 1951.

Crisp, L. F. *The Australian Federal Labour Party, 1901–1951*. London: Longmans, Green & Co., 1955.

deVyver, Frank T. "The Australian Way to Industrial Peace," *South Atlantic Quarterly*, Autumn 1958.

―――― "Australian Boards of Reference," *Labor Law Journal*, May 1959.

Ebbels, Robert Noel. *The Australian Labor Movement, 1850–1907*. Extracts from contemporary documents with additions by members of the Noel Ebbels Memorial Committee. Sydney: Noel Ebbels Committee in association with the Australia Book Society, 1960.

Eberhart, E. K. "Crisis in Australian Labor Relations," *Australian Quarterly*, December 1954.

Evatt, H. V. *Australian Labor Leader*. Sydney: Angus & Robertson, Ltd., 1945.

Evatt, H. V. "Control of Labor Relations in the Commonwealth of Australia," *University of Chicago Law Review*, June 1939.

Fitzpatrick, Brian. *A Short History of the Australian Labor Movement*. Melbourne: Rawson's Bookshop, 1944.

Flexner, J. A., et al. "Settlement of Industrial Disputes in Seven Foreign Countries," *Monthly Labor Review*, August 1946.

Foenander, O. de R. "The Achievement and Significance of Industrial Relations Regulations in Australia," *International Labour Review*, February 1957.

―――― "Aspects of Australian Trade Unionism," *International Labour Review*, April 1961.

―――― *Better Employment Relations, and Other Essays in Labour*. Sydney: Law Book Co. of Australasia Pty., Ltd., 1954.

―――― "The Commonwealth Court of Conciliation and Arbitration, A Brief Survey," *The Quarterly Journal of Economics*, August 1949.

―――― *Industrial Conciliation and Arbitration in Australia*. Sydney: Law Book Co. of Australasia Pty., Ltd., 1959.

Foenander, O. de R. *Industrial Regulation in Australia.* Carlton: Melbourne University Press, 1947.

—— *Studies in Australian Labour Law and Relations.* Carlton: Melbourne University Press, 1952.

—— *Trade Unionism in Australia: Some Aspects.* Sydney: Law Book Co. of Australasia Pty., Ltd., 1962.

Ford, H. A. J. "Aspects of Trade Union Law," *Twentieth Century,* Winter 1959.

—— "Trade Union Law and Aid to Political Parties," *Journal of Industrial Relations,* April 1960.

Galenson, Walter, ed. *Comparative Labor Movements.* New York: Prentice-Hall, 1952, Chap. 3, "Australia," by Kenneth Walker.

Glickman, D. L. "The Labor Movements in Australia and New Zealand," *Social Research,* June 1949.

"Government-Employer-Worker Collaboration in Australia," *International Labour Review,* February 1943.

Grattan, C. H. "Labor Problems in Australia," *Political Science Quarterly,* June 1944.

Hagger, A. "The Arbitration Court in the 1950's," *Australian Quarterly,* June 1958.

Heagney, M. A. *Arbitration at the Crossroads: Digest of Opinion on Legal Wage Fixation.* Melbourne: Muriel A. Heagney, 1954.

Heiser, R. O. "Money Wages and the Arbitration Commission," *Australian Quarterly,* September 1960.

Higgins, B. H. "Wage Fixing by Compulsory Arbitration: The Lesson of Australia," *Social Research,* September 1951.

Hughes, Larry. "Aims and Structure of Australian Trade Unions," *Employers' Review,* March 1954.

Isaac, J. E. "The Prospects for Collective Bargaining in Australia," *Economic Record,* December 1958.

Jones, L. I. "Industrial Arbitration in Australia," *Modern Law Review,* March 1945.

Kelsall, E. P. "Industrial Conflict in Australia," *Economic Record,* August 1959.

—— "The Decline of Conciliation in Industrial Relations," *Australian Quarterly,* June 1959.

Kuhn, James W. "Grievance Machinery and Strikes in Australia," *Industrial and Labor Relations Review,* January 1955.

—— "Strikes and Australia's Industrialization," *Australian Quarterly,* September 1956.

—— "The Demands of Politics and Job-Centered Unions," *Political Science Quarterly,* March 1957.

Laffer, Kingsley. "Problems of Australian Compulsory Arbitration," *International Labour Review,* May 1958.

"The Machinery of Arbitration," *Institute of Public Affairs Review,* July–September 1955.

Makin, Norman. *Federal Labour Leaders.* Sydney: Union Printing Pty., 1961.

Martin, Ross M. "Legal Enforcement of Union Security in Australia," *Industrial and Labor Relations Review,* January 1960.

Merrifield, Leroy S. "Wage Determination Under Compulsory Arbitration: The Basic Wage in Australia," *George Washington Law Review*, December 1955.

—— "Regulation of Union Elections in Australia," *Industrial and Labor Relations Review*, January 1957.

Monk, A. E. "Free Collective Bargaining Would Ease Strife," *Australian Financial Review*, January 29, 1959.

New South Wales. Laws, Statutes, etc. *Industrial Arbitration Act, 1940–1959*. Sydney: V. C. N. Blight, Government Printer, 1960.

Nolan, John Robert Walker. *Nolan and Cohen's Industrial Law: Annotated*. Sydney: Butterworth & Co., 1957.

Oxnam, D. W. "Industrial Arbitration in Australia: Its Effects on Wages and Unions," *Industrial and Labor Relations Review*, July 1956.

—— "Recent Changes in the Federal Arbitration System," *Australian Quarterly*, March 1957.

Perlman, Mark. *The Australian Arbitration System: An Analytical Description*. Honolulu: University of Hawaii, August 1951.

—— "An Industrial Problem: Australia's Longshoremen," *Labor Law Journal*, July 1953.

—— *Judges in Industry: A Study of Labor Arbitration in Australia*. Carlton: Melbourne University Press, 1954.

—— "Wage Regulation in Australia," *Labor Law Journal*, January 1953.

Portus, J. H. *The Development of Australian Trade Union Law*. Carlton: Melbourne University Press, 1958.

Queensland. Laws, Statutes, etc. *The Industrial Conciliation and Arbitration Acts, 1932 to 1955*. Brisbane: A. H. Tucker, Government Printer, 1955.

—— —— *The Industrial Conciliation and Arbitration Act of 1961*. Brisbane: S. G. Reid, Government Printer, 1961.

Rawson, D. W. "The Frontiers of Trade Unionism," *Australian Journal of Politics and History*, May 1956.

—— "Politics and 'Responsibility' in Australia Trade Unions," *Australian Journal of Politics and History*, November 1958.

Reminder from Trade Union Leaders, Opening Remarks by Labor Members at Opening of Australian Federal Parliament, February 1950: Need for Higher Production, Dealing with Communist Interference in Trade Unions. Brisbane: Queensland Institute of Public Affairs, 1950.

Ritter, A. S. "Australia's Labor Problems and Policies, 1951," *Monthly Labor Review*, July 1951.

—— and M. M. Smith, "Action Against Communism in Australia and New Zealand Unions," *Monthly Labor Review*, November 1950.

Ross, G. W. C. "The Constitutional History of Industrial Arbitration in Australia," *Minnesota Law Review*, December 1945.

Ross, L., and M. Weisz, "Conciliation and Arbitration in Australia and New Zealand," *Industrial and Labor Relations Review*, October 1948.

Rutherford, R. S. G. "Strikes in Australia: A Further Comment," *Economic Record*, November 1953.

Sawer, G. "Conciliation and Arbitration of Industrial Disputes," *Economic Record*, December 1947.

Sharkey, L. L. *The Trade Unions*. Sydney: Current Book Distributors, 1959.

Sharp, E. B. "The Australian Scene: Those Aspects of Australian Life Which Influence Industrial Relations and the Present State of Development of Personnel Management," *Journal of the Institute of Personnel Management*, May–July 1951.

Sharp, I. "Some Features of the Australian Industrial Relations Scene," *Journal of Industrial Relations*, April 1959.

Sutcliffe, James Thomas. *A History of Trade Unionism in Australia*. London: Macmillan & Co., 1921.

Sykes, E. I. *The Employer, the Employee and the Law*. Sydney: Law Book Co., 1960.

———— "The Role of Law in Industrial Relations," *Australian Quarterly*, June 1957.

———— *Strike Law in Australia*. Sydney: Law Book Co. of Australasia Pty., Ltd., 1960.

Thomson, D. C. "The Industrial Arbitration (Amendment) Act 1959," *Australian Lawyer*, September 1960.

Walker, E. R. "Wartime Labour Problems in Australia," *International Labour Review*, October 1941.

Walker, Kenneth F. "Arbitration in a New Key: The New Legislation in Perspective," *Economic Review*, April 1957.

———— "The Australian Labor Movement," *South Atlantic Quarterly*, Spring 1959.

———— "Conflict and Mutual Misunderstanding: A Survey of Union Leaders' and Business Executives' Attitudes to Industrial Relations," *Journal of Industrial Relations*, April 1959.

———— *Industrial Relations in Australia*. Cambridge: Harvard University Press, 1956.

———— *Research Needs in Industrial Relations*. Perth: University of Western Australia Press, 1960.

Walker, Kenneth F., ed. *Unions, Management and the Public*. Nedlands: University of Western Australia Press, 1955.

Weiner, Herbert E. "Communist-led Industrial Unrest in Australia and New Zealand," *Notes on Labor Abroad*, No. 19, March 1951.

———— "The Reduction of Communist Power in the Australian Trade Unions," *Political Science Quarterly*, September 1954.

Western Australia. Laws, Statutes, etc. *Industrial Arbitration Act, 1912–1952*. Perth: W. H. Wyatt, Government Printer, 1956.

Wilkes, John, and S. E. Benson, eds., *Trade Unions in Australia*. Sydney: Angus & Robertson, Ltd., 1959.

Workers' Education Association of South Australia, Inc. *Compulsory Arbitration and Collective Bargaining*. Adelaide: 1959.

CANADA

Alberta, Board of Industrial Relations. *Bulletin on the Board's Activities, April 1st, 1962 to June 30th, 1962*. n.p., 1962.

Bairstow, Frances, ed. *Research Frontiers in Industrial Relations Today*. Proceedings of the Fourteenth Annual Conference, Industrial Relations Centre, McGill University. Montreal: McGill University, 1962.

Boyle, J. E. "Law Lessening the Strike Evil: Canada's Industrial Disputes Investigation Act," *Barrow's*, October 12, 1931.

Boyle, Thomas. *Justice Through Power; A Study of Labor in Its Present Situation.* Toronto: Longmans, 1961.

Cameron, James C., and F. J. L. Young. *The Status of Trade Unions in Canada.* Kingston: Department of Industrial Relations, Queen's University, 1960.

Canada. Department of Labour. *Labour Legislation in Canada*, 1915–1923, 1928–1946, 1948. Ottawa: Department of Labour, 1917–1950.

————— ————— *Labour-Management Cooperation Through Joint Consultation.* Ottawa: Department of Labour, 1958.

————— ————— *Reports*, 1900/01–1916/17, 1918/19–1961/62. Ottawa: Queen's Printer & Controller of Stationery, 1902–1963.

————— ————— Research and Statistics Branch. *Strikes and Lockouts in Canada.* Ottawa: Department of Labour, 1957.

Canadian Congress of Labour Research Department. *A Handbook on Union Agreements.* Ottawa: 1945.

"Canadian Industrial Disputes Investigation Act Amendments," *Monthly Labor Review*, September 1925.

Carrothers, A. W. R. *Injunction Cases—Canada, 1946–1955.* Toronto: Canadian Commerce Clearing House, 1956.

Chartier, Roger. "Changing Collective Bargaining Problems and Their Challenge to Labour Mediation," *Labor Law Journal*, October 1962.

Comparative Canadian–U. S. Industrial Relations; Proceedings of the IRRA Spring Meeting, Montreal, Canada, May 6–7, 1963. Reprint from *Labor Law Journal*, August 1963.

"Compulsion in Australia and Canada," *Survey*, December 2, 1916.

"Constitutionality of Industrial Disputes Investigation Act of Canada," *Monthly Labor Review*, May 1925.

Craig, Alton W. "Arbitration of Labor-Management Disputes in Canada," *Labor Law Journal*, November 1961.

Crysler, Alfred C. *Handbook on Canadian Labour Laws.* Toronto: Carswell Company, 1957.

————— *Labour Relations and Precedents in Canada.* Toronto: Carswell Company, 1949.

Dodge, William. "Labour-Management Relations Today," *Canadian Labour*, February 1964.

French, Doris. *Faith, Sweat, and Politics; The Early Trade Union Years in Canada.* Toronto: McClelland and Stewart, 1962.

International Labour Office. *Grievance Procedure in the United States and Canada.* Geneva: International Labour Office, 1949.

————— *The Role of Government in the Field of Labor-Management Relations—Canadian Approach.* (Labour-Management Relations Series No. 1.) Geneva: International Labour Office, 1957.

Jamieson, Stuart. *Industrial Relations in Canada.* Ithaca: Cornell University Press, 1957.

Kovacs, Aranka E. "Compulsory Conciliation in Canada," *Labor Law Journal*, February 1959.

Logan, Harold A. *Canadian Government Policy, 1943–1954.* Toronto: University of Toronto Press, 1956.

Logan, Harold A. *Trade Unions in Canada—Their Development and Functioning.* Toronto: Macmillan Co. of Canada, 1958.

Lorentsen, E., and E. Woolner. "Fifty Years of Labour Legislation in Canada," *Labour Gazette,* September 1950.

Lorentsen, Edith. "Labour Mediation in the United States and Canada," *Labor Law Journal,* October 1962.

Montague, J. T., and S. M. Jamieson, eds. *Labour-Management Conference on Industrial Relations in British Columbia* (Proceedings). Vancouver: Institute of Industrial Relations, University of British Columbia, 1963.

National Industrial Conference Board. *The Canadian Industrial Disputes Investigation Act.* Boston: National Industrial Conference Board, 1918.

Queen's University. Industrial Relations Section. *Closed Shop and Other Union Security Clauses in Recent Canadian Collective Bargaining Agreements.* Kingston: Queen's University, Industrial Relations Section, 1944.

———— Department of Industrial Relations. *The Conciliation and Arbitration of Labor Disputes in Canada.* Kingston: Queen's University, Department of Industrial Relations, 1949.

Queen's University. Industrial Relations Section. *The Right to Organize.* (Industrial Relations Bulletin No. 8.) Kingston: Queen's University, Industrial Relations Section, 1943.

Scott, F. R. "Federal Jurisdiction Over Labour Relations: A New Look," *Proceedings of the Eleventh Annual Conference, Industrial Relations Centre, McGill University, 1959.*

Stewart, B. M. *Canadian Labor Laws and the Treaty.* New York: Columbia University Press, 1926.

"Unions and the Law," *Canadian Labour,* November 1962.

Williams, J. Earl. "Labor Relations in Public Telephone Systems of Canada," *Monthly Labor Review,* April 1962.

Woods, H. D. "Canadian Collective Bargaining and Dispute Settlement Policy: An Appraisal," *Canadian Journal of Economics and Political Science,* November 1955.

———— "Difficulties and Opportunities in Canadian Mediation," *Labor Law Journal,* October 1962.

———— and Sylvia Ostry. *Labour Policy and Labour Economics in Canada.* Toronto: Macmillan Co. of Canada, 1962.

———— ed. *Patterns of Industrial Dispute Settlement in Five Canadian Industries.* Montreal: McGill University, Industrial Relations Centre, 1958.

———— "United States and Canadian Experience: A Comparison," in Joseph Shister, Benjamin Aaron, and Clyde W. Summers, eds., *Public Policy and Collective Bargaining.* (IRRA Publication No. 27.) New York: Harper, 1962.

INDIA

"Adjudication of Industrial Disputes in India," *International Labour Review,* January 1944.

Advani, G. M. "State Intervention in Labor Relations: Canada and India," University of Toronto *Faculty of Law Review,* April 1961.

Aggarawala, O. P. *The Industrial and Labour Law Digest; 1960, Annotated.* Delhi: Metropolitan Book Co., 1962.

"The Ahmedabad Experiment in Labor-Management Relations," *International Labour Review,* April and May 1959.

Aiyar, A. N., ed. *Encyclopedia of Labor Law Legislation.* 6 vols. Delhi: Federal Law Department, 1957.

Asrawal, A. N. *Industrial Problems of India.* Delhi: Ranjit Partners & Publishers, 1952.

Banerjee, Pratap Kumar. *Basic Labour Problems.* Calcutta: Workers' Publication House, 1959.

Basu, Nrisinhadas. *The Arbitration Act, 1940.* Calcutta: Eastern Law House, 1948.

Bhasin, T. R. *Evolutionary Perspective of Labour Legislation and Policy in India, 1850–1956.* New Delhi: Industrial Legal Aid and Advice Institute, 1957.

Bose, S. N. *Indian Labour Code.* Calcutta: Eastern Law House, March 1957.

Brown, Irving. "Trade Unionism in India," *Indian Journal of Social Work,* December 1949.

Chakravarti, S. C. *Laws of Industrial Adjudications in India;* A Case-noted Commentary on the Industrial Disputes Act, 1947 and the Industrial Employment (Standing Orders) Act, 1946. 2nd ed. Calcutta: Eastern Law House, 1961.

Chatterjee, A. C. "Federalism and Labour Legislation in India," *International Labour Review,* April–May 1944.

"Conciliation and Arbitration in India: The Mysore Labor (Emergency) Act 1941," *International Labour Review,* January 1942.

Das, N. *Industrial Labour in India.* (Pamphlet No. 12.) New Delhi: Eastern Economist Ltd., 1952.

Daya, E. "Freedom of Association and Industrial Relations in Asian Countries," *International Labour Review,* April and May 1955.

"Decade of Labor Legislation in India, 1937–1948," *International Labour Review,* April and May 1949.

Devasagayam, A. "Employer-Employee Tension in Industry," *Indian Journal of Social Work,* December 1951.

Dias, Maurice V. "Industrial Relations in India," M.S. thesis, Loyola University, 1958.

Dutt, Rajani Palme. *Labour Movement in India,* Library of Congress, Microfilm No. 1965, Reel 7 HD, Mic 54–804.

Dutta, M. B. "Conciliation and Arbitration in Indian Labour Law," *Calcutta Review,* September 1948.

Gadgil, Dhanenjaya Ramchandra. *Regulation of Wages and Other Problems of Industrial Labour in India.* Poona: D. R. Gadgil, 1954.

Ganguli, Harish Chandra. "Indian Cooperatives: Various Causes of Industrial Conflict Against the Background of the Conditions in India," *Indian Journal of Social Work,* September 1955.

George, C. M. "The Importance of Labour Research in a Developing Economy," *Indian Worker,* June 11, 1962.

Giri, V. V. *Industrial Relations.* Bombay: N. M. Tripathi, Ltd., 1955.

Giri, V. V. *Labour Problems in Indian Industry.* Bombay: Asia Publishing House, 1959.

Goyal, Ramesh C. *Post-War Trends in Industrial Relations in India.* (Pamphlet No. 33.) New Delhi: Eastern Economist, Ltd., 1955.

Guha, S. R. "Collective Bargaining and Voluntary Arbitration," *Indian Journal of Social Work,* June 1959.

Haldar, Sadhausu Kumar. *Evolution of Labour-Management Relations and the Indian Law of Industrial Disputes.* Calcutta: Susama Press, 1953.

India, Department of Industries (Labour Department). *Labor Legislation in India Since 1937.* (Bulletin of Indian Industries and Labour, No. 74.) Delhi, 1945.

India (Republic). Labour Bureau. *Consultative Machinery in the Labour Field.* New Delhi: Government Press, 1959.

———— ———— *Current Problems of Labour in India.* Simla: Government Press, 1960.

———— Laws, Statutes, etc. *The Industrial Disputes Act, 1947 as Amended Up to 1952; The Industrial Disputes (Appellate Tribunal) Act, 1950.* Calcutta: Susama Press, 1951.

———— Ministry of Labour. *Annual Report.* Delhi: Manager of Publications, n.d.

———— ———— *Indian Labour Year Book.* 1950–51, 1951–52, 1952–53, 1953–54, 1954–55. Delhi: Manager of Publications.

———— ———— *Indian Labour Gazette.* (Annual.) Delhi: Manager of Publications, n.d.

———— ———— *Labour Bureau Industrial Awards in India: An Analysis.* Delhi: Manager of Publications, 1951.

———— ———— *Report on the Working of the Trade Union Act, 1926, during 1949–53.* Delhi: Manager of Publications, n.d.

———— ———— *Summary of the Proceedings of the Indian Labour Conference.* Delhi: Manager of Publications, n.d.

"Industrial Disputes in India," *Industry and Labour,* December 15, 1953.

"Industrial Labour in India," *Indian Affairs Record,* July 1959.

"The Institution of a Tripartite Labour Organization in India," *International Labour Review,* January 1943.

International Labour Organization. *Report to the Government of India on Labour-Management Relations and Some Aspects of Wage Policy.* (Labour-Management Relations Series No. 9.) Geneva, 1960.

Jagannadham, V. "Industrial Disputes in India," *Indian Journal of Economics,* October 1948.

Jain, Janeshwar Dass, and Parmeshwar Dass Jain. *Current Central Labour Code.* Containing commentary on the *Industrial Disputes Act, 1947;* complete and up-to-date acts, rules, orders, regulations and schemes enacted and framed under all central labour legislation. Delhi: Law Literature House, 1962.

———— ———— *Industrial and Labor Legislation, As Modified Up-to-Date.* Delhi: Industrial Advisory Service, 1957.

James, Ralph C. "Politics and Trade Unionism in India," *Far Eastern Survey,* March 1958.

Joman, R. J. *Peaceful Industrial Relations: Their Science and Technique*, Ahmedabad: Narajivan Publishing House, 1957.

Kapur, K. N. *Law Relating to Labour Disputes in India*. New Delhi: Karolbagh Publications, 1954.

Kennedy, Van Dusen. *The Conceptual and Legislative Framework of Labor Relations in India*. (Institute of Industrial Relations Reprint No. 114.) Berkeley: University of California, 1958.

———— *Problems of Indian Trade Unionism and Labor Relations*. (Institute of Industrial Relations Reprint No. 77.) Berkeley: University of California, 1955.

———— *The Role of the Union in the Plant in India*. (Institute of Industrial Relations Reprint No. 83.) Berkeley: University of California, 1956.

Kharbanda, M. L., and Chandan Gopal. *The Indian Disputes Act*. (Act IV of 1947.) Allahabad: Law Publishing House, 1955.

Kher, V. B. *Digest of Labour Law Cases*. Bombay: Thacher, 1956.

———— *Indian Trade Union Law*. 1st ed. Bombay: N. M. Tripathi, Ltd., 1954.

Krishnaswami, C. "Industrial Discipline Under Arbitral Review in the U. S. A. and India," M.S. thesis, Cornell University, 1956.

Kumar, Chakrapani B. *Development of Industrial Relations in India*. Bombay: Orient Longmans, 1961.

Lal, N. *Law of Arbitration in India*. Lucknow: Eastern Book Co., 1963.

Lattimore, Eleanor H. *Labor Unions in the Far East*. New York: Institute of Pacific Relations, 1945.

Lokanatham, P. S. "Industrial Disputes and Legislation," *Indian Journal of Economics*, April 1940.

"Machinery for the Administration of Labour Legislation in India," *International Labour Review*, April 1943.

Mahaseth, Satya Narain. "Industrial Relations in India," M.B.A. thesis, University of Pennsylvania, 1951.

Malik, P. L. *A Handbook of Industrial Law*. Lucknow: Eastern Book Co., 1953.

———— *The Industrial Law*. 5th ed. Lucknow: Eastern Book Co., 1961.

Mallik, A. N. "Labour Problems and Labour Legislation in India," *Indian Journal of Economics*, April 1940.

Mathur, A. S., and J. S. Mathur. *Trade Union Movement in India*. Allahabad: Chaitanya Publishing House, 1957.

Mathur, Jivan Narain. "Trade Unionism in India," *Ultara Bharti*, February 1957.

Mehta, Asoka. "The Mediating Role of the Trade Union in Underdeveloped Countries," *Economic Development Cultural Change*, October 1957.

Meyers, C. A. *Industrial Relations in India*. Bombay: Asia Publishing House, 1958.

———— *Labor Problems in the Industrialization of India*. Cambridge: Harvard University Press, 1958.

Morris, David. "Labor Discipline, Trade Unions and the State of India," *Journal of Political Economy*, August 1955.

Mukerjee, Radhakamal. *The Indian Working Class*. Bombay: Hind Kitabs, Ltd., 1951.

Mukhtar, Ahmad. *Trade Unionism and Labour Disputes in India.* London: Longmans, Green & Co., 1953.

Narayan, Braj K. "Compulsory Arbitration of Labor Disputes in India," M.S. thesis, Cornell University, 1956.

Ornati, Oscar. *Indian Trade Unions Since Independence.* (New York School of Industrial and Labor Relations Reprint Series No. 26.) Ithaca: Cornell University, 1954.

——— *Jobs and Workers in India.* Ithaca: New York State School of Industrial & Labor Relations, Cornell University, 1955.

——— *Legal Protection of Labor in Contemporary India.* (New York State School of Industrial & Labor Relations Reprint Series No. 33.) Ithaca: Cornell University, 1955.

——— *Problems of Indian Trade Unionism,* Ithaca: New York State School of Industrial & Labor Relations, Cornell University, 1957.

Pardasani, N. H. "The Bombay Industrial Disputes Act, 1938," *Indian Journal of Economics,* July 1940.

Patel, Vithalbhai B. *The Industrial Disputes Act, 1947.* Bombay: N. M. Tripathi, 1963.

Planalp, Sarl K. "Leading Principles in the Industrial Disputes Awards of India, 1951–54," M.S. thesis, Cornell University, 1956.

Punekar, S. D. *Industrial Peace in India: The Problem and Its Solution.* Bombay: Vora & Co., 1952.

Raj, Gopal T. A. *Industrial Disputes Act, 1947.* Banglore: Law of India, 1953.

Ramakrishnan, Peelamedu R. "Labor Legislation in India," M.S. thesis, Massachusetts Institute of Technology, 1953.

Rao, A. V. Raman, *Mediation, Conciliation and Arbitration; USA and India, a Comparative Study.* Bombay: Popular Prakashan, 1963.

Rao, Ganapathy M. R. "Industrial Peace and the 5-Year Plan," *Asian Economic Review,* May 1960.

Rao, Raghunath. *Wartime Labor Conditions and Reconstruction Planning.* Montreal: International Labour Office, 1946.

Rao, Venkoba K. "Indian Arbitration Law, *The Arbitration Journal,* Vol. 10, No. 3, 1955.

Ridgel, Gus T. "Government and Industrial Relations—India and the U. S. A.," *The Journal of the National Institute of Labour Management,* January-June 1956.

Row, C. M., and R. B. Sethi, *Law of Industrial Disputes.* Allahabad: Law Book Co., 1958.

Row, V. G. *Law Relating to Industrial Disputes.* Madras: Madras Book Agency, 1962.

Rustamji, R. F. *The Law of Industrial Disputes in India,* with an introduction dealing with "social legislation," etc. Allahabad: Law Pub. House, 1962.

Sarkar, P. C., ed. *Labour Laws in India.* Calcutta: S. C. Sarkar & Sons (Private) Ltd., 1956.

Sastri, L. S. *The Labour Manual.* Allahabad: Law Book Co., 1954.

Saxena, R. N. *Encyclopedia of Labour Laws.* Allahabad: Central Law Agency, October 1954.

Seshadri, S. "Communism in Indian Trade Unions," *Free Labour World*, January 1953.

Sethi, R. B. *Law of Trade Unions*. Allahabad: Law Book Co., 1958.

Shroff, Aloo Dinshaw. *The Conciliation and Arbitration of Industrial Disputes in India*. Bombay: Popular Book Depot, 1952.

Singh, S. D. *Law of Arbitration in India and Pakistan*. Allahabad: R. N. Lal, 1958.

"Social and Economic Proposals of India's Leading Trade Union," *Monthly Labor Review*, April 1955.

Srivastava, Gursharanlal. *Collective Bargaining and Labour-Management Relations in India*. Allahabad: Bookland, 1962.

Srivastava, Kerpa Kayal. *Commentaries on Industrial Disputes Act, 1947, Act No. XIV of 1947*. Lucknow: Eastern Book Co., 1960.

Srivastava, K. N. *Industrial Peace and Labour in India*. Allahabad: Kitab Mahal, 1954.

"Tripartite Labor Organization in India," *International Labour Review*, September–October 1944.

Trivedi, H. N. "Tripartite Labour Machinery in India," *Indian Worker*, January 29, 1962.

U. S. Department of Labor. Bureau of Labor Statistics. *Foreign Labor Information: Labor in India*. Washington, D. C.: Government Printer, 1956.

———— *Labor in India*. (BLS Report No. 188.) Washington, D. C.: Government Printing Office, 1961.

———— ———— *Summary of the Labor Situation in India*. Washington, D. C.: Government Printing Office, 1956.

Vaid, K. N., ed. *Labour-Management Relations in India; A Symposium*. (School of Social Work Publication No. 11.) Delhi: Delhi University, 1960.

Varma, Madhurendra Kishore. "Role of Legislation in Regulating Labor-Management Relations in India," *Labor Law Journal*, April 1957.

———— "Whither Industrial Relations in India?", M.S. thesis, Cornell University, 1956.

Vohra, D. N. *Law Relating to Strikes and Lockouts*. 1st ed. New Delhi: Labour Law Publishers, 1960.

Yudhisthira, B. A., and B. L. Munshi. *Labour Laws*, containing factories and labour laws, with up-to-date amendments, rules, case law and comments. Allahabad: Allahabad Law Agency, 1961.

JAPAN

Akuzawa, K. "Japanese Labor Law and Relations," *8 Japan Annual of Law and Politics*, 87–96 (1960).

Allen, George C. *Japan's Economic Recovery*. London: Oxford University Press, 1958.

"Amendment of Labor Legislation in Japan," *Industry and Labour*, February 1, 1950.

Ayusawa, Iwao. "Developments in Organized Labor," *Contemporary Japan*, 1952, Nos. 4–6, 7–9, 10–12.

Ayusawa, Iwao. "Japanese Trade Unions Today," *Oriental Economist*, January 1957.

——— "The Labor Problem in Japan," *Japan Quarterly*, October 1954.

——— *Organized Labor in Japan*. Tokyo: The Foreign Affairs Association of Japan, 1962.

——— "Organized Labor in Present-Day Japan," *Contemporary Japan*, March 1959, August 1959, December 1959.

——— *Post-War Developments in Organized Labor*. Tokyo: Foreign Affairs Association of Japan, 1953.

——— "Strike Wave Over Japan," *Oriental Economist*, January 1953.

——— "The Trade Union Act Enforced," *Oriental Economist*, February 16, 1946.

Azuma, M., ed. *Rodo Roppo* (Basic Statutes on Labor). Tokyo: Surugadai Shuppan-Sha, 1960.

Ballon, Robert T. *The Labor Movement in 1961*. (Sophia Industrial Relations Center Bulletin No. 4.) Tokyo: Sophia University, 1962.

Barrett, Ruth. "Japanese Labor Unionism: Hybrid Plant in Strange Soil," *Reporter*, November 24, 1953.

Camacho, Martin T. "The Administration of SCAP Labor Policy in Occupied Japan," Ph.D. thesis, Harvard University, 1954.

Daya, E. "Freedom of Association and Industrial Relations in Asian Countries," *International Labour Review*, April 1955.

Deverall, Richard. "Labor in Japan," *American Federationist*, March 1953.

——— "Japanese Post-War Labour Movement," *Asian Labour*, October 1949.

"Discharges of Communist Workers," *Notes on Labor Abroad*, No. 16, December 1950.

Edwards, Marie Alice. "Political Activities of Japanese Postwar Labor Unions," Ann Arbor: University of Michigan, 1956.

Farley, Miriam S. *Aspects of Japan's Labor Problems*. New York: John Day Co., 1950.

Fujibayashi, Keizo. *Bird's Eye View of the Labor Movement in Postwar Japan*. Tokyo: Nihon Taihuyo Mondai Chosakai, 1954.

"Functions and Activities of the Labor Relations Commissions," *Japan Labor Bulletin*, February 1960.

General Council of Trade Unions of Japan. *The Present Situation of Labor Movement in Japan*. Tokyo, 1954.

Gong, Wa. "Labor Movement in Japan," *Industry of Free China*, December 1959.

Japan. Central Labor Relations Commission. *Seventh Annual Report of the Labor Relations Commission*. Tokyo, 1953.

——— ——— *Eighth Annual Report of the Labor Relations Commission*, April 1953–March 1954. Tokyo, August 1954.

——— ——— *Labor Relations Commissions of Japan: What They Are, What They Do*. Tokyo, March 1956.

——— Laws, Statutes, etc. *Labor Union Law and Labor Relations Adjustment Law with Their By-Laws*. Tokyo: Trade Bulletin Corporation, 1955.

Japan. Laws, Statutes, etc. *Japan Labor Legislation, 1959.* Tokyo: Romu
Gyosei Kenkyusho, 1959.
——— Ministry of Labor. *Analysis of Japanese Labor Economy.* Tokyo,
1956.
——— ——— *Japan Labor Code 1952.* Tokyo, 1953.
——— ——— *The Japanese Labor Legislation.* Tokyo: N. Takehiko,
1950.
——— ——— *Japan Labor Legislation.* Tokyo, 1959.
——— ——— *Japan Labor Yearbook.* 1952–1957. Tokyo.
——— ——— *Progress of Labor Legislation.* Tokyo, 1952.
——— ——— "Summarized Results of 1953 Annual Survey of Labor
Unions," *Monthly Labor Statistics and Research Bulletin,* V, De-
cember 1953.
——— ——— *Yearbook of Labor Statistics.* 1952–1957. Tokyo.
——— ——— *Yearbook of Labor Statistics and Research.* 1949–1951.
Tokyo.
Japan Federation of Employers Association. *Labor Movement in Japan.*
Tokyo, 1958.
Japan Yearbook. 1933–1952. Tokyo, The Foreign Affairs Association of
Japan.
Karsh, Bernard, and Solomon B. Levine, "Present Dilemmas of the
Japanese Labor Movement," *The International Labor Scene,* Proceed-
ings of the Industrial Relations Research Association Spring Meeting,
1962. Reprinted from *Labor Law Journal,* July 1962.
Katayama, Tetsu. "Labour Dispute Adjustment Law," *Contemporary
Japan,* September–December 1946.
Katsunori, Rikutaro. "Labor Movement and Strikes," *Oriental Economist,*
December 7, 1946.
Kennard, A. "Strikes and the Japanese Labour Movement, *Nineteenth
Century,* September 1946.
Kikuchi, Isao. "Industrial Relations in Japan," *International Labour
Review,* August 1959.
Killen, J. S. "Report on Japan: Postwar Unionism Has Had a Rapid
Growth," *American Federationist,* August 1948.
"Labor Conditions in Japan," *Monthly Labor Review,* October 1945.
"Labor Legislation in Japan," *Notes on Labor Abroad,* October 1947.
"Labor Policy in Occupied Japan," *Labour Gazette,* October 1949.
The Labor Union Movement in Postwar Japan. Tokyo: Daily Labor Press,
Inc., 1954.
Lattimer, Eleanor H. *Labor Unions in the Far East.* New York: Institute
of Pacific Relations, 1945.
Levine, Solomon B. *Industrial Relations in Postwar Japan.* Urbana:
University of Illinois Press, 1958.
——— "Industrial Relations in the New Japan," *Pacific Affairs,* Sep-
tember 1957.
——— *Japanese Trade Unionism as a Model in Economic Development.*
(Paper presented at the Research Seminar on Comparative Labor
Movements, National Institute of Labor Education, Washington, D. C.,
November 1960.)

Levine, Solomon B. "Japan's Tripartite Labor Relations Commissions," *Labor Law Journal*, July 1955.

———— "The Labor Movement and Economic Development in Japan," *Annual Proceedings*, Industrial Relations Research Association, December 28–30, 1954.

———— "Labor Patterns and Trends," *Annals of the American Academy of Political and Social Science*, November 1956.

———— "Prospects of Japanese Labor," *Far Eastern Survey*, May 1954, July 1954.

Martin, Benjamin. "Reflections on Japanese Industrial Relations," *Far Eastern Survey*, August 1958.

McCoy, F. R. *Labor Policy in Japan*. U. S. Department of State Bulletin, 21:107–8, n.p., n.p., July 25, 1949.

McPherson, W. H. "Industrial Relations in Occupied Japan," in Colston E. Warne, ed., *Labor in Postwar America*. Berkeley: Remsen Press, 1949.

Meyer, Leonard. "Trade Unionism in Japan," Master's thesis, Columbia University, 1950.

Minakami, T. "Changing Patterns of Japanese Trade Unionism," *Asian Labour*, January 1951.

Miyamoto, Shozaburo. "The Labor Union Movement in Japan, 1950–1955," M.A. thesis, University of Hawaii, 1957.

Moran, W. T. "Labor Unions in Postwar Japan," *Far Eastern Survey*, October 19, 1949.

Muramatsu, Goro. "Development of Labor," *Contemporary Japan*. Nos. 10–12, 1955.

Nakayama, Ichiro. "Japanese Labor Trends," *Oriental Economist*, February 1955.

———— "Japan's Labor Movement," in *Japan's Problems*. Tokyo: Ministry of Foreign Affairs, August 1953.

———— *Japan's Labor Problems*. Tokyo: Ministry of Foreign Affairs, 1956.

"New Anti-Communist Federation of Industrial Unions to be Formed," *Notes on Labor Abroad*, May 1949.

"New Labor Relations Act in Japan," *Industry and Labour*, November 15, 1959.

Nihon Rodo Kyokai Zassi, April 1959.

Nihon Seisansei Hombu. *Industrial Relations in Japan, 1958*. Tokyo, 1958.

———— *The Status of Economic Research Organizations in Japan and Their Problems*. Tokyo, 1958.

Okochi, Kazuo. *Labor in Modern Japan*. Tokyo: Science Council of Japan, 1958.

Oriental Economist Yearbooks. 1955–1958. Tokyo: Oriental Economist.

Rosen, Anita Zenia. "Development of Japanese Labor Unions Under the American Occupation," M.A. thesis, Columbia University, 1955.

Sakurabayashi, Makoto. *Labor Unions in Postwar Japan*. Tokyo: Sophia University, Sophia Industrial Relations Center, 1960.

Saposs, David J. "Split Between Asian and Western Socialism," *Foreign Affairs Quarterly*, July 1954.

"Sohyo and Nikkeiren," *Oriental Economist*, November 1957.

Supreme Commander of the Allied Powers. *Japanese Labor Postwar Policies, Programs and Developments*. Tokyo: General Headquarters, 1949.

———— *Labor Developments in Japan*. Tokyo: General Headquarters, n.d.

———— *Labor Division Manual*. Tokyo: General Headquarters, 1949.

———— *Labor Division Report*. Tokyo: General Headquarters, n.d.

———— *Labor Policies and Program in Japan. Final Report of the Advisory Committee on Labor in Japan*. Tokyo: General Headquarters, 1946.

———— *Labor Union Statistics*. Tokyo: General Headquarters, 1946.

———— *Statistical Survey of Labor Unions and Federations in Japan, 31 December 1947*. Tokyo: General Headquarters, 1948.

Taira, Koji. "The Dynamics of Industrial Relations in Early Japanese Development," *The International Labor Scene*. Proceedings of the Industrial Relations Research Association Spring Meeting, 1962. Reprinted from *Labor Law Journal*, July 1962.

Takita, Minoru. "Reform in Trade Unionism," *Contemporary Japan*, March 1959.

"Text of Policy Directive in Japanese Trade Unions," *Notes on Labor Abroad*, May 1947.

Tiltman, Hessell. "Japanese Labor Faces Peace Abroad, A Battle at Home," *Reporter*, October 2, 1951.

"Trade Unions in Japan," *Oriental Economist*, July 1952.

"Trade Union Act," *Monthly Labor Review*, February 1947, October 1950.

"Trade Union Freedom in Japan," *Free Labour World*, May 1951.

"Trade Union Movement in Japan," *Monthly Labor Review*, October 1950.

U. S. Department of Labor. Bureau of Labor Statistics. *Summary of Labor Situation in Japan*. Washington, D. C.: Government Printing Office, 1955.

———— ———— *Summary of Labor Situations in Japan*. Washington, D. C.: Government Printing Office, 1958.

U. S. Foreign Economic Administration. *Trade Unions and Collective Bargaining in Japan*. Washington, D. C.: Government Printing Office, 1945.

Wada, Haruo. "Labor Movement Takes Two Forms," *Oriental Economist*, March 1955.

Weigert, O. "Labor Policies and Programs in Japan Under the Occupation," *Monthly Labor Review*, February 1947.

Yamada, Setsuo. "Postwar Labor Movement in Japan," *Oriental Economist*, October 1952.

NEW ZEALAND

Abbot, A. S. "Watersiders Expelled From Federation," *Notes on Labor Abroad*, March 1950.

"Action Against Communism in Unions," *Notes on Labor Abroad*, August 1950.

Brissenden, Paul F. "Disputes Settlement in New Zealand," *Industrial Relations*, February 1964.

Bucknell, D. W. "Industrial Tangles in a Commonwealth," *Wool*, 1958–1959.

Carter, John. "Where Tories Rule in New Zealand," *Labour Monthly*, October 1951.

"Change in Labor's Attitude Toward Compulsory Arbitration," *Monthly Labor Review*, December 1921.

"Conciliation and Arbitration in New Zealand," *International Labour Review*, March 1948.

Condliffe, John B. *The Welfare State of New Zealand*. London: George Allen and Unwin Ltd., 1959.

"The Court of Arbitration in New Zealand," *Economic Record*, June 1941.

Crowley, D. W. "Outline History of the New Zealand Labour Movement, 1894–1913," *Historical Studies: Australia and New Zealand*, May 1951.

————— "Critical Bibliography of the History of the New Zealand Labour Movement," *Historical Studies: Australia and New Zealand*, May 1951.

"Enforcement of the New Zealand Conciliation and Arbitration Act," *Monthly Labor Review*, March 1940.

Flexner, J. A., *et al.* "Settlement of Industrial Disputes in 7 Foreign Countries," *Monthly Labor Review*, August 1946.

Glickman, D. L. "The Labor Movements in Australia and New Zealand," *Social Research*, June 1949.

Hare, Anthony Edward Christian. *Report on Industrial Relations in New Zealand*. London: J. M. Dent & Sons, Ltd., 1946.

————— *Labour in New Zealand—1943*. Wellington: Victoria University College, 1944.

Hearnshaw, L. S. "Sound Industrial Relations," *Industrial New Zealand*, June 1947.

"Historical Summary of Arbitration Court from 1894 and Effect of 1936 and Later Legislation," *Monthly Labor Review*, August 1938.

"History of Wage Pronouncements of the Court of Arbitration," *Labour and Employment Gazette*, February 1952.

"Industrial Conciliation and Arbitration Act Consolidated," *Labour and Employment Gazette*, November 1954.

"Industrial Disputes in New Zealand," *Labour and Employment Gazette*, August 1959.

"Industrial Relations Machinery in Democratic Foreign Countries," *Monthly Labor Review*, November 1939.

"Industrial Unions: Their Constitutions, Government, Objects, Powers," *Labour and Employment Gazette* (Wellington), February 1953.

"Legality of Strikes: A Short Historical Summary of the Law in New Zealand," *Labour and Employment Gazette*, May 1954.

Lewin, J. P. "In Place of Arbitration," *Here and Now*, August 1952.

Luxford, J. H. "Survey of the Law of Arbitration," *Accountants' Journal*, June 1953.

Martin, R. M. "20 Years of Compulsory Unionism," *Political Science*, September 1956.

Mazengarb, Alfred John. *Industrial Laws of New Zealand.* Wellington: Butterworth & Co., 1947.

Miller, G. M. "Arbitration Court—Another View," *Here and Now,* June 1951.

New Zealand. *Report on Delegation from New Zealand at Geneva, 1950.* Wellington: 1950.

——— Asian Regional Conference of the ILO. *Report of Delegation from New Zealand to the 4th Regional Conference, New Delhi, Nov. 13–25, 1957.* Wellington: Government Printing Office, 1958.

——— Department of Labour. *Annual Awards, Recommendations, Agreements, etc., made under Industrial Conciliation and Arbitration Act and the Labour Disputes Investigation Act.* Wellington: Government Printer. ("Book of Awards.")

——— ——— *Annual Reports,* 1891–1963. Wellington: Government Printer.

——— ——— *Statutes Administered.* Wellington: Government Printer, 1945.

——— Department of Statistics. *New Zealand Official Yearbooks,* 1896–1960. Wellington: Government Printer.

——— ——— *Annual Reports on Prices, Wages and Labour Statistics of New Zealand,* 1946, 1957, 1958. Wellington: Government Printer.

O'Flynn, F. D., ed. *Mazengarb's Industrial Laws of New Zealand.* Wellington: Butterworth & Co., 1956.

"Organization of Employers and Workers Under the Industrial Conciliation and Arbitration Act, 1925," *Labour and Employment Gazette,* February and August 1951, February and August 1952, February 1953.

Oxnam, D. W. "New Zealand's Industrial Relations Act 1949," *Economic Record,* December 1949.

——— "Arbitration in Perspective—A Further Comment," *Economic Record,* April 1958.

Pauling, N. G. "Labour and Politics in New Zealand," *Canadian Journal of Economics and Political Science,* February 1953.

Riches, E. J. "The Restoration of Compulsory Arbitration in New Zealand," *International Labour Review,* December 1936.

Ritter, A. S., and M. M. Smith, "Action Against Communism," *Monthly Labor Review,* November 1950.

Rosenberg, W. *Compulsory Arbitration: Barrier to Progress?* Wellington: Modern Books, August 1952.

Ross, Lloyd, and Morris Weisz, "Conciliation and Arbitration in Australia and New Zealand," *Industrial and Labor Relations Review,* October 1948.

Scott, Sidney. *Outline History of the New Zealand Labour Movement.* Auckland: S. W. Scott, 1944.

Sorrell, G. H. "Industrial Relations in New Zealand," *Journal of Industrial Relations,* October 1961.

Sutch, William Ball. *The Quest for Security in New Zealand.* New York: Penguin Books, 1942.

"Trade Union Rift in New Zealand," *Christian Century,* May 31, 1950.

Tuck, W. R. "The Court of Arbitration in New Zealand," *Economic Record*, June 1941.

Tyndall, Arthur. "New Zealand System of Industrial Conciliation and Arbitration," *International Labour Review*, August 1960.

"Wage Regulation in New Zealand," *Industry and Labour*, November 15, 1950.

"Wartime Regulation of Labor on New Zealand." *Monthly Labour Review*, April 1942.

Webb, Leicester. "Trade Unions at the Crossroads," *New Zealand Journal of Public Administration*, March 1952.

Weiner, Herbert E. "Communist-led Industrial Unrest in Australia and New Zealand," *Notes on Labor Abroad*, March 1951.

"Where is Trade Unionism Heading? *New Zealand Economist and Taxpayer*, October 1950.

Wilson, M. W. "Strikes Continue in New Zealand," *Christian Century*, June 27, 1951.

"Work Stoppages and Related Disturbances Arising Out of Industrial Disputes: First 9 Months of 1950," *Labour and Employment Gazette*, February and August 1951.

"Work Stoppages and Related Disturbances Arising Out of Industrial Disputes: Summary for the Year 1952," *Labour and Employment Gazette*, August 1953.

"Work Stoppages and Related Disturbances Arising Out of Industrial Disputes: Twelve Months Ended September 30, 1952," *Labour and Employment Gazette*, February 1953.

"Work Stoppages and Related Disturbances Arising Out of Industrial Disputes: Disastrous Year Ends with One of the Quietest Periods on Record," *Labour and Employment Gazette*, August 1952.

"Work Stoppages in 1958 Lowest for 15 Years," *Labour and Employment Gazette*, May 1959.

UNITED STATES

Aaron, Benjamin. "Amending the Taft-Hartley Act: A Decade of Frustration," *Industrial and Labor Relations Review*, April 1958.

Arensberg, Conrad M., *et al. Research in Industrial Human Relations*. (IRRA Publication No. 17.) New York: Harper, 1957.

Aronson, Robert L., ed. *Industrial and Labor Relations Research in Universities: A United States Summary, 1953–54.* (N. Y. State School of Industrial and Labor Relations, Reprint No. 26.) Ithaca: Cornell University, 1954.

Barbash, Jack. *The Practice of Unionism*. New York: Harper, 1956.

Barkin, Solomon. "New Labor Relations Policies and Remedies Suggested by Different Industrial Settings," *Labor Law Journal*, February 1963.

Beal, Edwin F., and Edward D. Wickersham. *The Practice of Collective Bargaining*. Homewood: R. D. Irwin, 1963.

Bell, Daniel. "The Background and Development of Marxian Socialism in the United States," in Donald D. Egbert and Stow Persons, eds., *Socialism and American Life*, Vol. I. Princeton: Princeton University Press, 1952.

Bell, Daniel. *The End of Ideology: On the Exhaustion of Political Ideas in the Fifties.* Glencoe: The Free Press, 1960.

Berman, E. *Labor Disputes and the President of the United States.* New York: Columbia University Studies, 1924.

Bernstein, Irving, Harold L. Enarson, and R. W. Fleming, eds. *Emergency Disputes and National Policy.* (IRRA Publication No. 15.) New York: Harper, 1955.

Bloom, Gordon F., and Herbert F. Northrup. "Public Policy and Dispute Settlement," in Herbert G. Heneman, Jr., *et al.*, eds., *Employment Relations Research.* (IRRA Publication No. 23.) New York: Harper, 1960.

Blum, Albert A. *The Development of American Labor.* New York: Macmillan, 1963.

Braun, Kurt. *Labor Disputes and Their Settlement.* Baltimore: Johns Hopkins Press, 1955.

Brissenden, Paul F. "Public Policy on Collective Bargaining," *Labor Law Journal*, September 1951.

—— *Settlement of Disputes over Grievances in the United States.* Honolulu: Industrial Relations Center, University of Hawaii, 1965.

Bullen, Frederick H. "The Taft-Hartley and Emergency Defense Disputes," in Emanuel Stein, ed., *NYU 5th Annual Conference on Labor.* Albany: Matthew Bender, 1952.

Chamberlain, Edward H., *et al. Labor Unions and Public Policy.* Washington, D. C.: American Enterprise Association, 1958.

Chamberlain, Neil W. "The Problem of Strikes," in Emanuel Stein, ed., *NYU 13th Annual Conference on Labor.* Albany: Matthew Bender, 1960.

—— Frank C. Pierson, and Theresa Wolfson, eds. *A Decade of Industrial Relations Research 1946–1956.* (IRRA Publication No. 19.) New York: Harper, 1958.

Ching, Cyrus. *Review and Reflection: A Half Century of Labor Relations.* New York: B. C. Forbes, 1953.

Cole, David. "Emergency Labor Disputes," in Emanuel Stein, ed., *NYU 4th Annual Conference on Labor.* Albany: Matthew Bender, 1951.

—— "The Role of Government in Emergency Disputes," *Temple Law Quarterly*, Spring 1953.

Commons, John R., and Associates. *History of Labour in the United States.* 4 vols. New York: Macmillan, 1918.

Congress of Industrial Organizations. *Official Reports on the Expulsion of Communist Dominated Organizations from the CIO.* (Publication No. 254.) Washington, D. C.: CIO, 1954.

Cooper, R. Conrad. "The National Interest in Collective Bargaining," *Labor Law Journal*, November 1962.

Cox, Archibald. *Law and the National Labor Policy.* (Monograph Series No. 5.) Los Angeles: University of California Institute of Industrial Relations, 1960.

—— "Reflections Upon Labor Arbitration in the Light of the Lincoln Mills Case," in Jean T. McKelvey, ed., *Arbitration and the Law.* Washington, D. C.: Bureau of National Affairs, Inc., 1959.

Daugherty, Carroll R., and John B. Parrish. *The Labor Problems of American Society.* Boston: Houghton Mifflin Co., 1952.

Davey, Harold W. "Government Intervention in Labor Disputes," *Labor Law Journal,* November 1954.

Derber, Milton, and Edwin Young, eds. *Labor and the New Deal.* Madison: University of Wisconsin Press, 1957.

————— *et al.* "Union-Management Relations Research," *Industrial and Labor Relations Review,* April 1961.

————— and Rennard, Davis. "Research at the Industrial Relations Centers," *Annual Proceedings,* IRRA, 1962.

Elkouri, Frank. *How Arbitration Works.* Washington, D. C.: Bureau of National Affairs, Inc., 1952.

Evans, Hywell. *Government Regulation of Industrial Relations: A Comparative Study of U. S. and British Experience.* Ithaca: Cornell University, N. Y. State School of Industrial & Labor Relations, 1961.

Fanning, John H. "The New Taft-Hartley Amendments: A Preliminary Look," *Labor Law Journal,* November 1959.

Feinberg, I. Robert. "The Arbitrator's Responsibility Under the Taft-Hartley Act," *Arbitration Journal,* XVIII, No. 2 (1963).

Feinsinger, Nathan, *et al.* "The Role of the Law in Arbitration: A Panel Discussion," in Jean T. McKelvey, ed., *Arbitration and the Law.* Washington, D. C.: Bureau of National Affairs, Inc., 1959.

Fisher, Waldo E. *The Taft-Hartley Act as Amended in 1959; A Management Guide.* Pasadena: California Institute of Technology, Industrial Relations Section, 1960.

Fleming, R. W. *Emergency Strikes and National Policy.* (Institute of Labor and Industrial Relations, Reprint Series No. 84.) Urbana: University of Illinois, 1960.

Frankfurter, Felix, and Nathan Greene. *The Labor Injunction.* New York: Macmillan, 1930.

Freidin, Jesse. "Has Taft-Hartley Helped or Hurt the Achievement of Stable Labor Relations?" in Emanuel Stein, ed., *NYU 3rd Annual Conference on Labor.* Albany: Matthew Bender, 1950.

Galenson, Walter, and Seymour M. Lipset, eds. *Labor and Trade Unionism: An Interdisciplinary Reader.* New York: John Wiley & Sons, 1960.

Gomberg, William. "Government Participation in Union Regulation and Collective Bargaining," *Labor Law Journal,* November 1962.

Gregory, Charles O. *Labor and the Law.* New York: W. W. Norton & Co., Inc., 1958.

Grob, Gerald N. *Workers and Utopia: A Study of Ideological Conflict in the American Labor Movement, 1865–1900.* Evanston: Northwestern University Press, 1961.

Hanslowe, Kurt L. *Labor Law and the Public Interest.* Ithaca: Cornell University, N. Y. State School of Industrial and Labor Relations, 1962.

Henry, Edwin R. "Some Values of Research in Industrial Relations and Human Relations," *Annual Proceedings,* IRRA, 1958.

Henson, Francis A. "The Value of University-Sponsored Industrial and Human Relations Research to Labor Leaders," *Annual Proceedings*, IRRA, 1958.

Hood, Robert C. "Industry's Use of Outside Human Relations Research," *Annual Proceedings*, IRRA, 1955.

Hutchinson, John E. *Trade Unionism and the Communists: American and International Experience*. Berkeley: University of California, Institute of Industrial Relations, 1963.

Industrial Relations Counselors, Inc. *Behavioral Science Research in Industrial Relations*. (Industrial Relations Monograph No. 21.) New York: Industrial Relations Counselors, Inc., 1962.

Industrial Relations Research Association. *Interpreting the Labor Movement*. (IRRA, Publication No. 9.) Madison, 1952.

Kaltenborn, H. W. *Governmental Adjustment of Labor Disputes*. Chicago: Foundation Press, 1943.

Kampelman, Max M. *The Communist Party vs. The CIO: A Study in Power Politics*. New York: F. A. Praeger, 1957.

Kaufman, Jacob J. *Collective Bargaining in the Railroad Industry*. New York: King's Crown Press, 1954.

Killingsworth, Charles C. *State Labor Relations Acts*. Chicago: University of Chicago Press, 1948.

———— "The Taft-Hartley Act, Toward a New Labor Policy," in Walter Adams, ed., *The Structure of American Industry*. New York: Macmillan, 1950.

Ko, T. T. *Governmental Methods of Adjusting Labor Disputes in North America and Australia*. New York: Columbia University, 1926.

"Labor Dispute Settlement," *Law and Contemporary Problems*, Spring 1947.

Labor Study Group, *Public Interest in National Labor Policy*. New York: Committee on Economic Development, 1961.

Leiserson, William M. "The Role of Government in Industrial Relations," in *Industrial Disputes and the Public Interest*. Berkeley: Industrial Relations Institute, University of California, 1947.

Matthews, Robert E. *Labor Relations and the Law*. Boston: Little, Brown & Co., 1953.

McNaughton, Wayne, L., and Joseph Lazar. *Industrial Relations and the Government*. New York: McGraw-Hill Book Co., 1954.

Millis, Harry A., and Emily Clark Brown. *From the Wagner Act to the Taft-Hartley*. Chicago: University of Chicago Press, 1950.

Mueller, Stephen J., and A. Howard Myers. *Labor Law and Legislation*. Cincinnati: South-Western Publishing Co., 1962.

National Labor Relations Board. *Legislative History of the Labor-Management Relations Act, 1947*. Washington, D. C.: Government Printing Office, 1948.

———— *Legislative History of the National Labor Relations Act, 1935*. Washington, D. C.: Government Printing Office, 1949.

National Mediation Board. *Fifteen Years Under the Railway Labor Act*. Washington, D. C.: Government Printing Office, 1950.

Northrup, Herbert R., and Gordon F. Bloom. *Government and Labor; The Role of Government in Union-Management Relations.* Homewood: R. D. Irwin, 1963.

———— and Richard L. Rowan. "State Seizure in Public Interest Disputes," *Journal of Business,* April 1963.

O'Neill, Francis A., Jr. "Resolving Labor Disputes," *Labor Law Journal,* November 1962.

Perlman, Selig. *A Theory of the Labor Movement.* New York: Augustus Kelley, 1949.

Perry, Lewis. "The Legal Position of Communists in Labor Unions," *ILR Research,* IX, no. 2 (1963).

Prasow, Paul. "Preventive Mediation: A Technique to Improve Industrial Relations," *Labor Law Journal,* August 1950.

Radom, Matthew. "Industry's Contribution to Research in Industrial Relations," *Annual Proceedings,* IRRA, 1955.

Raffaele, Joseph A. "Collective Bargaining and the National Interest," *Labor Law Journal,* June 1963.

Reynolds, James J. "The Role of Government in Collective Bargaining Negotiations: The Public Interest," *Labor Law Journal,* November 1962.

Reynolds, Lloyd G. "Research and Practice in Industrial Relations," *Annual Proceedings,* IRRA, 1955.

Roberts, Harold S. "Compulsory Arbitration in Public Utility Disputes," *Labor Law Journal,* June 1950.

———— *Plant Grievances* (Source Book). Honolulu: Industrial Relations Center, University of Hawaii, 1952.

Rosenfarb, J. *The National Labor Policy and How it Works.* New York: Harper, 1940.

Samoff, Bernard. "Research on the Results and Impact of NLRB Decisions," *Labor Law Journal,* April 1957.

Saposs, David J. *Communism in American Unions.* New York: McGraw-Hill Book Co., 1959.

———— "The Course of Ideology in International Labor," *Monthly Labor Review,* October 1960.

———— "The Impact of Labor Ideology on Industrial Relations," *Monthly Labor Review,* October 1962.

———— *Labor Ideology Impact on Industrial Relations.* Honolulu: University of Hawaii, Industrial Relations Center, 1962.

———— *Left Wing Unionism.* New York: International Publishers, 1926.

Seidman, Joel. "Labor Policy of The Communist Party During World War II," *Industrial and Labor Relations Review,* October 1950.

Selekman, B. M. *Postponing Strikes.* New York: Russell Sage Foundation, 1927.

Shister, Joseph, Benjamin Aaron, and Clyde W. Summers, eds. *Public Policy and Collective Bargaining.* (IRRA Publication No. 27.) New York: Harper, 1962.

Silverberg, L., ed. *The Wagner Act—After 10 Years.* Washington, D. C.: Bureau of National Affairs, Inc., 1945.

Simkin, William E. *Role of Government in Collective Bargaining.* Washington, D. C.: U. S. Federal Mediation and Conciliation Service, 1962.

———— "The Third Seat at the Bargaining Table, the Role of the Federal Government in Collective Bargaining, A Government Point of View," *Labor Law Journal,* January 1963.

Slichter, Sumner H. *The Challenge of Industrial Relations.* Ithaca: Cornell University Press, 1947.

Smythe, Cyrus F. "Public Policy and Emergency Disputes," *Labor Law Journal,* October 1963.

Somers, Gerald. "Constancy and Change in Industrial Relations Research Programs," *Annual Proceedings,* IRRA, 1962.

———— *Labor Market and Industrial Relations Research.* (University of Wisconsin, Industrial Relations Center, Reprint Series No. 26.) Madison, 1961.

Special Research Seminar on Comparative Labor Movements, Washington, D. C., 1959–1960. *National Labor Movements in the Postwar World.* Evanston: Northwestern University Press, 1963.

Sturmthal, Adolf. *Some Thoughts on Labor and Political Action.* Urbana: University of Illinois, Institute of Labor and Industrial Relations, 1963.

Taylor, G. W. *Government Regulation of Industrial Relations.* New York: Prentice-Hall, 1948.

Teller, Ludwig. *The Law Governing Labor Relations and Collective Bargaining.* New York: Baker, Voorhis & Co., Inc., 1940. 3 vols.

Torff, Selwyn H. "A Reappraisal of the U. S. Collective Bargaining Process," *Personnel Administration,* January–February 1963.

U. S. Department of Labor. *Collective Bargaining in the Basic Steel Industry: A Study of the Public Interest and the Role of the Government.* Washington, D. C.: Government Printing Office, 1961.

———— Bureau of Labor Statistics. *National Emergency Disputes Under the Labor Management Relations (Taft-Hartley) Act, 1947–1961.* Washington, D. C.: Government Printing Office, 1962.

———— ———— *Report on the Work of the National Defense Mediation Board.* (BLS Bulletin No. 714.) Washington, D. C.: Government Printing Office, 1942.

U. S. President's Advisory Committee on Labor-Management Policy *Free and Responsible Collective Bargaining and Industrial Peace: Report to the President, May 1, 1962.* Washington, D. C.: Government Printing Office, 1962.

Van Arsdale, Harry. "The Role of Government in Collective Bargaining Negotiations," *Labor Law Journal,* November 1962.

Whyte, William F. *Needs and Opportunities for Industrial Relations Research.* (N. Y. State School of Industrial and Labor Relations Reprint No. 125.) Ithaca: Cornell University, 1962.

Williams, Jerre S. "Settlement of Labor Disputes in Industries Affected with a National Interest," *American Bar Association Journal,* September 1963.

Wirpel, Sander W. "Industrial Relations Research in Industry: Definition and Organizational Location," *Annual Proceedings,* IRRA, 1955.

Wirtz, W. Willard. "The Future of Collective Bargaining," *Monthly Labor Review*, November 1961.

—— *Labor and the Public Interest.* (Address . . . at the Ohio State University's 22nd Shepherd Memorial Lecture, Columbus, Ohio, April 11, 1963.) Washington, D.C.: U.S. Department of Labor, 1963.

Witney, Fred. *Government and Collective Bargaining.* Philadelphia: J. B. Lippincott Co., 1951.

Witte, Edwin E. "Government and Union-Management Relations: Past, Present and Future; Description and Analysis (Address)," *Michigan Business Review*, November 1959.

Wortman, Max S., Jr. "The Role of Collective Bargaining Research in Industrial Relations," *Labor Law Journal*, September 1961.

Yale University. *Unions, Management and the Public.* (Participants in a series of radio broadcasts: Neil Chamberlain, Clyde W. Summers, E. Wight Bakke, Chris Argyris, and Charles R. Walker.) (Yale Reports Nos. 248–250.) New Haven, 1962.

Yoder, Dale. "Practical Objectives in Industrial Relations Research," *Annual Proceedings*, IRRA, 1958.

Zon, Mary G. "Labor in Politics," *Law and Contemporary Problems*, Spring 1962.

INDEX

BY NAME

BY SUBJECT